בס"ד

To Rabbi Fried & Family

With respect and admiration for the positive השפעה you have on our קהילה

והצלחה ברוחניות וגשמיות

[illegible signature]

A Prayer for the Government

Ukrainian Research Institute, Harvard University
Harvard Series in Ukrainian Studies

Center for Jewish Studies, Harvard University
Harvard Judaic Texts and Studies

Cambridge, Massachusetts

A Prayer for the Government

Ukrainians and Jews in Revolutionary Times, 1917–1920

Henry Abramson

Distributed by Harvard University Press
for the
Ukrainian Research Institute and Center for Jewish Studies,
Harvard University

The publication of this monograph has been made possible by the generous support of the Peter and Emily Kulyk Publication Fund in Ukrainian Studies and the Leon I. Mirell Lecture Fund at Harvard University.

ISBN 0-916458-88-1 (clothbound); 0-916458-87-3 (softcover).

This book is printed on acid-free paper
Printed in Canada by Transcontinental Printing, Métrolitho Division

For editorial correspondence, please contact:
Publications Office, HURI
1583 Massachusetts Ave.
Cambridge, MA 02138 USA
617-495-3692 (tel.), 617-495-8097 (fax.)
huri@fas.harvard.edu

For Ulana

You are beautiful, my love, as Tirzah, enchanting as Jerusalem, terrifying as a bannered army. Turn your eyes from me, for they overwhelm me.

Song of Songs

Contents

Illustrative Material

Maps

Figures

Illustrations

Acknowledgments

Like the Sabbath, this section is "last in creation but first in conception." I take great pleasure in acknowledging the contributions that others have made to bring this work to its completion.

My wife Ulana shouldered countless burdens to give me the freedom to conduct my research. At an early stage of the research process, she postponed her own graduate education to support the family. Later, when scholarships and teaching positions provided the financial possibility for her to return to her studies, she managed to graduate with honors while remaining the primary caregiver of our children.

Many of these pages were written with one of our infants sitting on my lap as another scattered crucial notes all over the floor. Besides honing my powers of concentration, my children have given me tremendous insight into the enormous responsibility of parenthood. Their precious existences have made me appreciate the measure of what my parents, Jack and Ethel Abramson of Iroquois Falls, Ontario, have sacrificed on my behalf. I am also grateful to my wife's parents, Bohdan and Anne Zarowsky of Toronto. It was my father-in-law who provided me with the original impetus to study Ukrainian history.

Professor Paul Robert Magocsi, "a sealed vessel that loses not a drop" (*Avot* 2:11), has done far more than supervise the doctoral dissertation that is at the core of this work. He strove to inculcate in me a sense of responsibility to the discipline that would embrace all aspects of the historian's *Weltanschauung*. I recall with much fondness our contemplative strolls along Khreshchatyk and through Queen's Park.

This topic required research in four countries on three continents, and several institutions generously provided funding for this work. I gratefully acknowledge their contributions (in alphabetical order). The Academy of Sciences of Ukraine hosted my stay in Kyiv in 1990, together with the International Association of Ukrainianists, and enabled me to complete my studies at Kyiv State University. The Beth Tzedec Congregation of Toronto named me the Stephen Cooper Fellow for Jewish Leadership that same year, and the Canadian Foundation for Ukrainian Studies awarded me the Neporany Fellowship in 1992 to conduct research again in Kyiv. In Jerusalem I was affiliated with the Center for Research and Documentation of East European Jewry of the Hebrew University. On numerous occasions the Centre for Russian and East European Studies as well as the History Department of the University of Toronto extended research grants to facilitate my work, and later, the Jewish Studies Programme named me the Ray D. Wolfe Fellow for Advanced Research in Jewish Studies for 1992–1993. The Lucius N. Littauer Foundation contributed toward my research in New York City. The Petro Jacyk Educational Foundation, as well as the Petro Jacyk Centre for Historical Research at the Canadian Institute for Ukrainian Studies, University of Alberta, provided me with research grants. The transformation of the dissertation into a monograph was supported by the Program of Jewish Studies at Cornell University, where I served as the Slovin/YIVO Visiting Assistant Professor in 1995–1996. In 1993–1994 I held a Morris M. Pulver Memorial Fellowship in Jerusalem. The entirety of my doctoral research was generously supported by the Social Sciences and Humanities Research Council of Canada. Finally, the YIVO Institute for Jewish Research named me a Max Weinreich Fellow and hosted me for three summers in New York City.

I am grateful to the librarians of the Robarts Research Library at the University of Toronto, in particular the Inter-Library Loan Department. The National and University Library in Jerusalem, the Tsentral'na Naukova Biblioteka of Kyiv, the Gottesman Library of Yeshiva University, the Olin Library at Cornell University, and the New York Public Library were extremely helpful, and I received much assistance from Mr. Edward Kasinec, Head of the Slavic and Baltic Division of the New York Public Library. The library of the YIVO Institute is a treasure beyond comparison, both in its bibliographic and in its human resources—in particular, Ms. Dina Abramowicz, may she live to a hundred and twenty.

I was received with much courtesy at the Tsentral'nyi Derzhavnyi Arkhiv Hromads'kykh Ob'iednan' [Orhanizatsii] Ukraïny, the Tsentral'nyi Derzhavnyi Istorychnyi Arkhiv, the Tsentral'nyi Derzhavnyi Arkhiv Zhovtnevoï Revoliutsiï (Kyiv), and the Mahleket kitvei-yad shel bet ha-sefarim ha-leumi ve-ha-universitai (Jerusalem). The YIVO Institute (New York) provided a most congenial atmosphere in which to study the rich Tcherikower Archive, managed by Head Archivist

Marek Web. Mr. Myron Momryk of the National Archives of Canada (Ottawa) generously shared materials with me from the Zhuk collection.

Many individuals have contributed ideas and criticism which have improved the quality of this work. Its failings should in no way be imputed to their advice, which in some cases I stubbornly ignored—as the Ukrainian saying goes, який кухар, такий борщ. Professors Michael Marrus and Bennet Kovrig of the University of Toronto served on my dissertation committee. I was fortunate to have worked in close proximity to Professor Marrus's office, and learned much from his rigorous and disciplined methods. On many occasions he generously gave of his time and experience to advise me on issues beyond those related to this book. Others who provided comments on the text, suggested sources of information, or assisted with this research include Professors Robert Accinelli, Robert Johnson, Jacques Kornberg, Andrew Rossos, D. Schwartz, Joseph Shatzmiller, Danylo Husar Struk, and Piotr Wrobel of the University of Toronto, Professor Orest Subtelny of York University, Professors Zvi Gitelman of the University of Michigan and Roman Szporluk of Harvard University, Professors Mordechai Altshuler and Jonathan Frankel of Hebrew University, Dr. Lisa Epstein of the YIVO Institute, Professor Dominique Arel, Mr. Abraham Brumberg, Mr. Stuart Clarry, Rabbi Avraham Greenspoon, Mr. Myron Haluk, Professor Taras Hunczak, Professor Mark Levene, Rabbi David Lincoln, Professor Alexander Orbach, Professor Sam Revusky of Memorial University, Professor John-Paul Himka and Mr. Alan Rutkowski of the University of Alberta, Slawomir Tokarski of the Instituto Universitario Europeo, Dr. Arye Zaidman, and Professor Walter Zenner. *The Journal of Ukrainian Studies* generously allowed me to use a version of an earlier article as the bibliographic essay of this work. Ms. Ksenya Kiebuzinski, the Petro Jacyk Bibliographer at HURI's Research Library, provided help with the illustrations that was invaluable. I am especially grateful to Mr. Robert De Lossa, director of publications at HURI, who shepherded this work (and its author) through the complexities of publication with professionalism and patience.

Mr. Zachary Baker, Head Librarian of the YIVO Institute, wrote a valuable commentary on an early draft and also assisted with numerous bibliographic issues. Mr. Baker has a comprehensive grasp of the literature which makes him without doubt one of the most significant human resources for the study of Eastern European Jewry. Yohanan Petrovsky of Brandeis University read the entire text and provided valuable suggestions. My colleagues at the Chair of Ukrainian Studies, in particular Dr. Karel Berkhoff, created an intellectually challenging environment in which to write. Most recently, my colleagues here at Florida Atlantic University have provided much guidance and support.

On a more fundamental level, several families helped alleviate the frequent dislocations associated with this research. My second visit to Kyiv occurred in the context of political and social turmoil, and upon arrival I discovered that all my arrangements for lodging had collapsed. My friends Evgeny and Olena Antonovsky generously shared their one-bedroom apartment with me. In New York, Nosson and Tammy Schwab made our stay both possible and enjoyable. In Israel, Dan Aronovic and Rhonda Abramson-Aronovic, Brondie and Richard Levine, Asher and Chaya Kushnir, HaRav Daniel and Rivka Schloss, and Moshe and Malka Zeldman ensured that my family had all we needed and provided us with a supportive and stimulating community. I am grateful to HaRav Y. Uziel Milevsky זצ״ל for his guidance on the several occasions when the text raised questions in Jewish law. His untimely death is a loss that is keenly felt. In recent years HaRav Yerucham Bensinger has graciously shared his encyclopedic knowledge of Jewish law and tradition with me. Finally, my profoundest gratitude to the Source of all blessing, who has given me life, and preserved me, and enabled me to reach this time.

HMA
10 May 1999
24 Iyar 5759

Foreword

In the spring of 1917 the Russian Empire came to an abrupt end. With its disappearance, Jewish and Ukrainian political leaders in Kyiv attempted to bring about a *rapprochement* between two nationalities that had lived in intimate insularity for centuries. During the summer and autumn of that revolutionary year, as order disintegrated in the former Empire's center, this newborn friendship blossomed, resulting eventually in the appointment of the first Minister of Jewish Affairs in modern history. During much of 1918 this tenuous relationship was strained by the presence of German troops, but upon their departure it was immediately and enthusiastically renewed. By the spring of 1919, however, the experiment that once looked so promising ended in dismal failure, as Ukraine was submerged in a sea of violence that precluded such unprecedented cooperation between two traditionally antagonistic nationalities. One of the more systemic reasons for the failure of this *rapprochement* between Jews and Ukrainians was the fact that it did not have widespread support in all strata of society. The Ukrainian socialist parties could not communicate their liberal program to the peasantry, and the Jewish activists were too far removed from the ordinary Jew to mobilize grassroots support for the Ministry of Jewish Affairs.

This work is an examination of that grand failure. It examines why, perhaps against sound judgment, the *rapprochement* was attempted in the first place, and why this experiment ended so miserably, foiling future attempts at reconciliation for decades. On one level, it is a work of Ukrainian history. During this period, the Ukrainians, numerically dominant but long divorced from political power, attempted to establish a new, autonomous government in alliance with the Jewish political leadership. On another level, it is a bright chapter in the long history of the Jewish people, one in which the Jews were not only emancipated into a free state, but given privileges as a minority that exceeded even those in Western Europe and America, and as Kurt Stillschweig noted, "the historical significance of Jewish Autonomy in the Ukraine does not lie so much in its practical realization and functioning, as in its first complete fulfillment of national Jewish demands."[1] This period is also one of the darkest chapters of Jewish history, ending with a violent wave of pogroms, dwarfed only by the overwhelming brutality of the Holocaust. On the most basic level, this is a case study in relations between nationalities, examining how representatives of mutually antagonistic ethnic groups attempted to achieve a working political relationship, only to be betrayed by less enlightened attitudes among the general population.

The historiography has generally failed to rise above national agendas to address the crucial questions regarding the fate of Ukrainian-Jewish relations during the revolution. It has been exceptionally dichotomous since 1926, when Symon Petliura, a prominent Ukrainian revolutionary leader, was assassinated by a Jew named Samuel (Shalom, Sholem) Schwartzbard. In a verdict that attracted world attention, a Paris jury acquitted Schwartzbard of the crime. The trial has markedly influenced historical research, as scholars attempted either to justify or to condemn the outcome, and as a consequence, most studies have generally focused on either the anti-Jewish pogroms or the participation of Jews in the Ukrainian revolutionary movement. This work, which represents a synthesis of these two trends, attempts to achieve a more comprehensive understanding of the period.[2]

In truth, the Schwartzbard affair represents a discrete chapter in Ukrainian-Jewish relations quite separate from this work, yet it is impossible to evaluate the historiographical literature on the 1917–1920 period without understanding the ramifications of Petliura's assassination and its impact on subsequent studies of Ukrainian-Jewish relations. I have therefore appended a bibliographic essay that attempts to address the crucial questions raised concerning the literature and clearly states my evaluation of these often polemic sources. Readers well familiar with the topic may choose to read this essay first; otherwise, I recommend that they follow the story of 1917–1920 before they proceed to the events of 1926–1927.

I have avoided a general historical outline of events in Ukraine before and after the 1917 revolution, assuming that most of my readers will be familiar with that history. For those who are not, a brief explanation of a few institutions and terms is necessary. The Central Rada (Central "Council"—a term which in Ukrainian translates the Russian *sovet*, 'Soviet, council') arose in the turmoil following the abdication of Tsar Nicholas II in early 1917. At first the Rada acted as a representative of the Provisional Government in Petrograd, hoping for national autonomy within a federated state that would replace the Russian Empire. As the situation in Russia proper deteriorated, the Rada moved eventually to outright independence for Ukraine, which is described in Chapter 2. At this stage the chaos of the Civil War enveloped Ukraine. Bolshevik forces under Volodymyr Antonov-Ovsiienko and his infamous lieutenant Mykhail' Murav'ev invaded Ukraine in late 1917 in response to a clear lack of support for the Bolsheviks at the recent All-Ukrainian Congress of Soviets. By February 1918 two important events had occurred. First, Ukrainian representatives of the Rada had negotiated a treaty with the Central powers in Brest-Litovsk at the same time that Lenin's representatives signed their peace deal. At almost the same time, the Rada was forced to evacuate Kyiv to Murav'ev's forces. The Central Rada was able to regain control only by utilizing German and Austrian support—offered by them only in exchange for large-scale material support (mainly foodstuffs) for the Central Powers. As the Central Rada's ability to provide this support declined (which was natural given the countryside's reluctance to give up large food stores in the midst of the growing chaos), the Central Powers searched for a more efficient "provider" and found it in Pavlo Skoropads'kyi, who in late April 1918 dispersed the government of the Central Rada and formed the "Hetmanate," essentially a conservative dictatorship based on the support of landed interests and the occupying Austro-Hungarian and German powers. This government never had the support of the general population or the political left and its days were numbered once Central Power forces departed following the Armistice of November 11, 1918.

Soon after the withdrawal from Kyiv of German troops in November 1918, the city was taken by troops loyal to the "Directory" of the

Ukrainian National Republic, led by the writer Volodymyr Vynnychenko and the journalist Symon Petliura. The Directory remained in power for over a year, eventually to be subsumed by the Civil War, which raged until Bolshevik Soviet control was firmly entrenched in 1920. The actions of the troops ostensibly loyal to this Directory form the core of much of the investigation herein. For many reasons, Petliura himself is a pivotal figure, as I indicated above, during the period when the greatest violence against Jews occurred. One must remember, though, that Ukraine in 1919 was in a state of complete anarchy, in which no party ever exercised complete control over the nation. This certainly does not excuse or exculpate those forces responsible for the monstrous brutality that occurred. It does the reader well to remember how all-encompassing was the hellish pit into which Ukraine descended.

This study focuses on the experience of Jews and Ukrainians within the 1917 borders of the Russian Empire, specifically the nine provinces that were predominantly Ukrainian in ethnolinguistic character: Kharkiv, Katerynoslav, Poltava, Chernihiv, Kherson, Kyiv, Podolia, Volhynia, and Taurida (see Map 1, p. 11). It should be borne in mind that Ukrainian history, to a large degree separated from the overall history of the tsarist empire, would have been perceived as regional in character by the average nineteenth-century Jew, or even Ukrainian, given that the notion of a distinct Ukrainian state was still quite embryonic. One of the major coups of the nascent Ukrainian movement was its early success in winning the support of Jewish political activists away from their traditional Russotropism (see Chapter 1), and one of the major points upon which Ukrainian-Jewish cooperation turned was the maintenance of Ukrainian membership in a larger Russian political entity. When this failed, the *rapprochement* failed. Large Ukrainian and Jewish populations also lived in neighboring regions, notably in the Austro-Hungarian Empire, and an attempt was made to set up Jewish autonomy in Galicia. The experience of Austrian and later Polish rule, however, was so fundamentally different from the tsarist and later the Communist system that this topic is treated only briefly (see Chapter 5). A more comprehensive study is beyond the contours of this work.

Hebrew terms that appear in Yiddish texts or contexts follow Yiddish transliteration (*Akhdes*, not *Ahdut*; *shabes*, not *shabat*). In cases where a person is known to have used a particular spelling in the Latin alphabet, that form is generally used here (Tcherikower, not Cherikover or Tsherikover). In other cases the mother tongue of the individual has defined the transliteration. Names of places within Ukrainian ethnolinguistic regions are generally transliterated from the Ukrainian usage of 1917 (Proskuriv, not Proskurov or Khmel'nyts'kyi).

Until 1918 the lands of the former tsarist empire followed the Julian calendar, which by the twentieth century was thirteen days behind the Gregorian calendar used in the West. On January 31, 1918, the Soviet government switched to the Gregorian calendar, and the Ukrainian government followed suit on March 1. All dates cited in this work will be converted to the Gregorian, or "new style" calendar. The revolution that overthrew the tsar in early 1917 will therefore be referred to as the "March" Revolution, and not the "February" Revolution.

In an effort to avoid confusion, the term "national" has been rendered as "nationality" to denote an ethnic group rather than a state (*Natsional'nyi Soiuz* is translated "Nationality Union," *Natsional-rat* as "Nationality Council"). The Ukrainian word *zhyd* has been rendered as "Jew." As in Polish, the Ukrainian term does not necessarily carry any negative connotations, although in some contexts a harsher translation might be justified. The Russian word *zhid*, on the other hand, is unmistakably negative, the polite form being *evrei* (Hebrew).[3] Finally, the spelling "antisemitism" is used here rather than "anti-Semitism." The word was originally coined in the late nineteenth century to provide its practitioners with a respectable alternative to "Jew-hatred" and implies that there is such a thing as "Semitism," which one might oppose. In recent years many scholars have opted for the spelling "antisemitism" to denote the phenomenon itself rather than perpetuate its original meaning.

Finally, in the illustrations, I have asked the publisher to obscure the faces of the dead—Jewish, Ukrainian, and Russian alike. This is in accordance with Jewish law, which seeks to protect the dignity of the dead.

The Jewish Nationality Council, November 1918.
From: Shalom [Solomon] Goldelman, "Di Yidishe Natsionale Oitonomie in Ukrayne (1917–1920)," in *Yidn in Ukrayne*, 2 vols., New York: Shulsinger Bros., New York, NY, 1961, vol. 1, p. 130

Rabbi Hanina, the Deputy High Priest, said: "Pray for the welfare of the government, for were it not for the fear of it, people would swallow each other alive."

Avot 3:2

Chapter One

Ukrainians and Jews on the Eve of Revolutionary Times

Archaeological evidence places early Jewish settlement in Ukraine in antiquity, possibly several centuries BCE with the Greek colonization of the Black Sea coast. As legend has it, Jews entered Ukraine as early as the exile of the ten northern tribes (eighth century BCE) or the period of the Babylonian exile (sixth century BCE).[1] Comparatively little is known about the first thousand years of the Jewish presence in this area until the conversion of the Khazar empire to Judaism in the eighth century CE. The Khazars, a nomadic tribe from the east, had conquered much of what is now Ukrainian territory and subjugated it to their capital on the Caspian Sea. Faced with the emerging power of the Muslims to the south and the Christians to the west, the Khazar leadership decided to convert *en masse* to Judaism in 740.[2] The decline of the Khazar empire over the next two and a half centuries was roughly contemporary with the ascendance of Kyivan (Kievan) Rus'.

The influence of the Jewish Khazars on the early Slavic political entity was profound, as is indicated in the story of Grand Prince Volodymyr's conversion to Christianity in the tenth century. Interested in adopting a monotheistic faith, Volodymyr solicited the views of Muslims, Christians, and Khazarian Jews. According to the earliest surviving source referring to this meeting, Volodymyr might very likely have chosen Judaism as the faith of early Kyivan Rus'. He demurred only after learning that the Jews had been expelled from their native land by Divine wrath, saying "Do you expect us to accept that fate also?"[3]

The Jewish presence in early Kyiv (Kiev) was considerable. The city had both a Jewish quarter and a Jewish gate as early as the eleventh century.[4] One Moses of Kyiv is recorded as a member of the twelfth-century French analytical school of Talmud (Ba'alei Tosafot), while an

Isaac of Chernihiv, something of an early linguist, appears in the records of medieval English Jewry.[5] These rabbinic scholars were probably highly exceptional, since other sources describe a less well-educated Ukrainian Jewry. The twelfth-century traveler Petahia of Regensburg (Ratisbon) refers to Kyivan Jewry as "heretics," possibly indicating the presence of anti-Talmudic Karaites, and documents found in the Cairo geniza indicate a relatively high level of illiteracy among the Jewish population of Kyivan Rus'.[6]

Beginning in the fourteenth century, the bulk of Ukrainian ethnolinguistic territory came under the control of the rapidly expanding Grand Duchy of Lithuania, which in 1569 concluded an agreement of union with neighboring Poland to create the Polish-Lithuanian Commonwealth. Persecution of Jews in Western Europe, combined with incentives for settlement, drew waves of Jewish immigration to Ukrainian territory.[7] The Polish-Lithuanian authorities were eager to exploit their rich agricultural holdings in Ukraine yet loath to leave their comfortable lives in the heartland of the Commonwealth to do so. Using the Jews as their agents, however, the Polish and Lithuanian landlords were able to exact considerable income from their Ukrainian lands: under a system known as the *arenda*, they leased the right to collect various types of income from the Ukrainian peasantry to Jews, who passed a majority of the income along to the landlord and kept the remainder as profit. The *arenda* was generally based on the leasing of land and the right to distill alcohol, but it could also be extended to the collection of tolls on bridges and fish ponds, and to other types of duties and taxes.[8]

While acting essentially as tax collectors, the Jews also provided various services to the Ukrainian population. The lords' economic interests were comparatively narrow: they concentrated their energies on trade along the Vistula (Wisła) river and imported from other regions only large-volume and luxury goods. The Jews, on the other hand, were far more involved in local rural markets, and were willing to transport goods of use to the peasantry overland over vast distances. Whereas non-Jewish merchants were content to service the narrow business needs of the lords, Jewish merchants carried approximately 150 percent more kinds of products out of Ukrainian lands and brought back some 400 percent more kinds of products than their non-Jewish competitors.[9] Jews were also heavily involved in small crafts, and provided much-needed, although often resented, financial services to peasants in the form of petty moneylending.[10]

Given the nature of the economic relationship between Ukrainians and Jews, it is not difficult to imagine the tension between the two peoples. The absentee landlords, constantly cash-starved in their imitation of Western European opulence, strove to exact the greatest possible amount of income from their Ukrainian landholdings. Obtaining this onerous exaction, along with a commission, was the task of the Jewish agent. The absentee powers, moreover, often attempted to encroach not only on the economic well-being of the Ukrainian peasantry but also on their religious and cultural autonomy. It is hardly surprising that peasant rebellion became a recurring event and that Jews often felt the brunt of it.

The most significant of several rebellions was the uprising led by Bohdan Khmel'nyts'kyi in 1648–1649. Khmel'nyts'kyi successfully led a movement against three main targets: Poles, Jews, and those Ukrainian Orthodox who accepted the jurisdiction of Rome over Constantinople and a modified Byzantine rite through the Union of Brest in 1596 (called alternately Uniates, Greek Catholics, or Ukrainian Catholics depending on the period in question). The Uniates were despised by Khmel'nyts'ky and his forces—and treated ferociously—because they were considered heretics and agents of Polonization. With regard to the Jews, a medieval Jewish chronicle of these events entitled *Abyss of Despair* (an allusion to Psalms 69:3) recorded the suffering of Ukrainian Jewry with such pathos that parts of it were incorporated into the liturgy for *Tisha be-Av*, the day of mourning for the destruction of the two Temples in Jerusalem.[11] This Ukrainian tradition of rebellion against oppressive authorities and their Jewish agents was repeated in the eighteenth century with the Haidamak movement.

In contrast to the large-scale Jewish settlement of Ukrainian territory under the Polish-Lithuanian Commonwealth, virtually no Jews lived in tsarist Russia. Since the fifteenth-century affair of the mysterious "Judaizers," who had found sympathizers in high places (including that of Tsar Ivan III's daughter-in-law), Russia's borders were essentially closed to Jewish immigration.[12] With the eighteenth-century partitioning of Poland under Catherine II, the tsarist empire suddenly acquired one of the most numerically significant Jewish populations in the world. Although the tsarina seemed to be interested in allowing the Jews free movement within the empire to encourage trade, it was decided nevertheless that the old policy of exclusion should be retained for the prepartition borders. Thus, Jews were not allowed to move into Russia proper from the so-called "Pale of Settlement," which included much of present-day Ukraine, Belarus, and Lithuania.[13] The restrictions on settlement created an artificial, pressure-cooker atmosphere, and tensions between Jews and their neighbors increased throughout the last decades of the nineteenth century.

There are three basic truisms about Ukrainian Jewish society in the late Imperial period: it was a religious society, it was a gendered society, and it was a changing society. The religious, and to a certain degree gendered, aspects of Jewish society will briefly be discussed here. The dramatic changes Ukrainian Jewry faced will make up a large part of this work.

Avodas ha-Shem, literally "servitude to the Name [of God]," was the defining principle of religious Jewish life. For an adult Jewish male, a typical day would begin with morning prayers, either at dawn or shortly thereafter. The exceptionally pious would first immerse themselves in a ritual bath called a *mikveh*. This practice was especially prevalent among *Hasidim* ("Pious Ones"), followers of the teachings of the eighteenth-century Ba'al Shem Tov and his disciples. Prayers might be held in large synagogues, in study halls, and in numerous neighborhood locations, often private homes, anywhere that the required quorum (*minyan*) of ten males over the age of thirteen might gather. Some part of the day would be set aside for the study of traditional texts, usually accomplished in pairs or small groups. For ordinary working men, this study period might consist of only a few minutes to an hour, and would typically take place before or after prayers. Communities supported study in a variety of ways, however, and scholars would often spend the entire day immersed in the Talmud and other religious works. Morning prayers took approximately forty minutes (slightly longer on Mondays and Thursdays, when a portion of the Torah was read publicly), and afternoon and evening prayers roughly fifteen minutes each.

Women would rarely go to these fixed prayers, since traditional Judaism exempted them from the obligation to perform most positive commandments (i.e., "thou shalts") defined by time, such as morning prayers, which must be said exclusively in the morning. Unlike more Americanized practice, however, the center of religious activity was not the communal prayer halls but the home. There are three fundamental pillars of traditional Jewish ritual—observance of the dietary laws *(kashrus)*, of the laws governing marital relations *(taharas hamishpoche*, literally "purity of the family"), and of the Sabbath (*shabes*)—and all of them revolve primarily around the home, not the synagogue. In this highly gendered society, women's observance and supervision of Jewish ritual were taxing enterprises, albeit with the potential of great spiritual meaning and fulfillment.

Daily observance of Jewish law was all-pervasive, from the ritual hand washing upon waking to the set order of dressing and the required recitation of some one hundred blessings each day: a series before and after meals and snacks, before smelling fragrances, after seeing lightning, hearing thunder, receiving good or bad news, even after performing bodily functions. Although women were not required to observe the rigid schedule of communal prayers, Jewish law did require them to spend a certain amount of time in personal prayer, the general themes of which were sentiments praising God, followed by personal requests and concluding with an expression of gratitude. Women were free to create their own spontaneous personal prayers or petitions (*tekhines*); many of these were recorded for others and are among the most moving examples of Jewish spirituality.[14]

Contact between men and women was highly circumscribed. With the exception of blood relatives, men and women were not to touch each other physically, nor were they to be secluded in certain types of private locations. Husbands and wives observed a monthly cycle of separation revolving around menstruation, the conclusion of which was marked by the wife's ritual immersion in the *mikveh* and the resumption of marital relations. Although traditional Judaism limited sexual expression to the right person (one's spouse) and the right time (after immersion in the *mikveh* but before the next menstrual cycle) and to a lesser extent to the right place, sexuality was viewed as an intrinsic and healthy part of the Jewish lifestyle.

The Jewish week revolved around *shabes*, the Sabbath. Preparations for *shabes* would begin earlier in the week, since many common household tasks, such as cooking, laundering, lighting fires, and so on, are prohibited on *shabes* itself. Men would finish their work early Friday afternoon in order to have time to bathe and dress for the evening prayers, which would welcome the "Sabbath Queen," while women would prepare the home and begin *shabes* with the ritual lighting of candles. Three festive meals would be served (one on Friday evening and two on Saturday), and Jewish families would relax from their weekday cares in singing, feasting, and discussing the portion of the Torah that was read at Saturday morning prayers. The entire family would often go to synagogue on Saturday morning, and the communal gathering provided an opportunity for increased social bonding. The numerous restrictions on work encouraged the family and community to set aside their responsibilities and come together, increasing their cohesion and bolstering their group identification. *Shabes* was truly the mainstay of Jewish communal existence. Besides this weekly festive day, Jews observed a rich cycle of feast and fast days throughout the year.

Jewish culture, having adapted to many different contexts during the two millennia since the expulsion from Israel, was self-sufficient and self-enclosed. This, together with a long and mournful history of persecution, gave Jews a tendency to view non-Jews with mistrust and sometimes contempt. Rabbinic sources occasionally refer to non-Jews in less than complimentary terms, and these passages (albeit often distorted or taken out of context) are a staple of antisemitic literature.[15] To take one example, the morning liturgy includes a blessing expressing gratitude that one "was not made a non-Jew."[16] There are many Rabbinic justifications for this blessing that make it more palatable to modern sensibilities,[17] but it is probable that the average Jew in Ukraine understood these words in a rather blunt, straightforward manner.

This contempt of non-Jews should not be confused, on the other hand, with more Christian notions of the damned and the saved. According to Jewish tradition, Jews were given 613 commandments to observe, whereas non-Jews were given seven.[18] There is absolutely no reason for a non-Jew to observe more than these basic seven commandments, for example to refrain from non-kosher foods such as shellfish. Any non-Jew, moreover, who faithfully observes these seven commandments is credited with a place in the world to come. Like many monotheistic faiths, Judaism regards itself as the only "true" belief. Unlike many others, however, it does not require non-Jews to conform to Jewish practice to achieve reward, a theological attitude that also dulled any vestigial missionary impulses that might have been directed at Ukrainians.

It should also be noted that traditional Judaism places many other restrictions on social intercourse with non-Jews. Sexual contact is of course proscribed, the laws regarding kosher diet make eating together awkward, and the fact that *shabes* is on Saturday and not Sunday makes socializing less convenient. The only extensive contact between Jews and non-Jews was in the commercial sphere, as Ukrainian peasants came to trade in the local marketplace. Ukrainian-Jewish contacts in this area were quite broad, particularly in tsarist Russia's poorly developed "horizontal relationship" economy[19]. Despite all the centrifugal forces separating Jews and Ukrainians, this daily business contact resulted in considerable mutual influence, particularly in Jewish adaptations of things Ukrainian. This is most apparent in linguistic borrowings.

The Ukrainian language belongs to East Slavic, which includes three modern languages that developed out of Common Slavic (the other two are Belarusian and Russian). It shares many features of both Russian and Polish (a neighboring West Slavic language) and is written in a Cyrillic alphabet that differs from the Russian Cyrillic. The very existence of the Ukrainian language was hotly denied by those opposed to the development of Ukrainian national aspirations. Volodymyr Vynnychenko records in his memoirs the opinion of one expert on the Russian language: "the Ukrainian language never was, is not, and can never be."[20]

The vernacular of Ukrainian Jewry was Yiddish, and an overwhelming 97 percent of Jews in Ukraine declared it as their mother tongue in the 1897 Imperial census.[21] A composite language, Yiddish is based primarily on several Middle High German dialects, with significant influences from Hebrew, Aramaic, and the Romance and Slavic languages; it is written in the Hebrew alphabet from right to left. The Yiddish spoken by Jews living in Ukrainian ethnolinguistic territory may be clearly distinguished from the Northeastern dialect (characteristic of Belarus, Lithuania, and Latvia) and the Central dialect (characteristic of Poland and west Galicia).[22]

Only 1.2 percent of Jews by religion at that time declared Russian as their mother tongue, and a tiny 0.05 percent of Jews by religion claimed Ukrainian.[23] Nevertheless, the Yiddish spoken in Ukraine is profoundly marked by the influence of the Ukrainian language. In terms of grammar, for example, Yiddish shows evidence of a form of Ukrainian verbal aspect that is absent from Middle High German (*ikh hob geshribn*, I have written, versus *ikh hob ongeshribn*, I have completed writing). Yiddish has also absorbed a multitude of Ukrainian conjunctions, prepositions and adverbs, such as *i...i* and *nu* ('both...and'; 'well'). The rich variety of Ukrainian diminutives was adapted to Jewish names (*Khayimke*, diminutive of *Khayim*), and Ukrainian names were sometimes given to Jewish children, particularly girls (e.g., *Badane*, from *Bohdana*). The Yiddish vocabulary has also been enriched by countless Ukrainian words such as *khreyn* (from *khryn*, horseradish), *zeyde* (from *did*, grandfather), *nudnik* (from *nudnyi*, boring; annoying), and others. While Ukrainian influence on Yiddish is clearly evident, the reverse is harder to detect, since many terms that may have been taken from Yiddish could also have come from similar or identical German roots. Hebrew loan words are much more readily identified in Ukrainian, yet it is less likely that they were taken into Ukrainian as a result of the grass-roots contact of the two peoples. Words such as the Ukrainian *subota* (Saturday) are certainly borrowed from the Hebrew (*shabat*), but this was probably due to Church influence rather than Jewish mediation.

Other aspects of daily life, such as the culinary arts, also show evidence of significant cultural interchange. Many traditional Jewish foods are of Slavic origin, such as noodle pudding (Yiddish *lokshin kugel*, Ukrainian *lokshyna zapechena*), potato pancakes (*latkes*, *selians'ki kartoplyanki*), and cabbage rolls (*holuptsi, holubtsi*). While the recipes have been changed to meet Jewish tastes—they tend to be considerably sweeter, for example, and pork products are naturally omitted—the similarities are striking.[24] It is worth noting the influence of Ukrainian not only in "kitchen" vocabulary but also in even more intimate aspects of family life. Jewish children, for example, called their grandmothers *Bobe*, from the Slavic *Baba* and not from the Hebrew *Savtah* or German *Oma*. Similarly, father was known as *Tate*, from the Ukrainian

Tato, not the Hebrew/Aramaic *Aba* or the German *Vater*, and countless other terms and endearments. While the *Weltanschauungen* of the two peoples could hardly be more dissimilar, it is clear that on a more basic level Ukrainian and east European Jewish culture had much in common. Frequent contact, particularly between women, was the likely conduit for such cross-cultural exchanges.[25]

Although the most recent census prior to the March 1917 revolution was taken in 1897, it has been estimated that the rate of Jewish emigration during this interval was roughly equal to the natural rate of increase, so that figures from that census may be considered reasonably accurate to the outbreak of World War I.[26] According to the 1897 census, Ukrainians constituted roughly three-quarters of the twenty-three million people living in the nine provinces that would later constitute the bulk of the territory claimed by the Ukrainian National Republic. Jews, Russians, Poles, and other minorities accounted for the remaining quarter.[27] When the German front lines cut off Polish and Lithuanian Jewry from the lands of the former tsarist empire in 1917, Ukrainian Jewry accounted for roughly 60 percent of Jews remaining in the Pale of Settlement and some 17 percent of Jews worldwide (see Figure 1.1).[28] The Jewish and Polish populations were concentrated in the right-bank provinces (that is, west of the Dnipro [Dnieper] River), whereas the prominent minority in the left-bank provinces was Russian (see Figure 1.2).

The urbanization patterns of the roughly 17 million Ukrainians and the 6.5 million minority inhabitants of the area differed markedly. Less than 6 percent of Ukrainians lived in cities and towns, where 80 percent of Jews made their homes.[29] Ukrainians thus constituted only one-third of the inhabitants in the urban sector, while Jews accounted for another third, and the bulk of the remainder was Russian. Ukrainians constituted a narrow majority of the urban population in only two provinces (Poltava and Kharkiv), and a plurality in one (Chernihiv). In all other provinces, the urban landscape was dominated either by Jews or by Russians (see Figure 1.3). In some towns, "the police and all the functionaries and workers as well were Jewish."[30]

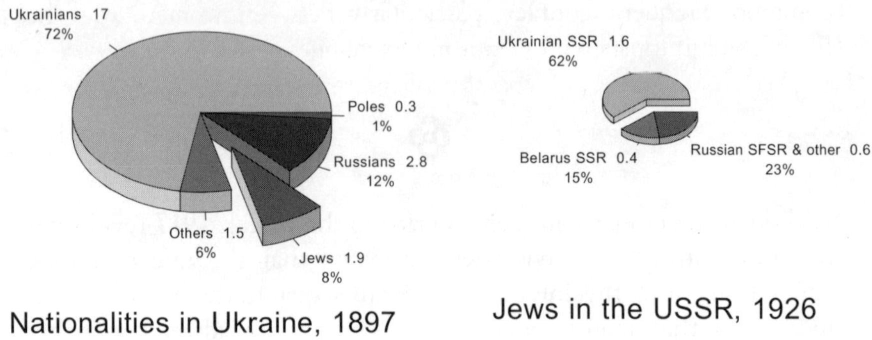

Figure 1.1. Jews in Ukraine and the Soviet Union (millions)
Source: Perepis'; Lestschinsky, *Sovetishe idntum*, p. 75.

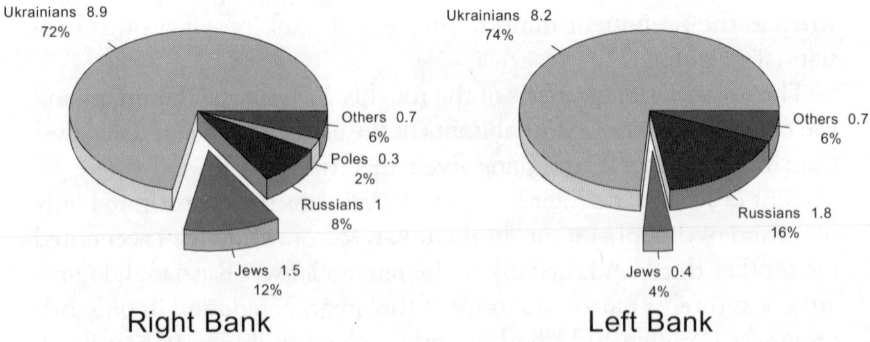

Figure 1.2. Nationalities in Ukraine, 1897 (millions)
Source: Perepis'.

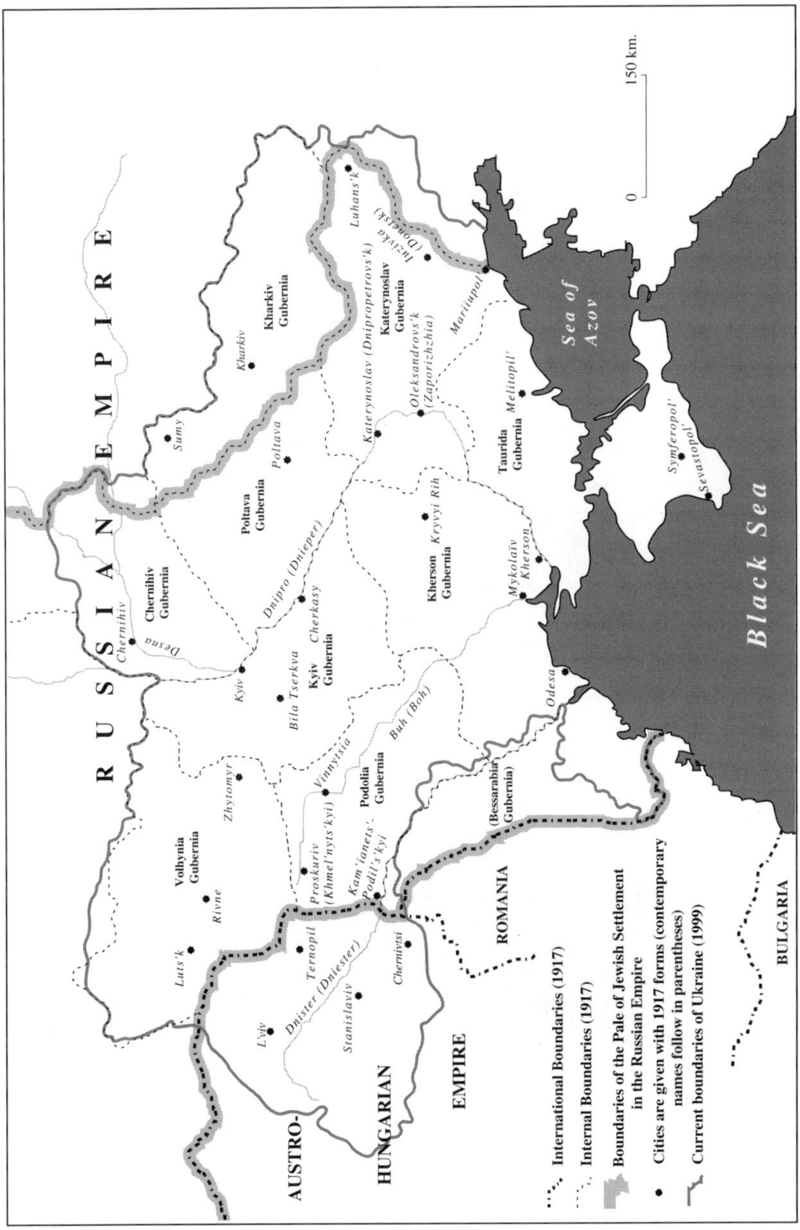

Map 1. Ukrainian Provinces (Gubernias) and the Pale of Jewish Settlement in the Russian Empire, 1917

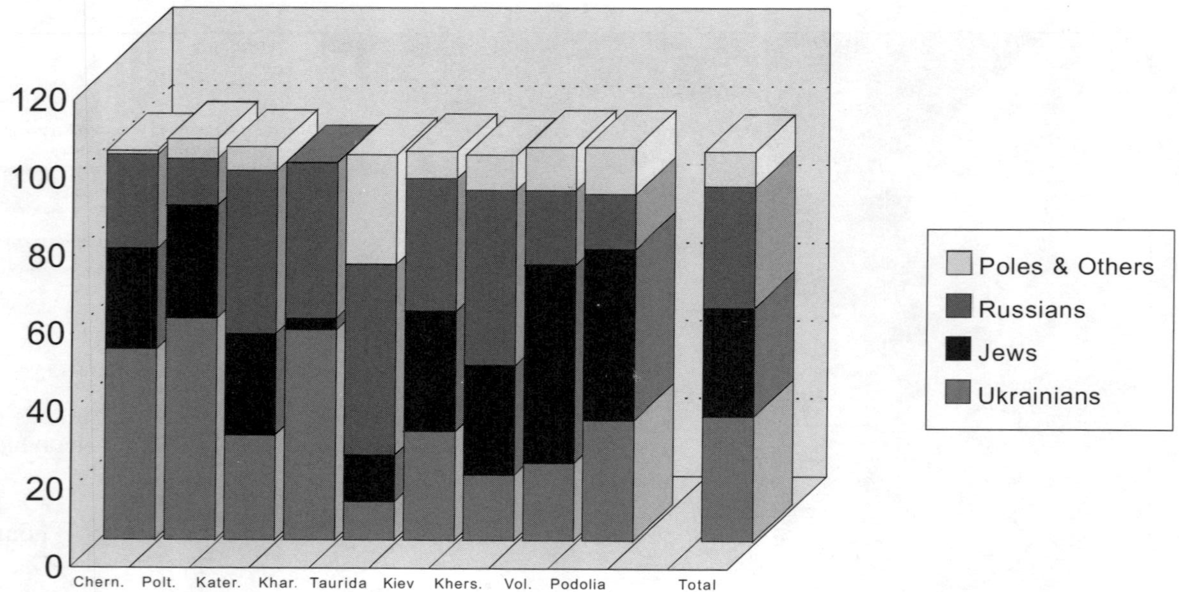

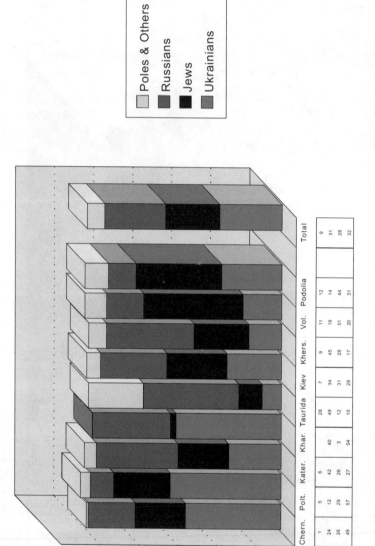

	Chern.	Polt.	Kater.	Khar.	Taurida	Kiev	Khers.	Vol.	Podolia		Total
Poles & Others	1	5	6		28	7	9	11	12		9
Russians	24	12	42	40	49	34	45	19	14		31
Jews	26	29	26	3	12	31	28	51	44		28
Ukrainians	49	57	27	54	10	28	17	20	31		32

Figure 1.3. Urban Population in Ukraine, 1897 (percent)
Source: Lestschinsky, "Sotsial," p. 88; Borys, *Sovietization*, p. 66. Some data incomplete.

The small number of self-identifying Ukrainians in the urban sector was exacerbated by the fact that many ethnic Ukrainians were assimilated to Russian culture; over 25 percent preferred to call themselves "Little Russians" (*malorosy*). To a large extent this was the inevitable result of a policy of Russification encouraged by the tsarist government, which prohibited the establishment of a Ukrainian-language press in the empire until 1905 and did not allow any level of state schooling in that language.[31] An interesting illustration of Ukrainian attempts to counter Russification is provided by a pamphlet on an unrelated topic published by the Ukrainian Library (*Ukraïns'ka Knyharnia*) in 1918 in Kherson province. The text appears in full in both Ukrainian and Russian to make it more comprehensible to the russified Ukrainian, and unfamiliar words in the Ukrainian text are translated in footnotes. It is interesting that many of the translated words, such as "work" (Ukrainian *pratsia*, Russian *trud*) and "time" (Ukrainian *chas*, Russian *vremia*), are very common, which seems to indicate a serious lack of familiarity with the language among the russified population.[32]

Furthermore, the proportion of Ukrainians was diminishing in the cities as these urban areas experienced a population boom in the last half of the nineteenth century. Kyiv, for example, doubled in size, from 247,723 in 1897 to 506,000 in 1917. The number of Russians in the city doubled, and the number of Jews tripled, but the number of Ukrainians increased by only 60 percent. Ukrainian cities, often described as "Russian-Jewish-Polish islands" in the "Ukrainian sea," would become even more isolated in the twentieth century.[33]

In 1917, when the population of Kyiv included roughly equal proportions of Jews and Ukrainians, Ukrainians were predominantly proletarian (42.3 percent of Ukrainians) but with a significant white-collar population (23.3 percent).[34] Roughly the same proportion of Jews worked in white-collar jobs (27.2 percent), yet far more Jews than Ukrainians were involved in business (29.7 percent of Jews, 10.0 percent of Ukrainians). Ukrainians were more heavily represented in the servant class (15.1 percent, Jews 2.1 percent) and less in the liberal professions (5 percent, Jews 12.6 percent) (see Figure 1.4).

Looking at the tsarist empire as a whole, the economic profiles of Jews and Ukrainians tended to follow urbanization patterns: the majority of Ukrainians were involved in agriculture, while the majority of

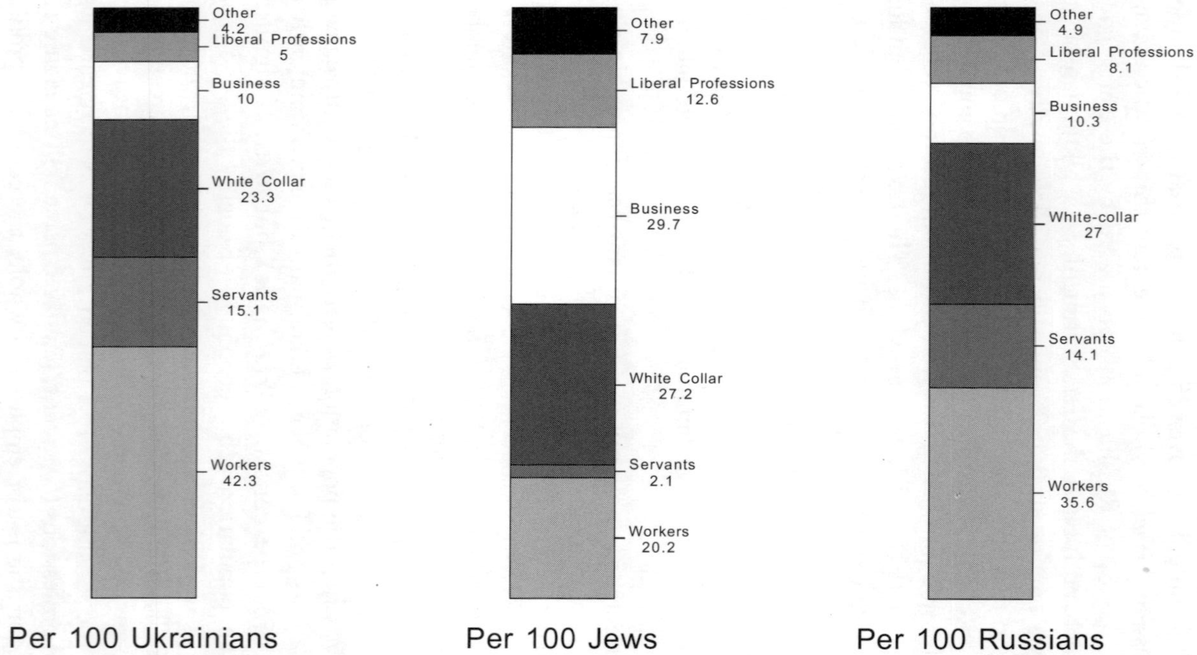

Figure 1.4. Occupational Structure of Ukrainians, Jews, and Russians in Kyiv, 1897
Source: Krawchenko, "Social Structure," p. 104.

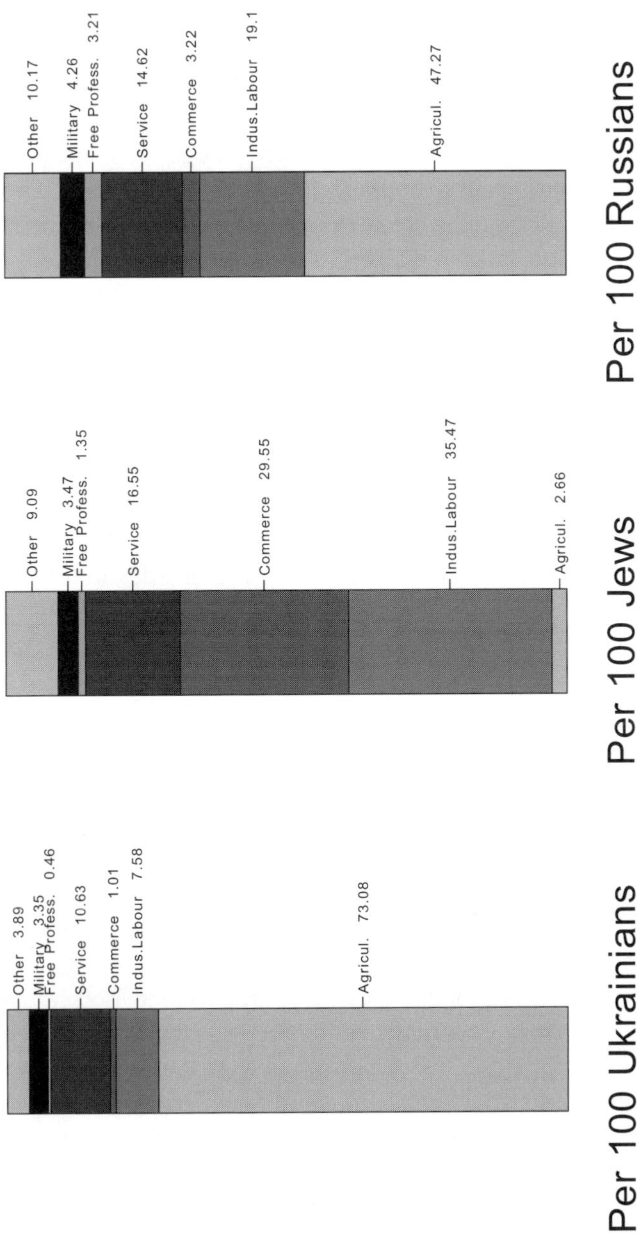

Figure 1.5. Occupational Structure in the Tsarist Empire, 1897
Source: Bauer, *Nationalitäten*, vol. 2, pp. 167–70.

Jews were involved in commerce and industry (see Figure 1.5). In 1917 roughly 80 percent of the total Ukrainian population lived in the countryside, and constituted 97 percent of all peasants. Of these, half were classified as "poor," that is, holding less than 3 *desiatyns* (3.3 hectares) of land.[35] Ukrainian Jewry was also impoverished. A large segment of the population was popularly known as *luftmenshn*, literally, "air people," since they existed without any recognizable means of support. In 1898, almost fifty thousand Jewish families, some 20 percent of the total in Ukraine, were so poor, they required assistance in purchasing *matse*, the unleavened bread for the Passover holiday.[36] Just over half of all Jews were literate, but less than 20 percent of Ukrainians. Jewish literacy was particularly prominent in rural areas (see Figure 1.6).

The changing atmosphere in late tsarist Russia caused tensions to increase between Ukrainians and Jews. Before 1881, anti-Jewish violence in Ukraine rarely developed past the level of temporary, localized conflicts, the major exceptions being the rebellions of Khmel'nyts'kyi (1648–1649) and Gonta (1768), which were themselves separated by over a century. Following the assassination of Tsar Alexander II in March 1881, however, anti-Jewish violence became a disturbingly regular phenomenon in Ukrainian ethnolinguistic territory. More ominously, the degree of brutality also increased: the Jews killed in 1881–1884 numbered in the tens, in 1903–1906 in the thousands, and in 1919, in the tens of thousands.[37]

In his study of "middleman minorities,"[38] Walter Zenner argued that minorities often blend into societies by filling otherwise vacant economic niches, a characterization that certainly held true for early modern Ukrainian Jewry. When a given minority moves out of its niche—due to either economic pressures or internal disintegration—and begins to compete with the majority, there are two likely outcomes. If the economy is strong and can support this increased competition, the minority may eventually assimilate into the larger society, which is how Zenner describes American Jewry. If the economy is incapable of sustaining this competition, and here Zenner refers to the example of interwar Poland, violence may be directed at the minority. The case of Ukrainian Jewry might also be paradigmatic for Zenner's analysis, since in the late nineteenth century, impoverishment increased just as Jews were moving beyond their traditional pursuits.

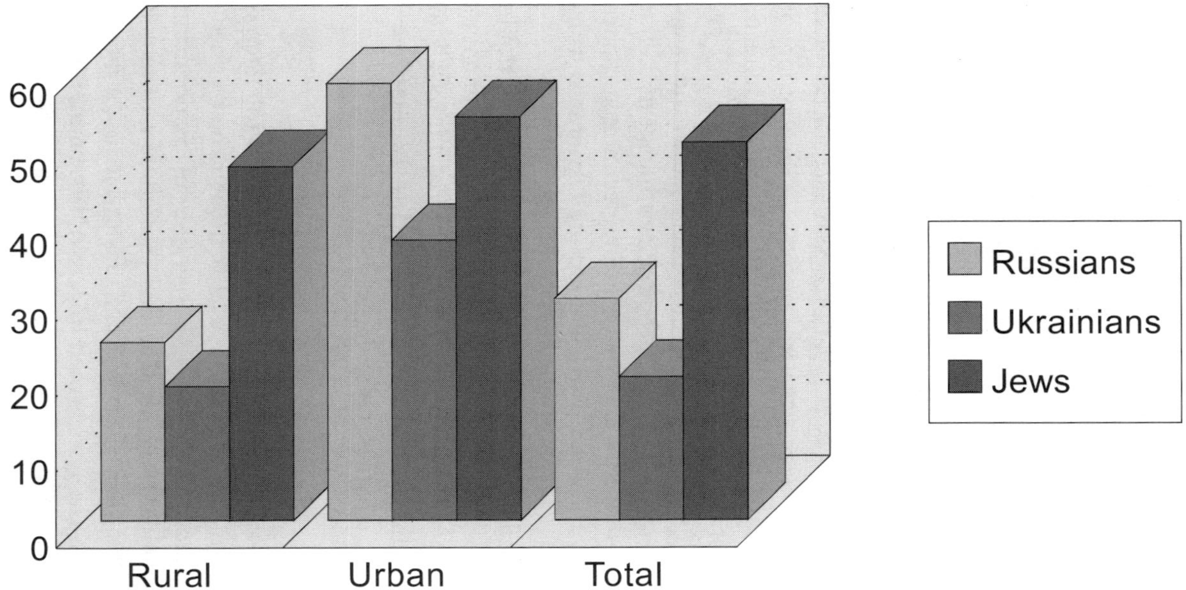

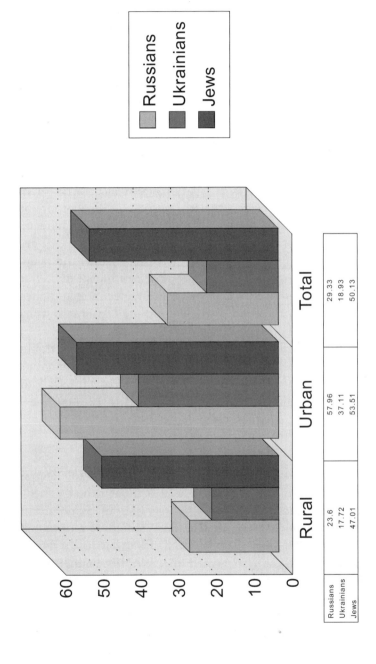

	Rural	Urban	Total
Russians	23.6	57.96	29.33
Ukrainians	17.72	37.11	18.93
Jews	47.01	53.51	50.13

Figure 1.6. Literacy in the Russian Empire, 1897 (percent: respondents over age 10, with regard to any language)
Source: Bauer, *Nationalitäten*, vol. 2, pp. 107–110.

Tsarist legislation, from the creation of the Pale of Settlement to the regime's miscellaneous decrees, impeded the free growth of the Jewish economy: Jews were prevented, for example, from maintaining warehouses near railroads, forcing Jewish merchants to export raw timber rather than processed wood products and to use inefficient river transportation. At the same time, the sheer scope of the changes occurring at the end of the nineteenth century actually provided enterprising Jews with a wide array of opportunities for economic advancement. The only major exception to this general pattern of growth was the market for consumer goods, a field in which Jews were already heavily involved; despite increasing business opportunities, a large segment of the Jewish population was tied to a sector of the economy that did not keep pace with the times.[39] In addition, during the nineteenth century, the Jewish population increased dramatically. At the beginning of the century Jews constituted some 6 to 7 percent of the population of the Pale of Settlement, but by 1897 this figure had increased to 12 percent.[40] Thus, late nineteenth-century Ukrainian Jewry increasingly moved out of its traditional economic niches and into competition with others, particularly those Ukrainians struggling to move into middle-class trades and the industrial labor force.[41] Even more significant perhaps was the internal disintegration of the Jewish community, the loosening of traditional bonds of communal affiliation. Modernity invaded even the Torah-centered life of Ukrainian Jewry, and more and more young Jews looked to Western modes of thought and political expression.

Before the 1905 revolution, little political activity was tolerated in the autocratic empire of the tsars, but socialist thought had gained wide currency among underground political organizations. Some antisemitic tendencies were evident in early Ukrainian socialism, most notably in the call of the Ukrainian "People's Will" (*Narodnia volia*) movement for pogroms against the Jews, which hoped in this manner to incite a mass rebellion against the tsarist authorities. The general trend of socialist thought, however, emphasized class conflict rather than nationality conflict. In the late nineteenth century, the common Russian interpretation of socialism held that the preservation of nationality differences was counterproductive, and served only to keep the masses blinded to their "true enemies," the exploiting classes of capitalists, industrialists, and speculators.[42]

This critique of nationalism, however, was unpalatable to socialists who wished to retain some of their national distinctiveness, in particular, the rights to their own language. Here, Ukrainian and Jewish socialists found a common ground for dialogue. Neither Ukrainian nor Yiddish was considered a full-fledged language in some circles. Many Russians regarded Ukrainian as a quaint southern dialect and called Yiddish, quite literally, "jargon." This meeting of minds found its greatest expression in the poorly defined political theory generally known as Autonomism.

Autonomism can be seen in many ways as a transitional model directed at societies moving from a medieval hierarchical structure to the modern notion of individual citizenship without regard to religious or ethnic identity. This trend in Western politics, at least in terms of the Jews, can be traced to the French Revolution, with its slogans of *liberté, égalité, fraternité*, which in theory applied to the Jews as well as to the Catholic French. For centuries, the Jews had been tolerated as a separate group within European countries and accorded the special privileges and disabilities associated with being *servi camerae*, immediately subservient to the royal court. Jews were often given exclusive rights to pursue certain occupations, particularly in trading and moneylending, although a share of the profits went to the king's treasury. In this position, Jews were granted residence privileges only on the good will of the king. Any realignment of church-state relations, for example, or a special charter given to a particular town, could potentially result in mass expulsion.[43]

The French Revolution initiated a movement to reform Jewish status. Emancipation and full civil rights were first extended to the French-speaking Sephardi Jews in Bordeaux, and shortly afterward to the more "foreign" Yiddish-speaking Ashkenazi population.[44] In response to popular opposition, however, in the early nineteenth century Napoleon was forced to reexamine the situation. With his typical taste for actions on a grand scale, he decided to "reconvene" the *Sanhedrin*, the Jewish high court, which had not met since the Temple era some two thousand years earlier. Napoleon posed a series of questions to this body aimed at determining the relationship of the French Jewish community to the new country and hoped to receive a definitive, authoritative answer. In essence, he asked if French Jews regarded themselves primarily as French citizens of the Jewish faith or as Jews who happened to reside in French territory. The *Sanhedrin* duly answered to Napoleon's satisfaction. Thus, a European Jewish community for the first time committed itself to being a religious community of national citizens (here French), rather than one of Jews with residence privileges.[45]

The problem was different in Eastern Europe. Eastern Jews were generally far more numerous, religious, and insular than in the west.[46] Furthermore, the Western-oriented Jewish enlightenment, or *Haskalah*, was far less influential in the east. Unlike the relatively homogenous ethnicities of Western Europe, the eastern regions were typically multinational, with large groups of different peoples living within one empire. Although granting of full citizenship and equality to every inhabitant was seen as a positive measure, the problem of maintaining nationality rights within these large states required special attention. The Jewish political leadership found a solution in Autonomism.

The ideological roots of Autonomism are often traced to the Austrians Karl Renner and Otto Bauer.[47] Neither Renner nor Bauer, however, regarded the Jews as a nationality deserving special status.[48] Both thinkers were considerably antedated by the Ukrainian Mykhailo Drahomanov (Dragomanov),[49] who devoted energy specifically to the Jewish question. He has sometimes been labeled, incorrectly, as an antisemite, but this is clearly the result of a misunderstanding of his thought.[50] A thoroughgoing socialist, Drahomanov deplored the sometimes exploitative economic practices of Ukrainian Jewry, yet as early as 1875 he argued for the preservation and encouragement of their national distinctiveness.[51] In 1880 Drahomanov published a pamphlet by a mysterious "Rodin," who claimed to be writing "On Behalf of a Group of Jewish Socialists," calling on them to abandon Russian in favor of the vernacular Yiddish for their press (some fifteen years before Jewish socialists adopted a similar measure) and suggesting an alliance between Jewish and Ukrainian socialists.[52] The basis for this alliance was to be the mutual support of each other's national distinctiveness, to be expressed for Jews in the form of self-government at the local level, the essential unit of all later theories of autonomy.[53]

Individual thinkers, including Chaim Zhitlowsky, spread these concepts to the Jews of the tsarist empire over the next few decades, but with only partial success.[54] Beginning in 1897, a series of articles by the renowned historian Simon Dubnow (1860–1941) was published in the influential Russian-Jewish journal *Voskhod*, which significantly increased the popularity of the idea of Jewish national autonomy among politically active Jews.

Dubnow, whose three-volume *History of the Jews in Russia and Poland* and ten-volume *Weltgeschichte des jüdisches Volkes (World History of the Jewish People)* remain classics of Jewish historiography,[55] had spent years studying a Jewish institution that undoubtedly inspired his political theory: the early modern "Council of Lands." The Council of Lands (also known as the Council of Four Lands) was an unusual institution for its time, and it is no surprise that the period of its existence coincided with the golden age of Eastern European Jewry. The Council of Lands acted as a guarantor of the growing Jewish community in ways both physical and spiritual, and served to ground Jewish civilization in the region for centuries. The Council was basically an umbrella organization stretching from the Baltic to the Black seas that encompassed all the local Jewish municipalities and acted as an extended form of Jewish self-government within the larger Polish-Lithuanian Commonwealth.[56]

Jews, it should be recalled, constituted a highly distinct minority in Eastern Europe and were distinguished from their neighbors by religion, language, economic profile, and a host of other measures. To preserve the religious and social aspects of this civilization, Jews have historically organized themselves into local self-governing bodies known as *kehiles*, which center on a rabbinical court *(beis din)* for the resolution of disputes and a network of self-help organizations *(khevres)* to administer to the needs of the community. The *kehile* leadership regulated all aspects of Jewish life, from the conferring of religious honors and privileges in the synagogue to the establishment of economic regulations. All Jews were members of the *kehile*, and in exchange for its governing activity, they paid regular taxes, which were assessed by the representatives of the *beis din* or took the form of a surcharge for religious necessities such as *shabes* candles or kosher meat. Nonconformance with the rulings of the *beis din* was perilous, since the court had the right to impose a series of sanctions that varied from a temporary ban (*kherem, nidui*) to the denial of vital services such as burial.

The power of the *kehiles* was guaranteed by the authority of the Polish-Lithuanian Commonwealth. Most significantly, the *kehiles* formed an overall governing body that regulated standards for all of the various *kehiles* in the Commonwealth, effectively making the Council a type of Jewish parliament within the structure of the non-Jewish state. The Council was free to pass legislation, in conformance with Talmudic law, which affected all the Jewish citizens of the region. As the Commonwealth declined, however, the Council suffered a similar dissolution and did not survive the tumultuous eighteenth century. Tsar Nicholas I dealt the *kehiles* terrible blows in 1844 with legislation that severely limited their activity.[57] Nevertheless, the far-reaching authority of the Council at its peak prompted late nineteenth-century Jewish thinkers to look to it as an inspiration and a model for new forms of Jewish self-government in the modern era.

Under the provocative title "Letters on Old and New Judaism," Dubnow argued that nationalism was essentially a transient, evolutionary phenomenon linked to the relative maturity of a people.[58] The first of three stages of nationalism, according to his theory, was tribal in nature and dated from prehistoric times. A group of individuals linked together by common ancestry would form a rudimentary political framework to coordinate their activities. Later this group would evolve into a political-territorial nationalism by conquering or being conquered by other clans in the vicinity, and the object of group loyalty would shift from the extended family to the territory in which the group lived. The vast majority of national identities in the early twentieth century corresponded to this second stage, with one exception. The Jews, for Dubnow, represented the pinnacle of national development, and their lack of sovereignty was precisely the reason. The Jews had succeeded in attaining the third and highest level, "cultural-historical" or "spiritual" nationalism, and learned to maintain a national culture without sharing a common language or territory.[59]

> There is...[a] rigid test for the maturity of a nation. When a people loses not only its political independence but also its land, when the storm of history uproots it and removes it far from its natural homeland and it becomes dispersed and scattered in alien lands, and in

> addition loses its unifying language; if, despite the fact that the external national bonds have been destroyed, such a nation still maintains itself for many years, creates an independent existence, reveals a stubborn determination to carry on its autonomous development—such a people has reached the highest stage of cultural-historical individuality and may be said to be indestructible, if only it cling forcefully to its national will. We have many examples in history of nations that have become dispersed among other nations. We find only one instance, however, of a people that has survived for thousands of years despite dispersion and loss of homeland. This unique people is the people of Israel.[60]

Dubnow's philosophy affirmed the exile of the Jews, preserving a Jewish nationalism without succumbing to assimilation or demanding political-territorial power, both of which Dubnow considered a step backward. Often referred to as extraterritorial autonomy, it posited the creation of local centers of self-government for Jews without affecting the overall state apparatus. Politically, Dubnow argued for the development of institutions that would promote Jewish cultural, educational, and religious activities within a larger, multinational state. The practical application of this philosophy of Autonomism was a matter of considerable debate. In general, however, it was seen as a resurrection of a sort of the Council of Lands but with one important distinction: while the Council was led by religious authorities, the Jewish national autonomy was to be secular.

This theoretical Jewish national autonomy would comprise four structural components: the local *kehiles* elected by the local Jewish population; a Jewish parliament whose delegates represented each of the *kehiles* and/or the Jewish political parties; a Nationality Council (*Natsional-Rat*), the executive body or cabinet of the Jewish parliament; and a Minister of Jewish Affairs in the state parliament. The candidate for this latter post would be appointed either by the Nationality Council or by the state parliament with the approval of the Nationality Council.

Jewish national autonomy—as an institution—would perform two basic functions. As an umbrella group of the *kehiles*, it would coordinate activities and standardize policies for all the members of the Jewish population. Second, it would act as the major point of liaison between the Jewish community and the greater state apparatus, lobbying for Jewish interests and administering some state functions to the

Jewish community. The relationship between the Jewish national autonomy and the government was mutually beneficial, as both sides could work to support each other's policies. Besides lending financial and legal support to the activities of the Jewish community, for example, the state could enforce compliance, both Jewish and non-Jewish, with the decrees of the Jewish national autonomy. In return, the Jewish national autonomy could assist with all state-related affairs such as conscription, taxation, and so on. In a manner similar to the corporate structure of the medieval government, the state would deal with its Jewish population not directly but rather through the institution of the Jewish national autonomy. In theory, this sharing of power would work to the advantage of both the multinational state and the individual nationalities within it.

❁

As the folk expression "two Jews, three opinions" suggests, there was to be little agreement on the particulars of Jewish national autonomy. Nevertheless, it is significant that despite the vast ideological rifts separating the various Jewish political parties, all agreed in principle to the desirability of some form of autonomy. The parties, which were usually Ukraine-based branches of international political movements, can be broadly grouped into four categories: Zionists, socialists, Diaspora nationalists, and religious parties, each of which will be elaborated upon below.[61] By way of general introduction, however, it is important to note that Ukrainian Jewish political activity was on the periphery. The epicenter and birthplace of Jewish political activity in the tsarist empire was Vilna (Vilnius), the "Jerusalem of Lithuania."

The "Jewish map" of the tsarist empire was divided into three major areas: Lithuania (which included much of Belarus), Poland, and the "South and Southwest"—meaning Ukraine. These demarcations reflected many fine distinctions in religious ritual, language, and a host of cultural biases and prejudices. The stereotypical *Litvak*, for example, was considered to be cold, rational, and disdainful of the unlettered; if he were religious he would likely be a *misnaged*, or "opponent" of the Hasidic movement. The stereotypical Ukrainian Jew, on the other hand, was jovial, with a tendency to drink and an aversion to serious Talmudic study. These stereotypes have a long and undistinguished history in the evolution of Jewish sub-cultures, and many of their unstated preconceptions had an impact on the development of political infrastructures in the region.[62]

Lithuania enjoyed several social and economic features, many of which were not present in Ukrainian regions, that accelerated the development of Jewish political activity. Lithuanian Jews were far more active in small-scale industry such as craftwork, which employed greater numbers of unskilled laborers and thus accelerated proletarianization, leading to greater levels of trade union activity. In contrast, Jewish politics in Ukraine developed relatively late—primarily in the first two decades of the twentieth century—under the direct influence of Lithuanian activists and for the most part in Kyiv.[63]

As the name implies, the primary goal of the various Zionist parties was to establish a Jewish state in Zion. The major differences between them were related to the particular admixture of socialist or religious ideologies. These Zionist parties, which later proved to command the majority of politically active voters in Ukraine, were by and large united under the direction of the General Zionists, and were in turn part of the World Zionist Organization (WZO), which had been meeting periodically since 1897. Initially, the WZO had been hesitant to deal with the idea of autonomy, since it essentially constituted a diversion of Jewish energies from the Zionist task of rebuilding a homeland in Palestine. After the revolution of 1905 and the waves of pogroms that followed, however, the need for increased Jewish civil and communal rights in the Russian Empire became increasingly evident. At the 1906 meeting of the WZO in Helsingfors (Helsinki), Finland, the delegates approved a resolution affirming the desirability of autonomy.[64] The resolution provided for the eventual establishment of a form of *kehile*-based autonomy, active mainly in the areas of education, health, communal self-help, and religious affairs. Although most Zionists preferred to develop the ancient Hebrew language, the resolution called for the judicial recognition of Yiddish as well, both languages to be acceptable "in the school, at court and in public life."[65] The Tseire Tsion ("Young Zion"), a moderately socialist Zionist party that grew out of a youth group, also supported autonomy.[66] One of the most prominent Jewish supporters of Ukrainian national aspirations was Vladimir Jabotinsky, of the Revisionist Zionist movement.[67]

On the opposite end of the spectrum was the Bund, or General Jewish Workers' League, the most popular of the Jewish socialist parties. Initially formed in 1897, the Bund was openly assimilationist in its early years until it discovered the value of propagandizing the Jewish proletariat in the Yiddish vernacular. In 1899 Chaim Zhitlowsky's article arguing for the whole-hearted acceptance of the "jargon" as a legitimate language of the Jewish people was published in the Bund organ, sparking a huge debate on the orientation of the Bund to autonomy in general and Jewish identity in particular. For years the Bund was divided, since many of its members viewed autonomy for a specific nationality as an impediment to the general socialist movement. The concept was finally accepted at the fifth convention in Zurich in 1903.[68] The term "national-cultural autonomy" was adopted since it seemed to imply a narrower scope than "national-personal" and had none of the separatist connotations of "national-political autonomy."[69] With the revolutions of 1917, the Bund reiterated this position in the first brochure it distributed after the revolution. Autonomy was to include extending full emancipation to Jews and allowing the use of Yiddish in state organs, while reserving power to the central authorities to make decisions that might affect the Jewish population.[70]

The major ideologue of the Bund's view of Jewish nationalism was Vladimir Medem (1879–1923), who developed a curious political theory known as "Neutralism." Seeing nationalism as, on the one hand, detrimental to the development of class consciousness because it set up artificial barriers between proletarians of different nationalities and, on the other hand, as an expression of a vague "general culture" in a specific linguistic and cultural environment, Medem argued for a "neutral" stance vis-à-vis Jewish nationalism. While regarding nationalism as an undesirable phenomenon, Medem argued that it should be tolerated in a way that would allow Jews to acquire revolutionary consciousness, in the hope that in the days of world socialism Jewish nationalism would eventually fade away. The Bund saw Jewish national autonomy, therefore, as restricted to linguistic and cultural spheres alone, and although the *kehile* would form the basic unit, its activities were restricted to cultural affairs.[71] The Bund was also the party with the most distinguished revolutionary heritage, having been formed years before the others. In a survey of 102 of the 106 delegates attending the August 1917 conference of Bund in Kyiv, 41 percent had joined the party previous to the abortive 1905 revolution, another 37 percent between then and the March Revolution, and a further 22 percent in the five months afterward. Moreover, forty-one of the delegates had been arrested a total of 136 times; one particularly unlucky delegate had been arrested twenty times.[72]

The other major Jewish socialist parties were not willing to agree that assimilation was a desirable alternative for the Jews, and argued for a more positive vision of Jewish national identity in the socialist future. Most significant among these parties was the Poale-Tsion ("Workers of Zion"), which combined Zionism with socialism at a 1906 convention in Poltava.[73] In the same year, the Poale-Tsion formulated a platform on national autonomy that was broadly similar to the Zionist idea. The next year, the party defined this as territorial autonomy in Palestine and national-personal autonomy elsewhere.[74] The Poale-Tsion, also known as the Jewish Social Democratic Workers' Party, was consistently allied with the socialist bloc during the years of the Ukrainian revolution until the party split in 1919.

The third broad category of Jewish political parties was that of the Diaspora nationalists, who, unlike the Zionists, saw a positive future for Jews in the Diaspora to the possible exclusion of a Jewish state in Palestine. In contrast to the Bund, however, the Diaspora nationalists saw intrinsic value in the preservation and development of a Jewish national consciousness. In short, these parties were the most likely champions of Jewish national autonomy, and it is not surprising that they provided the future Ministry of Jewish Affairs with much of its leadership. Ideologically the most significant of these parties was the People's Party (Folkspartey, not to be confused with the Folksgruppe), founded by Simon Dubnow in 1906, which followed the ideology he had earlier formulated in his "Letters on Old and New Judaism."[75] Despite his contribution to Jewish political theory, however, Dubnow's party failed to gain a significant measure of popularity.

Another Diaspora nationalist party, the United Socialist Jewish Workers' Party (Fareynikte, sometimes transliterated as Faraynigte or Faraynikte), was more successful. This party was created by the merger, in May 1917, of the Zionist-Socialist Workers' Party (which was not Zionist at all, despite the name) and the Jewish Socialist Workers' Party (SERP-Seymists). The latter was only moderately socialist in ideology, basically following Dubnow's conceptions of autonomy; its merger with the more Marxist Zionist-socialists placed it squarely in the socialist bloc of parties even as it assumed the leadership of the Diaspora nationalists.[76] The party also proved to be quite popular with the merger, claiming between 13,000 and 15,000 members in 1917.[77]

The religious parties constitute the fourth and final category of Jewish political groupings. Although one party (Mizrahi) claimed a specific Zionist orientation, these parties were more explicitly concerned with the defense of traditional Judaic practice. The Agudas Yisroel ("Assembly of Israel"), formed in 1912 as a reaction to the Zionist movement, was actually quite anti-Zionist and viewed the establishment of a Jewish state by human means to be an insult to the divine plan.[78] Faced with the growing success of the atheistic socialist parties, however, the Agudas Yisroel joined Akhdes Yisroel ("Unity of Israel"), a coalition of religious parties allied with the Zionist bloc.[79]

Although the discussion has to this point focused on the specifically Jewish parties, that is, parties that were devoted to Jewish interests primarily or exclusively,[80] Jews were also members of general political parties in Ukraine, but their activities in relation to the Jewish community (and often their affiliations with the Jewish community) were minimal. Indeed, it is well known that Jewish Communists commonly distanced themselves from their Jewish origins as much as possible.[81] Leon Trotsky, for example, was described by his friend Max Eastman as being "as little bothered about, or influenced by, his being a Jew as any Jewish person I ever knew," to the point of denying his father a Jewish burial.[82] The Jewish share of these parties was usually disproportionate to the percentage of Jews in the overall population, a phenomenon probably related more to Jewish urbanization patterns than to Jewish ethnicity.[83] Nevertheless, they constituted only a small minority of the parties under consideration, virtually all of which were dominated by Russians. Figures for the Communist party in Ukraine, for example, clearly indicate this phenomenon. Partial statistics from 1917, before the influx of Jews, indicate that although Jews constituted roughly 4 percent of the membership of the Communist (Bolshevik) Party in the former tsarist empire, this amounted to 964 Jews, only some of whom may have come from Ukraine.[84] The Bund, in contrast, had reported a membership of 30,000 a dozen years earlier.[85]

It is also worth noting that while the percentage of Jews in the Communist Party of Ukraine (UkCP) was somewhat disproportionate to their percentage in the total population, their relative weight in the

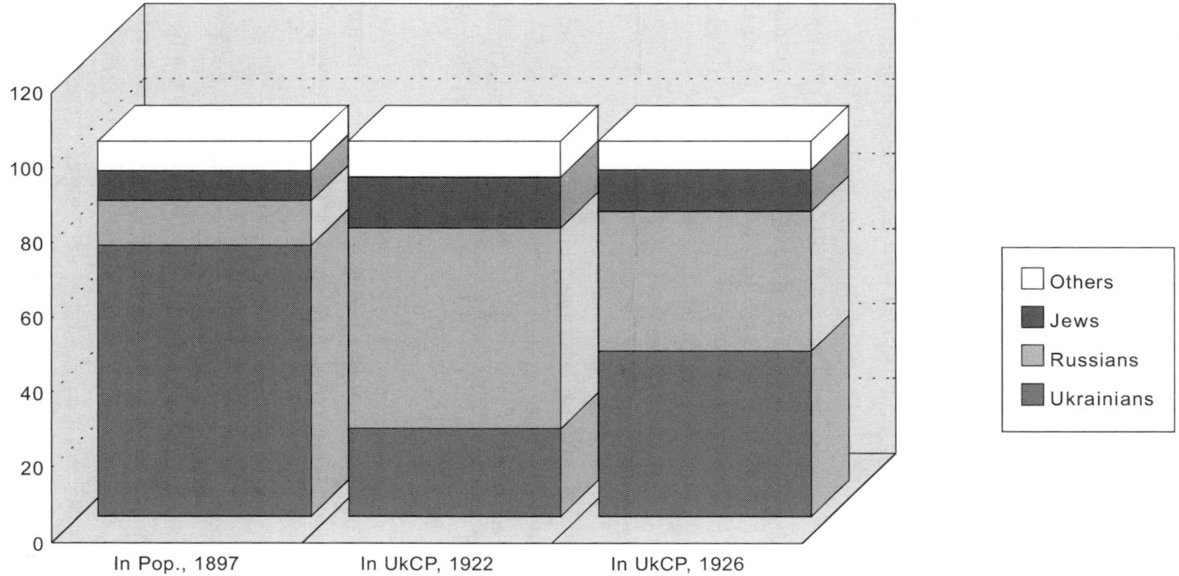

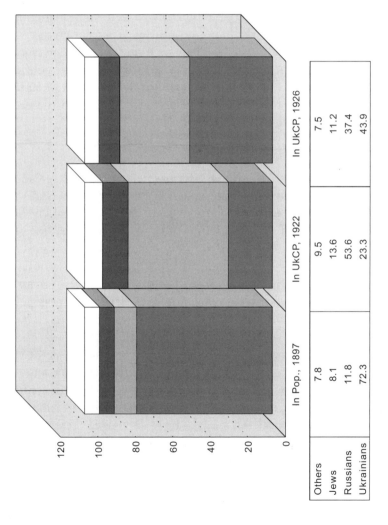

	In Pop., 1897	In UkCP, 1922	In UkCP, 1926
Others	7.8	9.5	7.5
Jews	8.1	13.6	11.2
Russians	11.8	53.6	37.4
Ukrainians	72.3	23.3	43.9

Figure 1.7. National Composition of the Communist Party of Ukraine, 1922–1926 (percent)
Source: Perepis'; Borys, *Sovietization*, p. 89.

party steadily declined after the revolution with the influx of Ukrainians (see Figure 1.7). In 1922, Jews were 13.6 percent of the UkCP (Russians 53.6 percent, Ukrainians 23.3 percent), but by 1926 Jews had been reduced to 11.2 percent and Russians to 37.4 percent, while Ukrainian membership had increased to 43.9 percent. Even in 1927, when the percentage of Jews in the party as a whole was still high (20,306 members, some 12.1 percent of the CPSU), this accounted for only 129 party members out of every 10,000 Jews in Ukraine.[86] Despite these statistics, Jews were often perceived as revolutionaries and generally as agents of corruption in tsarist Russia, a perception that will be discussed in greater detail in Chapters 4 and 5. Another crucial caveat is the fact that, despite the wide spectrum of Jewish political movements, most Ukrainian Jews were politically quiescent or, at the very least, disinclined to register their political leanings in the elections to the Jewish pre-parliament (see Chapter 3 below).

The notion of Ukrainian antisemitism has become so widespread in popular thinking that it is quite common for North Americans to associate Ukrainians with antipathy to Jews. This is particularly true for the second half of the twentieth century, as attention has focused on Ukrainians who collaborated with the Nazis. Despite this proverbial antisemitism, however, remarkably few scholarly studies of it have appeared.[87] The reality of Ukrainian-Jewish relations was far more complex, and many factors have gone into shaping the current popular attitude. Two may be noted briefly here. First, the twentieth century represents the nadir of Ukrainian-Jewish relations. Although there have been notable moments of cooperation (including some of the events described in this work, for example, and the years surrounding the collapse of the Soviet Union), more Jews have died in this century as a result of Ukrainian violence than during the rest of Ukrainian-Jewish history as a whole. Ukrainians have also suffered tremendous devastations in this century, both in terms of actual human losses in the famine of 1932–1933 and in the Second World War, and in terms of cultural and political oppression. The latter is often attributed, at least in the popular Ukrainian *mentalité*, to the activity of Jewish Communists such as Lazar Kaganovich. In the latter half of the twentieth century, Jews and Ukrainians have historical precedent for perceiving each other with mistrust. Second, these hostile attitudes are particularly strong in the West, since the postwar children of emigrés have a less sophisticated view of the Eastern European reality than their immigrant parents and grandparents. Elements of coexistence are forgotten in the context of episodic violence. In sum, Zvi Gitelman has identified a phenomeon of "Jewish Ukrainophobia" as "a historical myth [that has] been created and effectively transmitted...there is a readiness to believe in Ukrainian anti-Semitism, a historically shaped mind-set that can understand and interpret Ukrainian actions and characteristics."[88]

Premodern Ukrainian antisemitism, which persisted well into the twentieth century, was basically socioeconomic in nature. It should be distinguished clearly from the more religiously inspired antisemitism of medieval Western Europe, and the more political and racial versions of the late nineteenth century. Ukrainians were so ignorant of these "developments" in antisemitic theory that the anonymous author of a 1919 pamphlet who used the term *antysemityzm* felt the need to be explicit and define it as "anti-Jewish" (*proty ievreiska*).[89]

This is not to say that elements besides the social and the economic were totally without precedent in Ukrainian antisemitism. Jews figure prominently, and negatively, in the earliest Church writings in Ukraine. One scholar noted that "we find, rather appallingly, that they are engrossed by the problem of Judaism...it is the only theological subject which is treated...at length, with never tiring attention."[90] Particularly, though not exclusively, illustrative of early Church attitudes toward Jews is this passage from the biography of Feodosyi:

> The blessed one [Feodosyi] had the custom of getting up at night without anyone's knowledge and going out to the Jews to argue with them about Christ, reproaching and reviling them, and calling them rebellious and lawless, because he wanted to be killed preaching about Christ.[91]

Legal documents from this period record several examples of anti-Jewish legislation, including a ban on sexual contact between Jews and Christians. Henrik Birnbaum's conclusion that the anti-Jewish attitudes of this era represent a type of antisemitism "with its modern, that is, racist, implication and not merely its connotation of religious intolerance,"[92] seems, however, difficult to accept. Much of this legislation might also be explained as intended to protect less well-versed Christians from exposure to Jewish ideas and practices thought potentially corrosive to their faith, in short, as a theological matter with social implications.

In reality, the essence of the Ukrainian grievance against Jews in the premodern era is based in their economic relationship. Prior to the Khmel'nyts'kyi rebellion, many Jews were active participants in the Polish policy of exploiting Ukrainians. Simon Dubnow's famous characterization of the Jews as caught "between hammer and anvil"—that is, between the demands of the Polish lords and the anger of the Ukrainian peasants—is simply misleading.[93] For Ukrainians, the Jews were very much a part of the "hammer," the economic machinery that extended and enforced Polish control over Ukraine. This fact was obvious to the earliest chroniclers of the massacre. Nathan of Hannover's *Yeven Metsulah* described Polish oppression with scriptural allusions that even compared the Ukrainians to the Jews under Egyptian bondage:

> ...[the Ukrainians] were looked upon as lowly and inferior beings and became the slaves and handmaids of the Polish people and the Jews... "their lives were made bitter by hard labor, in mortar and bricks" [Exodus 1:14]...so wretched and lowly had they become that all classes of people, even the lowliest among them [i.e. Jews] became their overlords.[94]

Ukrainian attacks on Jews during the Khmel'nyts'kyi rebellion and during Gonta's uprising of the next century must be seen as essentially anti-Polish and anti-Catholic uprisings.[95] These massacres of Jews, while horrific, were epiphenomenal to the central aspects of the conflict. The period under discussion in this study, however, marks a significant change in the nature of the Ukrainian-Jewish conflict. Medieval antisemitism in Ukraine was primarily confined to the religious arena, an elevated theological dispute with rare outbursts of communal violence. Premodern antisemitism in Ukraine, which extended to the beginning of the twentieth century in many regions, was primarily social and economic in nature, reflecting the pressure points in the castelike division of labor as market forces were increasingly brought to bear in Ukrainian society. With the Ukrainian revolution, however, the conflict takes on unmistakably *political* overtones.

Chapter Two

The Establishment of Jewish Autonomy

On March 8, 1917, a starving woman participating in a march commemorating International Women's Day threw a stone through a baker's window in Petrograd (St. Petersburg), the capital of the huge Russian Empire.[1] According to the British military attaché, this was what started all the "trouble." As the food riot quickly spread throughout the city, popular discontent was directed against the last of the tsars, Nicholas II, and his repressive autocracy. Within days the rock that shattered the baker's window also succeeded in destroying what was then the world's largest state: the corpulent, bureaucratic Russian Empire. Often referred to as the February Revolution, using the Julian calendar followed in the Russian Empire until 1918, the successful insurrection marked the end of several centuries of Romanov rule.

The fall of the last tsar was marked not by the immediate succession of the Communists, but by an attempt at liberal democracy in the form of the Provisional Government, which was hastily cobbled together by the members of the largely redundant Russian parliament. For a brief nine months (March to November 1917) the Provisional Government and its last chairman, Aleksandr Kerenskii, desperately attempted to maintain the political and spiritual unity of the far-flung territories of the empire, many of which had been proceeding along their own centrifugal paths for decades.

Kyiv, long a provincial outpost of the tsar in St. Petersburg, found itself momentarily rudderless when a telegram arrived on March 13 reporting on the revolution in the capital.[2] In those first confusing days, leadership of the city centered in City Hall, where the representatives of the old guard vied with previously disenfranchised elements for control. A compromise was reached in the formation of the Council of United Community Organizations of Kyiv (*Sovet Obedinennykh*

Obshchestvennykh Organizatsii goroda Kieva, abbreviated here as CUCO), which brought together representatives from various political, cultural, and ethnic groups, including Jews and Ukrainians. Dominated by Russians, CUCO was recognized by the Provisional Government as its authoritative representative in Kyiv.[3]

Initially, Jewish organizations were attracted to the Provisional Government in general and to CUCO in particular. The Provisional Government had been quick to promise sweeping democratic reforms while preserving order among the remnants of the tsarist empire. With the announcement of its formation on March 14, the Provisional Government declared the "abolition of all class, religious, and national restrictions," which implied the destruction of the hated residency laws that confined the Jews to the Pale of Settlement.[4] Even the tradition-oriented Orthodox Jews, after a waiting period to ensure that the revolution was in fact final, greeted the Provisional Government with enthusiasm.[5]

It was not long before Jewish political opinion shifted, however, in favor of the Ukrainian Central Rada (Council), another newly established institution that rivaled CUCO for leadership of all Ukraine. Headed by Professor Mykhailo Hrushevs'kyi, the dean of Ukrainian historical scholarship and a political moderate, the Rada initially demanded only limited autonomous rights within a federated Russia, particularly, though not exclusively, in cultural and linguistic matters. In the early days of the revolution, the Central Rada seemed more like a special-interest lobbying group than an effective governing body. In their first statement to the Ukrainian people, for example, the Central Rada tentatively asked for private donations to support its activities.[6] Nevertheless, the Rada became the focus of all Ukrainian-oriented political activity within a short time and eventually succeeded in winning the support of the traditionally Russocentric Jewish community.

The groundwork for the Ukrainian-Jewish *rapprochement* had been prepared by Ukrainian political movements in the prerevolutionary period. The influence of Mykhailo Drahomanov was critical in bringing the significance of the Jewish presence to the attention of early Ukrainian activists and, as noted in Chapter 1, some Ukrainian political circles adopted Jewish autonomy as a platform even before the

Jewish parties themselves came to support it. Ukrainian political theory in the early twentieth century was clearly moving in the direction of harmonious cooperation with national minorities, especially Jews.

The incentive for the establishment of the Central Rada came from a small party called the Ukrainian Party of Socialist-Federalists (USF), originally known as the Society of Ukrainian Progressives. It was a moderately socialist party distinguished primarily by its leader, Mykhailo Hrushevs'kyi, considered by many to be the father of modern Ukrainian nationalism.[7] As a historian, Hrushevs'kyi had devoted considerable attention to the millenial Jewish presence in Ukraine. During the revolutionary period, he consistently advocated tolerance of minorities in his vision of a democratic, multinational Ukraine.[8] Hrushevs'kyi was later elected president of the Central Rada.

Also significant for the leadership of the Central Rada was the Ukrainian Social Democratic Labor Party (USDLP). The most prominent members of this party were the playwright Volodymyr Vynnychenko and the journalist Symon Petliura. Their occupational background was typical of many of the early political activists, since the repressive atmosphere in the tsarist empire had created a situation in which "literature became more a carrier of national consciousness and a surrogate for political action than a form of art."[9] The USDLP had long agitated for cultural independence from its larger brother, the Russian Social Democratic Labor Party, and had developed considerable sympathy for subjugated nationalities.[10] Another leading member of the USDLP, Mykola Porsh, has been credited with being "the intellectual bridge between the vague concept of minority rights and the concept of national-personal autonomy," based on his 1907 pamphlet advocating the decentralization of power in the tsarist empire.[11]

The most popular party was the Ukrainian Socialist Revolutionary Party (USRP). Like the USDLP, the USRP was affiliated with a Russian party, the Russian Socialist Revolutionary Party. Although USRP members were less prominent among the leadership of the Ukrainian movement, the party remained a staunch advocate of Jewish autonomy from well before the revolutionary period and had published many works advocating this platform, including some writings of Chaim Zhitlowsky.[12] By way of contrast, the Russian Socialist Revolutionary Party did not resolve in favor of national-personal autonomy until the summer of 1917.[13]

Taken together, the appointment of Hrushevs'kyi to the presidency of the Central Rada and the prominence of the USDLP with the support of the popular USRP effectively silenced any antisemitic voices in the early months of the Ukrainian revolution. This is not to deny their presence. The right-wing Ukrainian Party of Socialist-Independentists (UPSI) often took an anti-Jewish position. Led by Mykola Mikhnovs'kyi (1873–1924), a long-standing Ukrainian national activist, the UPSI followed a definition of Ukrainian citizenship that was based on narrow ethnic grounds. His ideas were particularly relevant to the development of interwar integral nationalism among Ukrainians, but during the revolution he was not successful in mobilizing wide-spread support.[14] The UPSI was composed primarily of soldiers or veterans who, in the words of Jurij Borys, were "determined separatists...[a] little group of fanatical nationalists."[15] The Ukrainian political leadership had come to realize the desirability of coming to terms with the Jewish population, however, and these more radical opinions remained a small, if distinct voice in the early days of the Ukrainian revolution.[16]

There were three basic reasons for Ukrainian support for Jewish autonomy.[17] First, the concept was very much in keeping with the general utopian tenor of socialist ideology, which envisioned a democratic paradise where the working classes of all nationalities would work in harmony to build a democratic, socialist future. Second, and more pragmatically, the overwhelmingly agrarian Ukrainians lacked a native bourgeoisie. Volodymyr Vynnychenko referred to this in his memoirs:

> Where are the forces which would constitute these organs...[of government]? Well, there is a need for thousands of experienced, educated, and nationally-conscious people in order to fill all the governmental positions and all the institutions, beginning with the ministers and ending up with the secretaries in the offices. Where are these people? Where could they be found, when we did not have our own schools and when we had no possibility of having our own mass intelligentsia from which we could select these experienced, educated, and nationally conscious people? Well, there are probably enough for the ministers, but after that?[18]

The cities, as noted previously, were Russian-Jewish-Polish islands in a Ukrainian sea. Although a significant number of Ukrainians lived in major cities such as Kyiv, the Jewish presence in middle-sized towns and villages, particularly on the right-bank, was often a heavy majority.[19] Jews in these rural areas had a literacy rate of 47 percent, far higher than that of the Ukrainians (18 percent) or the Russians (24 percent) (see Figure 1.6). Ukrainians had depended on Jewish commercial activity for centuries, and early Ukrainian activists realized that this dependence would have to be maintained, at least until the demographic imbalance changed. Furthermore, while Russians and Poles also formed a significant segment of the commercial community, they were likely to be less sympathetic to the Ukrainian movement than were Jews. They could look north and west to large numbers of powerful co-nationals, while Jews were minorities wherever they lived and were therefore more eager to establish harmonious relations with the local authorities.

Finally, the extension of national-personal autonomy to Jews became a stick with which to beat the Provisional Government in St. Petersburg.[20] While the Ukrainians were demanding territorial autonomy, that is, limited self-rule intended to increase the level of Ukrainian national and cultural activity, the Russian center was attempting to inflate the power of the minorities in Ukraine beyond their proportion in the population. By granting national-personal autonomy, the Ukrainians could effectively address the concerns of the Provisional Government and bring minorities into the debate on the Ukrainian side.[21] In short, Jewish autonomy proved to be desirable to the Ukrainian movement for ideological, practical, and strategic reasons.

It is not surprising that the initial impulse of the organized Jewish community was to align itself with the traditional sources of authority in Kyiv, specifically with the City Hall, revitalized as CUCO. The orbit of politically conscious Jews traditionally revolved around the Russian-dominated cities and not the Ukrainian countryside. The maintenance of the *Rechtsstaat*, a lawful society that could adequately guarantee order and peace, was controlled by the tsarist authorities and not their Ukrainian subjects. To be sure, Jews had little sympathy for the tsarist government, which increasingly adopted antisemitic policies. Russian antisemitism was fueled by the appearance of the fraudulent "Protocols of the Elders of Zion," which claimed to reveal the existence of a Jewish conspiracy for world domination.[22] Between 1905 and 1916, over fourteen million copies of nearly three thousand antisemitic works were published, and Nicholas himself is alleged to have contributed over twelve million rubles for this purpose.[23] Nicholas also firmly believed that the Jews were at the forefront of the revolutionary movement and he financially supported the notorious Union of Russian People, popularly known as the Black Hundreds (*Chernye sotni*).[24] Side by side with the government, the Black Hundreds agitated in favor of the infamous trial of Mendel Beilis (in Kyiv, 1911–1913). The trial revolved around a young boy who had been found murdered. An innocent Jew was accused of slaughtering him to use his blood in Jewish ritual (the infamous "blood libel" that dates from medieval times).[25] At the boy's funeral, the Black Hundreds distributed a leaflet that proclaimed:

> Orthodox Christians! The Jews have tortured to death the little boy Andrei Iushchina! The Jews torture to death several dozens of young boys every year before their Pessah [*sic*], for adding their blood to the Mazza [*sic*]. The Jews do this to remind them of the suffering of the Savior whom the Jews tortured to death by crucifying him... [gruesome details left out here]. Russians! If the life of your children is dear to you, beat the Jews! Beat them until there is not a single Jew in Russia. Have mercy on your children. Take revenge for the innocent sufferers! It is time, it is time.[26]

Beilis was eventually acquitted by a jury of Ukrainian peasants, but Jews continued to be treated with contempt by the government. Their loyalties suspect, they suffered when Nicholas continued a long-standing tradition of abrupt expulsions by forcing some 600,000 Jews to leave areas near the front lines, causing tremendous hardship.[27]

Despite these drastic measures, Jews were more concerned with maintaining law and order than risking social upheaval through a radical change of authority. Several Jewish organizations, therefore, sent representatives to CUCO, and a delegate was appointed to its Executive.[28] Over the summer, however, the mood of Jewish political opinion shifted dramatically, from a Russian to a Ukrainian orientation. There were three basic reasons for this shift. First, as the Ukrainian movement rapidly demonstrated its popular strength, the Provisional Government looked increasingly frail and ephemeral. The Jewish political leadership began to realize that the Ukrainian hand was stronger and might eventually exercise effective control over the region, possibly through some form of self-rule.[29] Ukrainian strength was demonstrated in a march in Kyiv on April 1, which drew some 100,000 participants marching under 320 yellow and blue flags.[30] Similar congresses and demonstrations became more frequent, and when the Ukrainian National Congress was convened in mid-April, it was evident that Jewish politicians had taken notice of this dark horse.

The Jews formed a Council of Jewish Organizations in late March, in part to come to grips with the possibility that the Ukrainians might be successful in realizing their territorial demands.[31] The Council decided to continue relations with the young Rada and later greeted the Ukrainian National Congress on April 21 with the traditional salutation, *slava* (glory).[32]

The Ukrainians also impressed Jewish political activists with their devotion to the principle of autonomy, although the definition of the term was yet to be clearly articulated. The principle of autonomy required the recognition of nationality rights as well as personal rights, including, for example, culture-specific education. The Provisional Government maintained its commitment to general emancipation yet refused to advocate any type of national rights for any particular nationality.[33] The Ukrainian movement, on the other hand, stressed territorial autonomous rights for the Ukrainian nationality within a federated Russian Republic, and a transition eventually granting extraterritorial autonomy to Jews seemed natural. The most fervent advocate of minority rights, after all, was the president of the Ukrainian Central Rada, Mykhailo Hrushevs'kyi. In a series of articles published in local newspapers, Hrushevs'kyi consistently promoted the development of the multinational concept, "with broad popular representation in the government and no discrimination on the basis of ethnic, religious, or social criteria."[34]

Along with the growing strength of the Ukrainian movement and its overt devotion to the principle of autonomy, the third and final reason for the shift in Jewish opinion was the firm stand the Ukrainian movement initially took in favor of the continued political unity of the former lands of the Tsarist Empire. Ukraine was to take its place as an autonomous entity in a new, federated Russian Republic.[35] The maintenance of political unity was a *sine qua non* for the Ukrainian-Jewish *rapprochement*, and when this plank was dropped from the Ukrainian platform in early 1918, cooperation between Ukrainians and Jews began to founder. This principle was important to Ukrainian Jews for several reasons. For socialists, the preservation of the political integrity of the territory was especially important for maintaining the broadest possible "revolutionary front," while for Zionists it meant the potential mobilization of the largest mass of Jewry for their own political ends. It should be noted that Jewish political parties in Ukraine were invariably branches of larger, all-Russian parties, but even more important was the fact that the very concept of a *Ukrainian* Jewry was almost totally absent from the *Weltanschauung* of the Jews of the Russian Empire.

A specifically Ukrainian Jewish identity had failed to develop in Ukraine, even though the history of Jews in the region stretches back some two millennia and the population reached roughly two million at the beginning of this century.[36] It is true that a Jew from, say, Odesa would recognize distinctive "national" characteristics in a coreligionist from Vilnius. The Yiddish dialect would be slightly different, the clothing could be quite different, and even the liturgy of the thrice-daily prayers might be different. Yet beyond their regional identities these Jews would clearly identify themselves as Russian Jews rather than as Ukrainian or Lithuanian, particularly in emigration. (The concept of, for example, a "Midwestern Jew" only makes sense in a place where there is a concept of "the Midwest." There is not much point in referring to oneself as a Midwestern Jew in Bangkok, where the less precise yet still correct term "American Jew" suffices.) While maintaining a highly distinctive Jewish culture well into the twentieth century, for all intents and purposes Ukrainian Jews defined themselves nationally as Russian, a position that affected the relations of all three nationalities significantly.

There are three readily identifiable reasons for this Russotropism. First, the attitude of Ukrainian Jews was typical of minorities living in multinational states. The ruling power is usually the body most able to guarantee minority interests and is therefore likely to command their loyalties. This orientation has a long-hallowed tradition in Talmudic law. Second, the modern Jewish intelligentsia was far more attracted to Russian literary and social culture than to its Ukrainian counterpart, which was not as well developed in the last decades of tsarist era. Finally, antisemitism was associated with the peasantry, even if it was also evident at higher levels of society and the state bureaucracy. Taken together, these factors served to stunt the development of a Ukrainian Jewish identity.

As noted earlier, minorities are concerned more than anything else with maintaining a *Rechtsstaat*, a society governed by law, as the precondition for their peaceful existence in a potentially hostile environment. It is even acceptable if these laws are moderately discriminatory, just so long as their rights and privileges are clearly defined, and there is some means of legal redress if these limited freedoms are impugned. As a "nonterritorial" minority, the Jews had no independent state in the region (or even a contiguous population concentration) to which they could appeal for assistance in times of need.

The Jews took this loyalty to the ruling powers as, quite literally, a religious concept. The Mishnah, the body of Jewish law codified from oral tradition in the second century, adjures Jews to "pray for the welfare of the government, for were it not for the fear of it, people would swallow each other alive" (*Avot* 3:2). Laws passed by non-Jewish governments are recognized as valid under the Talmudic principle *dina d'malkhuta dina* ("the law of the state is the law," *Bava Kama* 113a; some exceptions apply). Modern prayer books include a blessing for the state that is generally recited every Sabbath. Typical is this text, taken from a nineteenth-century prayer book for the High Holidays:

> The One who gives salvation to kings...may He bless, guard, preserve, aid, raise up, make great, and elevate our lord The Tsar Alexander Nikolaevich, may his glory be exalted, with his wife the honored Tsarina Maria Aleksandrovna and his son the inheritor Nicholas Aleksandrovich, and his sons and daughters. The King who is King over kings, in His mercy may He grant him life, and guard him from all distress and anxiety and harm and rescue him...may his enemies fall before him and make all that he attempts successful. The King who is King over kings, in His mercy may He place mercy in [the Tsar's] heart and in the heart of all his advisors and ministers to do good with us and with all Israel...so that Israel may dwell in security, and may a redeemer come to Israel, let it be His will, and let us say, Amen.[37]

Noteworthy are the dedication to the Tsar's welfare, both personal and national, and the prayer that he deal "mercifully" with the Jewish community. Even if the Tsar were to fulfill this wish, however, it would not be considered an ideal arrangement for the Jews, since the prayer concludes, "and may a redeemer come to Israel," that is, may the Messiah come and remove Jews from this oppression as quickly as possible. In the final analysis, however, earthly kingship is regarded as a privilege that is Divinely apportioned to particular families or individuals.

The fictitious rabbi in *Fiddler on the Roof* teaches that the correct blessing for the Tsar is "May God bless and keep the Tsar—far away from us!" According to authentic Jewish law, however, there actually is such a blessing: "Blessed are You, Lord our God, who has given of His honor to flesh and blood."[38] The Tsar's honor stems directly from the King who is King over kings and commands loyalty as a religious precept. The masses of Ukrainian Jewry, therefore, followed a religious tradition in supporting the Tsar. Their support was primarily passive, and whenever possible more active forms, such as military service, were avoided. The Jews, like other minorities such as the Old Believers, were required to pay a double tax, which "many considered only a compensation for the exemption from military service."[39]

Two very different Jewish intelligentsias coexisted during the late tsarist period. The traditional Talmudic elite headed by individuals such as Rabbi Yisrael Meir Kagan (the *Hafets Haim*) and others, which was respected by the masses of religiously observant Jews,[40] approached the growing Ukrainian movement according to the traditional lines already described. This source of religious authority was being rapidly eclipsed, however, by the increasing popularity of the *Maskilim*, those Jews who supported the *Haskalah* (the Jewish enlightenment). They were abandoning religious observance in favor of nationalist (Zionism), Jewish socialist (mainly Bundism), and assimilationist (e.g., Menshevism, Communism) ideologies. These movements were all essentially European in character and used the political and social vocabulary of modern, particularly Western, Europe.

If Russian culture had achieved a recognized place in the canon of European society, Ukrainian culture had to prove first that it existed at all, then that it was not some subset of Russian culture, and finally, that it was worthy of study and respect. Ukrainian language and literature, which contended with oppressive censorship in the Russian Empire, relied on comparatively few authors, such as Taras Shevchenko (1814-1861) and Ivan Franko (1856–1916), to justify its paternity; a good portion of its literature consisted of peasant-oriented oral traditions collected by nineteenth-century enthusiasts. When the *Maskilim* looked to non-Jewish European cultures, Russian seemed far more attractive. Ukrainian Jews were already familiar with the language, which promised a huge Jewish readership, and Russian culture was the most convenient (if not the least encumbered) means of access to the larger European world of ideas. Although the Zionists struggled to reestablish ancient Hebrew as a vernacular language, and the Jewish Socialists eventually came to exploit Yiddish as a propaganda tool, Jewish scholarly and cultural work was published increasingly in Russian. Ukrainian language and culture simply had too little to offer the *Maskilim*.

The widespread notion that antisemitism was a form of primitive prejudice that could be eliminated, or at least greatly alleviated, through higher education encouraged the *Maskilic* orientation to the Russians. Many Zionists, however, took exception to this attitude, as did the religious masses, who understood antisemitism as a permanent feature of reality with metaphysical implications. In this sense, the poorly educated peasantry was seen as the source of anti-Jewish attitudes. Bureaucrats and other nonpeasants who held antisemitic attitudes suffered from a rather harmful form of ignorance and nothing more. Insofar as Ukrainians were overwhelmingly involved in agriculture, this preconception did little to foster the development of Ukrainian-Jewish ties. The Russians had a large peasant population, but they also had a much larger, sophisticated intelligentsia. The Ukrainian intelligentsia, in contrast, occupied only a thin stratum of Ukrainian society, and many were still undecided about whether to be "Ukrainians" or "Little Russians." When *Maskilim* in Ukraine identified themselves as "Russian Jews," they were not identifying with the entire Russian people, but with that segment of Russians who held modern, Western views in common with their own. They encountered precious few Ukrainians who fit this description.

By guaranteeing the creation of a *Rechtsstaat* within a federated Russian Republic, the Ukrainian movement was able to satisfy Jewish concerns and draw the political leadership into a new and unprecedented alliance. This achievement was useful to the Central Rada, since it was able to rely on Jewish support in its increasingly confrontational relationship with the Provisional Government in Petrograd. In June 1917, after several months of debate, the Central Rada issued its First Universal (proclamation), which read in part:

> Let Ukraine be free! Without separating from all of Russia, without breaking with the Russian state, let the Ukrainian people have the right to manage its own life on its own soil…
>
> No one can know better than we what we need and which laws are best for us…
>
> We thought that the Central Russian [Provisional] Government would extend its hands to us in this task, that in agreement with it, we, *the Ukrainian Central Rada*, would be able to provide order for our land.
>
> But the Provisional Russian Government rejected all our demands; it pushed aside the outstretched hand of the Ukrainian people…
>
> And now, Ukrainian people, we are forced to *create our own destiny*. We cannot permit our land to fall into lawlessness and decline. Since the Russian Provisional Government *cannot* provide order for us, since it *does not want* to join us in this great task, then we must take it upon ourselves. This is our duty to our land and to the peoples who live on our land.
>
> That is why we, *the Ukrainian Central Rada*, issue this Universal to our entire nation and proclaim: from this day forth we shall build our life.[41]

The Universal also contained a passage directed specifically to minorities:

> In cities and those areas where the Ukrainian population lives alongside other nationalities, we urge our citizens to quickly *come to agreement and understanding with the democratic elements of those nationalities*, and jointly begin preparation for a new, orderly existence.
>
> *The Central Rada* hopes that the non-Ukrainian peoples living on our territory will also care for order and peace in our land, and that in this difficult time of disorder in the entire state, they join us in a united and friendly fashion to work for the organization of an *autonomous Ukraine*.[42]

The Bund was the only Jewish party to react negatively to the First Universal. Its Southern Bureau issued a statement claiming that the Universal "places the Ukrainian national movement on the road to a break with revolutionary democracy and establishes the conditions for the internal friction among the population of Ukraine."[43] The Central Rada reacted quickly to this criticism, however, and proposed that a multinationality commission (composed of seventy-one Ukrainians, eleven Russians, eight Jews, two Germans, and six representatives of other nationalities) be formed to draft a constitution, for the time being mollifying the Bund.[44]

At this point the Rada was heavily involved in heated negotiations with the Provisional Government in St. Petersburg. Despite its rather moderate demands, the First Universal posed a unique challenge to the unstable government in the capital of the defunct Tsarist Empire. The Rada took a major step toward the goal of territorial autonomy with the creation of an executive body called the General Secretariat to assume administration of Ukraine. Heading this new body was Volodymyr Vynnychenko (USDLP); the cabinet he presided over included Symon Petliura (USDLP) as General Secretary for Military Affairs and Serhii Iefremov (USF) as General Secretary for "Internationality Affairs."[45] Several days later Aleksandr Kerenskii, the chairman of the Provisional Government, led a delegation to Kyiv to negotiate with the Rada. Although Kerenskii may have hoped to win a better bargain, external political pressures forced his hand, and he acceded in principle to the moderate requests of the Rada. The results were announced in the Second Universal on July 16, 1917, which was issued in four languages: Ukrainian, Yiddish, Polish, and Russian.[46] It stated, in essence, that the Provisional Government would now recognize the Ukrainian Central Rada (which was to be reformed and expanded to include a wider cross-section of the population) as the legitimate authority and representative of the Provisional Government in Ukraine. Although little detail was provided, the Universal clearly indicated that the national minorities of Ukraine would be involved in drafting the legislation that would define the political and administrative structure of the newly autonomous Ukraine.[47]

The Jewish socialist parties were the first to take up the Ukrainian offer. Although the Zionists were by definition dedicated to the principle of national self-determination, it seems that the elderly Ukrainian leadership of the movement (the "Bnei Tsion") vacillated, waiting for instructions from leaders in Moscow and St. Petersburg.[48] The socialists, on the other hand, saw the moment as one ripe with opportunity. The minutes of the local Poale-Tsion in Kyiv reflect this change in attitude. Their meetings in the early spring were informal and haphazard, but by April they had set up a full-time office with a staff of two, and later that month they were self-consciously referring to each other by their formal surnames, a rather strained practice given their former casual terminology.[49] The Rada itself was dominated by socialists, and the First Universal in fact contained an implicit invitation directed at non-Ukrainian socialists in the phrase "democratic elements," which, in the shorthand of the day, meant "socialist parties."

Tensions within the Jewish establishment had erupted in May, when a nonpartisan Regional Jewish Conference was convened. Despite the "Regional" title, over three hundred delegates from several provinces were in attendance to discuss such topics as "On Uniting and Organizing the Jewish Population," "On the Rights of National Minorities in Russia," and "On Autonomy and Federation." According to one of the few memoirs of the period, the man invariably at the center of the controversy was Moshe Rafes, the leader of the Bund, who consistently opposed measures promoted by the Zionist contingent. The conference nearly came to an abrupt end when Rafes and his followers refused to accede to a resolution to symbolically honor the Torah. The resulting brouhaha was contained only when the delegate Sh. An-skii assuaged the intensely anticlerical Bund by suggesting they honor the Torah as a symbol of Jewish culture only.[50] Rafes frequently aroused the ire of his Zionist opponents, invoking many protests against his behavior.[51]

The Jewish socialist parties had also expressed their separatist inclinations by boycotting the nonpartisan Council of Jewish Organizations and forming their own Council.[52] For their part, the Poale-Tsion refused to participate, first because they would be forced to work together with nonsocialist ("bourgeois") elements, and second, because as a small minority on the Council, they would have little opportunity to exercise their own policies, always being compromised by the majority.[53]

The Jewish socialist parties were comparatively well represented in the Ukrainian government, which consisted of three organs. The largest was the Central Rada proper, which met only infrequently. The working body of the Central Rada was the Mala Rada ("Little Coun-

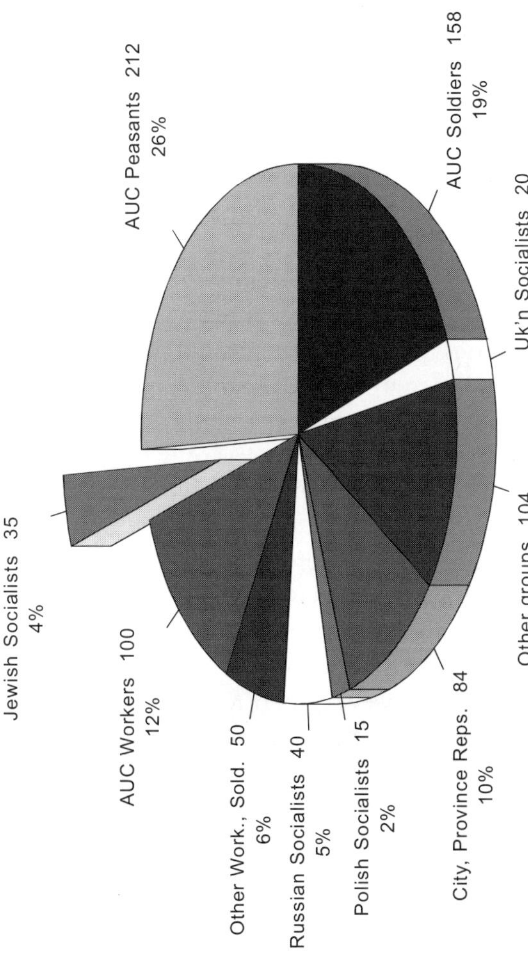

Figure 2.1. Composition of the Central Rada, 1917 (AUC = All-Ukrainian Council)
Source: Doroshenko, *Istoriia Ukraïny*, vol. 1, p. 123.

cil"), a parliament that held frequent and regular deliberations. The executive (cabinet) of the Mala Rada was called the General Secretariat. The Jewish socialist parties were allocated thirty-five seats in the Central Rada, or 4 percent of its total membership (see Figure 2.1, previous page). This was roughly half the proportion of Jews in the region as a whole, but it compared favorably with the number of seats given to the socialist partics of other nationalities: Ukrainians received only 20 seats (2 percent), Russians 40 (4 percent), and Poles 15 (1 percent). Despite the small number of seats given to Ukrainian socialists, Ukrainians still constituted a majority of the Central Rada as representatives of congresses of workers, soldiers, and other groups.[54]

All together, the seats officially reserved for socialist parties in the Central Rada accounted for 13 percent of the total membership. The bulk were held by representatives of other Soviets (Councils) of workers, peasants, and soldiers. The Jewish share of the Central Rada was increased by the presence of deputies appointed by other organizations, most notably in the cities, where Ukrainians did poorly in local elections held that summer. Even in Kyiv, the capital and center of Ukrainian political activity, Ukrainian parties garnered only one-fifth of the seats for the local city government. This was only slightly more than the "Russian Bloc," with their slogan of "Down with Ukraine and Ukrainianization!" (see Figure 2.2, below), and the pattern was repeated in cities all over Ukraine, where Ukrainian parties (sometimes in coalition with Russian parties) received only 27 percent of recorded votes (see Figure 2.3, below).[55] Complete figures for all election results are not available. If the figure for Jewish success in the Kyivan election is generalized for all cities, however, then roughly one-quarter of the city and provincial deputies in the Central Rada would have been Jewish representatives. The Jewish share in the Central Rada would thus be increased to approximately 7 percent, only slightly less than their proportion of the population as a whole.

In the more significant sitting parliament called the Mala Rada, Jews received a much larger share of seats. Of the 199 places, Jewish parties were entitled to 50 (see Figure 2.4, below). Minorities were given a greatly disproportionate share of the seats in the Mala Rada (125 seats, or 63 percent) due to the pressure of the Provisional Government, which feared Ukrainian domination of the region. Even given this disproportionate representation of minorities, it is noteworthy that

First General Secretariat, Central Rada, late 1917 (Standing from left: Pavlo Khrystiuk, Mykola Stasiuk, Borys Martos; Sitting from left: Ivan Steshenko, Fedir Baranovs'kyi, Volodymyr Vynnychenko, Serhii Iefremov, Symon Petliura)
Photo courtesy of the Bohdan Krawciw Collection at the Research Library of the Harvard Ukrainian Research Institute

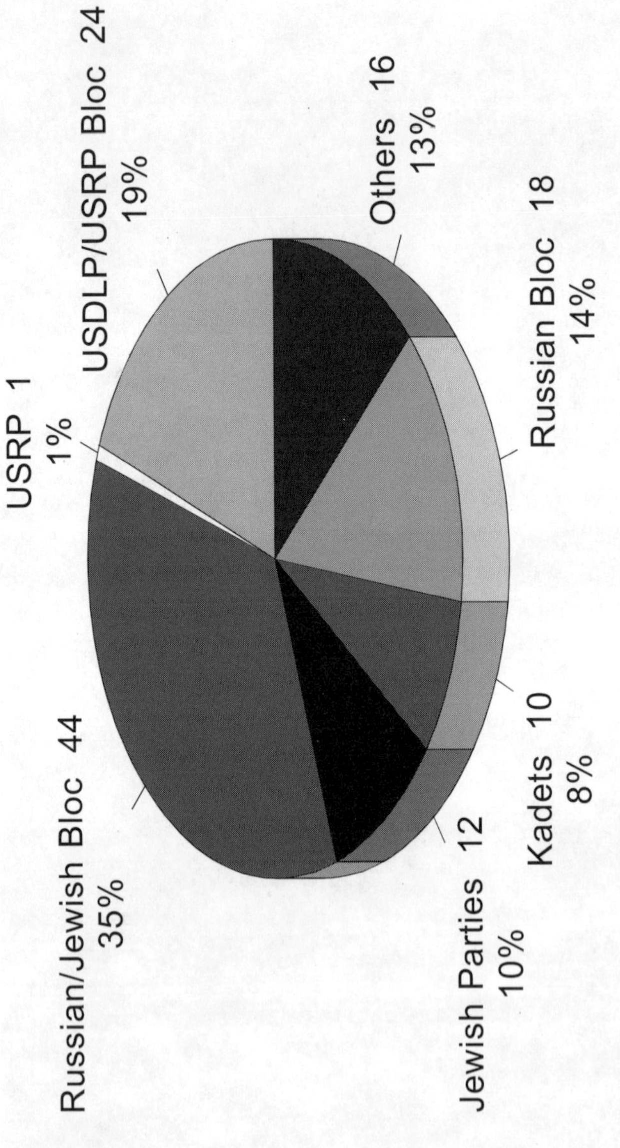

Figure 2.2. Elections to the Kyiv City Government, 1917
Source: Doroshenko, *Istoriia Ukraïny*, vol. 1, p. 143.

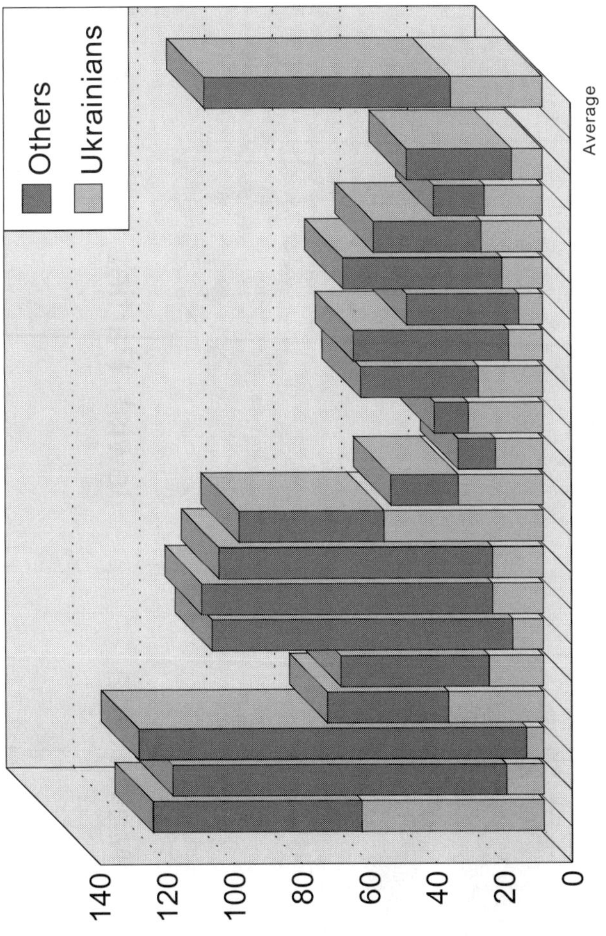

Figure 2.3. Ukrainians Elected to City Governments, 1917
Source: Doroshenko, *Istoriia Ukraïny*, vol. 1, p. 144. Some Ukrainians in coalition parties. See Doroshenko for data on individual locations.

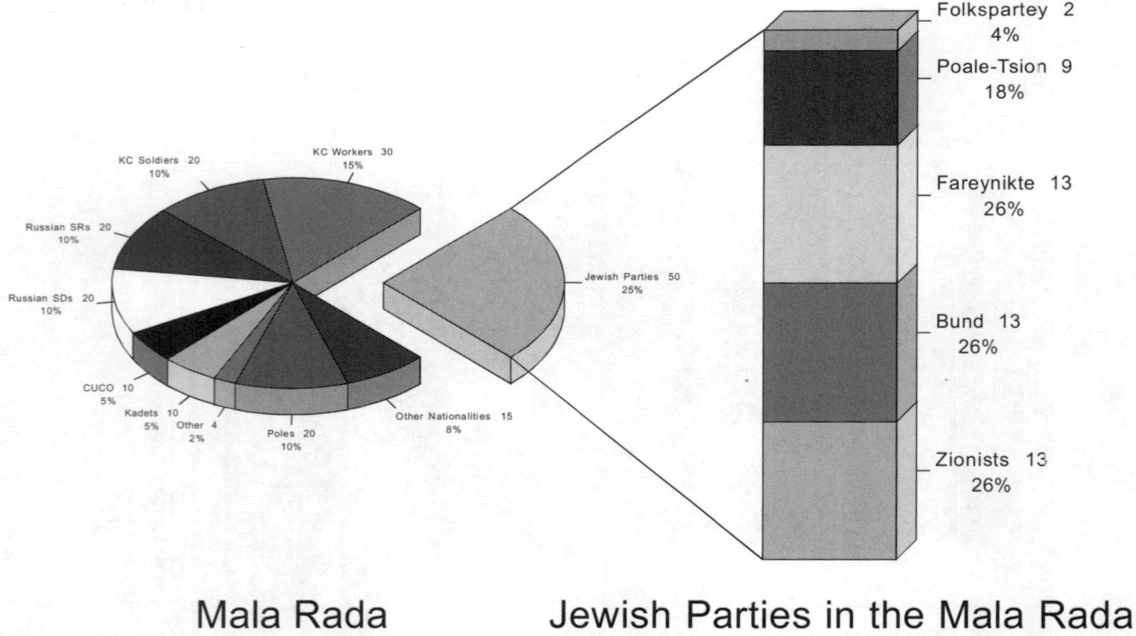

Figure 2.4. Composition of the Mala Rada, August 12, 1917 (KC = Kyiv Council)
Source: Doroshenko, *Istoriia Ukraïny*, vol. 1, p. 123 (for full members); Zaidman, "Ha-avtonomiah," p. 43

Jews were given the largest share (33 percent) of these minority seats. The proportions of representation gave the larger Jewish parties (Zionists, Bund, Fareynikte) equal weight, with thirteen seats each. The Poale-Tsion received nine seats and the Folkspartey received two.

It was representation of Jews in the executive body called the General Secretariat, however, that caused the most controversy. The nature of this representation, both in quantity and in quality, was a major source of conflict in the negotiations between the Rada and the Provisional Government during the summer and early autumn of 1917. Although heated and often bitter, these negotiations ended with the establishment of the Vice-Secretariat for Jewish Affairs.

Shortly after Kerenskii's visit, the Central Rada appointed Serhii Iefremov (USF) to the newly created post of General Secretary for Inter-Nationality Affairs (*Mizhnatsional'nykh sprav*).[56] The head of the General Secretariat, Volodymyr Vynnychenko, issued a statement defining the nature of the new office. This Secretariat was to perform two distinct functions, namely, "to campaign for accord with other minority peoples in the Russian Empire with the aim of transforming it into a federative state; [and]...to campaign for accord among all nationalities in Ukraine, with the aim of forging a political consensus of all peoples living within its boundaries in the upcoming battle for [territorial] autonomy."[57] The structure of the office was further elaborated upon in the "Statute for the Higher Government [*Vyshchoho Upravlinnia*] of Ukraine," which was submitted to the Provisional Government for approval on July 16 :

> 4. The General Secretariat will consist of 14 General Secretaries, including: Internal Affairs, Finance, Defense...Nationalities...
>
> Remark: The Secretariat of Nationality Affairs will include three Vice-Secretaries [*tovaryshi sekretary*]—from the Russians, Jews, and Poles. The Vice-Secretaries have the right to make presentations and participate in debates in the General Secretariat on matters which have relevance to their nationalities. The Vice-Secretaries for Nationality Affairs will be confirmed by a Committee of the Rada.[58]

Having successfully weathered an attempted Bolshevik coup in July, the Provisional Government issued an "Instruction" that severely cut back Ukrainian demands, reducing Ukrainian territory and limiting the size of the General Secretariat to nine.[59] The third point of the Instruction required, in addition, that four of the nine positions be filled by non-Ukrainians. The Provisional Government consistently attempted to increase the proportion of minorities in order to minimize the power of the Ukrainian movement, while limiting the competencies of the Vice-Secretaries as far as possible, presumably because the Rada would hand-pick these Vice-Secretaries to support its policies.[60]

The Instruction was received with great bitterness by the Ukrainians, who felt that the Provisional Government had dealt in bad faith by severely limiting the power of the Central Rada. The Jewish members of the Mala Rada echoed that sentiment. In a session devoted to discussing whether or not the Instruction should be accepted, the Jewish parties protested vehemently yet urged acceptance, in order to maintain the political integrity of the Russian federated republic, which was to replace the defunct Russian Empire. The Zionist Syrkin "was critical of the Instruction, which gave national freedom in hourly tablespoon doses." Moshe Rafes of the Bund even proposed that the proportion of seats given to minorities be reduced to three to correspond to their proportion in Ukraine.[61] Vynnychenko himself noted that the non-Ukrainian members of the Central Rada were "more daring" in their criticism of the Instruction, but in the end, the motion in favor of accepting the Instruction carried, and the protest of the minorities against it was registered in the resolution.[62]

With the Instruction accepted, the Rada finally had firm legal footing on which to begin the construction of the Secretariat for Nationality Affairs, now under the leadership of O. Shul'hyn (USF).[63] The change of name from "Inter-nationality" to "Nationality," intended to reduce the significance of the office, was retained.[64] The Rada had originally planned to appoint the delegates of their own choosing to the posts in nationality affairs, but the Polish parties announced without ceremony that they would supply a candidate based on their own criteria. Not surprisingly, the Jewish parties subsequently made the same demand. After some negotiation, it was agreed that the Rada would appoint the Secretary for Nationality Affairs, and the nationality parties would provide their own candidates for the respective Vice-Secretariats.[65] On July 13, 1917, the Rada appointed candidates for two of the Vice-Secretariats: Moshe Zilberfarb for Jewish Affairs and M. Mickiewicz for Polish Affairs. Several months later it added M. Odinets for Russian Affairs.[66] Zilberfarb, a longtime political activist known under the pseudonym "Bazin," was born to a wealthy Hasidic family in Rivne in 1876. Until the age of fourteen he received a traditional religious education, but later went on to study law in Kyiv, Berlin, and Berne, where he earned a doctorate, with a dissertation entitled "Die Verwaltung der jüdischen Gemeinden in Russland: Historisch und dogmatisch dargestellt." He was active in socialist politics in Kyiv., and was a founding member of the Vozrozhdenie circle there.[67]

Plans were laid for a Congress of Nationalities held in September, which served to bolster the efforts of the Rada in nationality relations. Ninety-two delegates representing twenty different nationalities were present (see Figure 2.5). The Congress, which was presided over by Hrushevs'kyi, resolved in favor of "extra-territorial personal autonomy," specifically mentioning the Jews. All nationalities, however, were to be eligible for this right, which would be based on democratic elections. The state should also guarantee, the resolution continued, full use of the minority languages in official organs.[68]

The primary task of the new General Secretariat for Nationality Affairs, meanwhile, was to define itself. After several months of debate, a lengthy "Statute" describing its structure and competencies was confirmed by the Rada and sent to the Provisional Government in October for final confirmation.[69] In the first paragraph, under the heading "General Principles," the General Secretariat for Nationality Affairs stated as its purpose the protection of the national rights of all the peoples of Ukraine. The second paragraph expanded on this in a more concrete fashion:

> 2) The competency of the General Secretary for Nationality Affairs includes:
>
> a) the creation of legislative proposals, which should firmly establish and protect the national rights of the peoples, which live in Ukraine, and carrying out these laws in life;
>
> b) taking measures and disseminating them among the local government institutions and offices...with the goal of establishing good relations between the nationalities;
>
> c) collecting, editing, and disseminating materials, which have relevance to the solution of the nationality question in Ukraine.

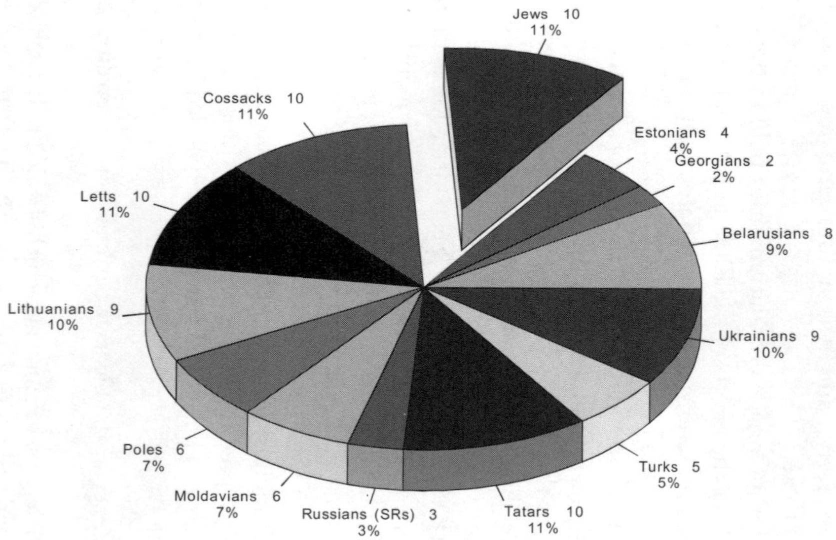

Figure 2.5. Composition of the Congress of Nationalities, September 1917
Source: Stoiko, "Z'ïzd narodiv," p. 15.

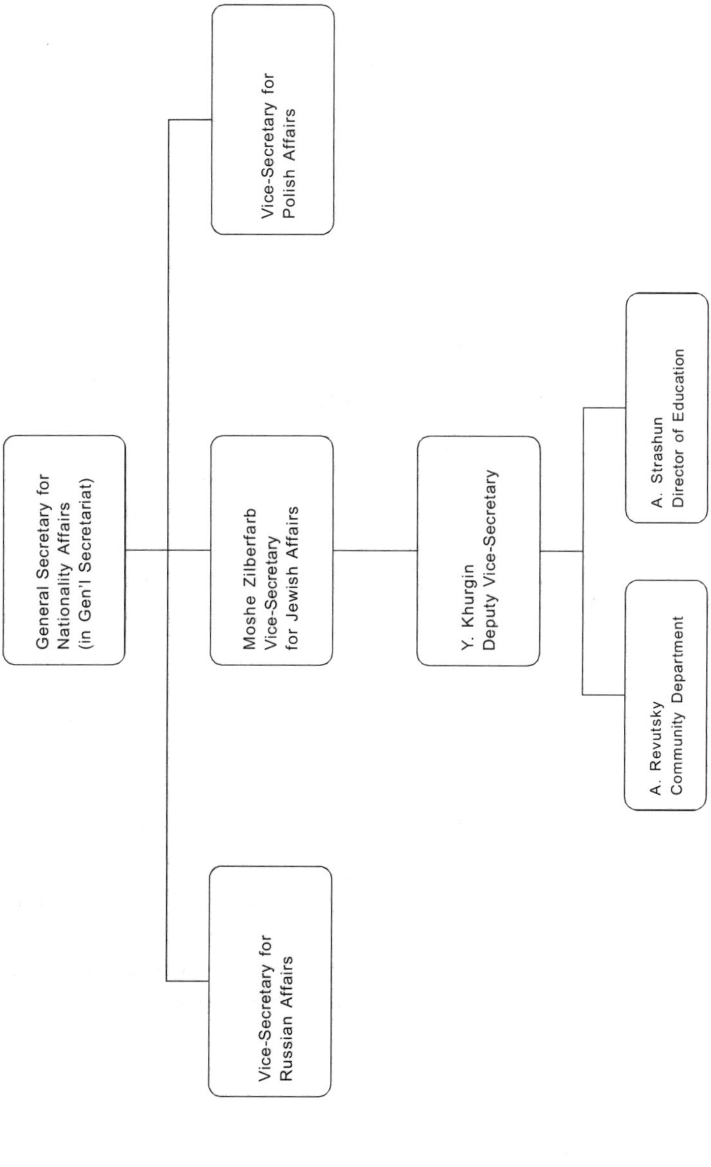

Figure 2.6. Structure of the Secretariat for Nationality Affairs, July–November 1917
Source: Zilberfarb, *Idishe*, p. 22.

The Secretariat had two basic functions: to organize the nationality life of the peoples of Ukraine, and to promote harmony among these nationalities. The nature of nationality life was to be defined by the Secretariat and its organs. As indicated in Article 6, "specifically, the Vice-Secretariat should create and effect measures which are relevant to the people's education." With the Zionist emphasis on teaching in modern Hebrew, the Bundist emphasis on teaching in Yiddish, and the religious preference for teaching Rabbinic Hebrew and Aramaic texts in the Yiddish vernacular, this proved to be a gargantuan task.

Section II of the Statute outlined the structure of the Secretariat (see Figure 2.6, previous page). Under the Secretary for Nationality Affairs were the three Vice-Secretaries for the Russian, Jewish, and Polish minorities, each with its own staff. The Russian Vice-Secretariat never really got off the ground, and the Polish Vice-Secretariat existed for only a few months. Zilberfarb's Vice-Secretariat was much more organized and long-lasting.

In addition to the officers in the Vice-Secretariats, each nationality was to have its own Nationality Council, a type of parliament, although the exact nature of the relationship between them was not defined. One interpretation held that the Vice-Secretary was accountable to the Nationality Council, another that the Nationality Council was to act merely as a consultative body for the Vice-Secretary, allowing him to sound out new policies and prepare to carry them out. This distinction formed the foundation of the conflict between the Zionists and the Socialists (see Chapter 3). Articles 4 and 5 of the Statute, however, indicated that the Secretary for Nationality Affairs was to be responsible for the policies of the Vice-Secretaries, and also that these Vice-Secretaries had to be confirmed by the Central Rada. The Secretary thus had veto power, which limited the ability of each nationality to arrange its own affairs.

Article 7 was directed specifically at the Jews, authorizing the revitalization of the *kehiles*, local Jewish self-governments that had been stripped of almost all their powers and virtually banned by Tsar Nicholas I in 1844.[70] Poles and Russians were not given similar rights, presumably because they lacked the centuries-old tradition of the *kehiles*. The Vice-Secretaries were allowed to participate in all discussions of the General Secretariat, but could cast a vote and present briefs to the meetings only on issues of direct relevance to their nationality (Article 8). On such issues, however, they had effective veto power, since laws affecting their nationality had to be countersigned by the respective Vice-Secretary (Article 9).

The problems inherent in such a system were obvious. When did an issue only have direct relevance to one nationality? Taxation and conscription were relevant to general state interests as well as each nationality. Therefore either the provenance of each Vice-Secretary would have to be carefully circumscribed, to education or perhaps religious affairs alone, for example, or the requirement of a countersignature would have to be ignored in case of a dispute. These issues were never resolved in practice, however, as political events proceeded too rapidly for the Statute to be put into effect as originally accepted.

Article 10 declared that the official language of the Vice-Secretariats would be their own, that is, Russian, Polish, or Yiddish, and Zilberfarb's Vice-Secretariat earnestly attempted to put this into effect, translating all documents whenever necessary. But this arrangement, which effectively declared that Ukraine had four official languages and three alphabets (one of which was written from right to left), caused bureaucratic chaos. With few exceptions, this law was ignored "for technical reasons" and most laws were published in Ukrainian alone.[71]

Section III of the Statute dealt with possible controversy and deadlocks within or between the Vice-Secretariats. The Secretary for Nationality Affairs was charged with ensuring harmonious relations between the nationalities, and was given several powers to form various committees to this end. Section IV indicated just how weak the entire structure was: while calling for the appointment of local officers and Commissars of Nationality Affairs, the Statute identified these positions as honorary; only travel and sundry expenses would be paid for by the state.

The Provisional Government never had a chance to respond to this Statute. On November 7, the Bolsheviks took power from the Provisional Government in St. Petersburg, which put an end to Russia's efforts to create a parliamentary democracy. The Rada did not hesitate to respond to the new political situation, issuing its Third Universal, a strong declaration of increased autonomy:

> Ukrainian people and all peoples of Ukraine!
>
> A heavy and difficult hour has fallen upon the land of the Russian Republic. In the capitals to the north a bloody civil struggle is raging; the Central Government has collapsed, and anarchy, lawlessness, and ruin are spreading throughout the state.
>
> Our land is also in danger. Without a single, strong national authority, Ukraine may also fall into the abyss of civil war, slaughter and ruin.
>
> Ukrainian people! You, together with other fraternal peoples of Ukraine, have placed us to…create order…and we, the Ukrainian Central Rada, by your will, and in the name of establishing order in our country in the name of saving all of Russia, do now proclaim:
>
> From this day forth, Ukraine becomes the Ukrainian People's [National] Republic.
>
> Without separating from the Russian Republic and maintaining its unity, we shall stand firmly on our own soil, in order that our strength may aid all of Russia, so that the whole Russian Republic may become a federation of free and equal peoples.[72]

The Third Universal also sent a message to the minorities in Ukraine, offering to enshrine the institutions of autonomy in a new law of "national-personal autonomy":

> The Ukrainian people, who have fought long years for their national freedom and have won it today, shall firmly defend the free national development of all nationalities residing in the Ukraine, therefore, we proclaim: The Great-Russian, Jewish, Polish and other peoples in Ukraine are granted national-personal autonomy to guarantee their own self-government in all matters of their national life; and we charge our General Secretariat for National[ity] Affairs to present to us, within the shortest possible time, legislative drafts for national-personal autonomy.[73]

The Polish minority balked at the Third Universal, since it also called for sweeping agrarian reform that would rapidly dispossess the landowning Polish inhabitants. Mickiewicz resigned his post immediately. Shortly thereafter, Vynnychenko met with the Poles and several other influential figures and promised to delay implementation. Reassured, Mickiewicz resumed his post.[74]

All the Jewish parties, on the other hand, voted in favor of the Third Universal, which was regarded as "something like a test of their loyalty to the Ukrainian cause."[75] Their consistent support of the Rada reached its apex with this Universal because the Rada had addressed their two major concerns: 1) nonseparation from the lands of the former Russian Empire, and 2) the establishment of Jewish autonomy. The legal basis for the Statute, however, rested on the existence of the Provisional Government in Petrograd, and with the disappearance of the Provisional Government, the Statute of the Secretary for Nationality Affairs was rendered instantly obsolete just weeks after its acceptance by the Rada.

Tension between the Jewish and Ukrainian politicians mounted during the last weeks of 1917 and the beginning of 1918. The Soviet government to the north was increasingly belligerent, and open hostilities eventually broke out. Meanwhile, pogroms had begun to occur in the western regions, further straining relations between Jews and Ukrainians. It was in this charged atmosphere that Zilberfarb and his colleagues were faced with the task of preparing a new Law of National-Personal Autonomy to replace the now obsolete Statute.

After much effort, a piece of draft legislation for the Law of National-Personal Autonomy was eventually completed. This document implicitly accepted most of the conclusions laid out in the earlier Statute, and the greater authority of its tone anticipated Ukrainian independence.[76]

Articles 1 and 2 dealt with the issue of which nationalities were eligible for national-personal autonomy. Although autonomy was referred to as the "irrevocable right of nationalities," only three of Ukraine's minorities (Jews, Russians, and Poles) were specifically named as having this "right." Several other minorities were named as having the potential to acquire national-personal autonomy upon acceptance by the state of a petition signed by ten thousand members of the nationality. Nationalities not specifically mentioned in the law were also to be eligible for national-personal autonomy, subject to prior examination by the state.

Article 3 called for the creation of a Nationality Union: every person declaring membership in the said nationality was to sign a Nationality Register, or *kadaster*, which would be published and made available to the general public. Individuals could have their names added or removed (it was not indicated if this could be done repeatedly). The implied basis for this membership was the same as in Article 2: anyone over the age of 20, "without any distinction as to sex or

Універсал Української Центральної Ради.

Народе Український і всі народи України.

Тяжка і трудна година впала на землю Республіки Російської. На півночі в столицях йде межиусобна і кривава боротьба. Центрального Правительства нема і по державі шириться безвластя, безлад і руїна.

Наш край так само в небезпеці. Без власти, дужої, єдиної, народньої Вкраїна теж може впасти в безодню усобиці, різні, занепаду.

Народе Український! Ти, разом з братніми народами України, поставив нас берегти права, здобуті боротьбою, творити лад і будувати нове життя на нашій землі. І ми, Українська Центральна Рада, твоєю волею, во ім'я творення ладу в нашій країні, во ім'я рятування всеї Росії, оповіщаємо:

Однині Україна стає Українською Народньою Республікою.

Не одділяючись від Республіки Російської і зберігаючи єдність її, ми твердо станемо на нашій землі, щоб силами нашими помогти всій Росії, щоб уся Республіка Російська стала федерацією рівних і вільних народів.

До Установчих Зборів України вся власть творити лад на землях наших, давати закони і правити належить нам, Українській Центральній Раді, і нашому правительству—Генеральному Секретаріатові України.

Маючи силу і власть на рідній землі, ми тою силою і властю станемо на сторожі прав і революції не тільки нашої землі, але і всеї Росії.

Отож, оповіщаємо:

До території Народньої Української Республіки належать землі, заселені у більшости Українцями: Київщина, Поділля, Волинь, Чернигівщина, Полтавщина, Харьківщина, Катеринославщина, Херсонщина, Таврія (без Криму). Остаточне визначення границь Української Народньої Республіки, як що до прилучення частини Курщини, Холмщини, Вороніжчини, так і суміжних губерній і областей, де більшість населення українська, має бути встановлено по згоді організованої волі народів.

Всіх же громадян сих земель оповіщаємо:

Однині на території Української Народньої Республіки існуюче право власности на землі поміщицькі та инші землі нетрудових хазяйств сільсько-господарського значіння, а також на удільні, манастирські та церковні землі—касується.

Признаючи, що землі ті єсть власність всього трудового народу і мають перейти до нього без викупу, Українська Центральна Рада доручає Генеральному Секретареві по Земельних Справах негайно виробити Закон про те, як порядкувати земельним комітетам, обраним народом, тими землями до Українських Установчих Зборів.

Праця робітництва в Українській Народній Республіці має бути негайно упорядкована. А зараз оповіщаємо:

На території Народньої Республіки України з сього дня встановлюється по всіх підприємствах вісім годин праці.

Тяжкий і грізний час, який переживає вся Росія, а з нею і наша Україна, вимагає доброго упорядкування виробництва, рівномірного розприділення продуктів споживання і кращої організації праці. І через те приписуємо Генеральному Секретарству Праці від сього дня, разом з представництвом від робітництва **встановити державну контролю над продукцією України, пильнуючи інтересів як України, так і цілої Росії.**

Четвертий рік на фронтах ллється кров і гинуть марно сили всіх народів світу. Волею і іменем Української Республіки ми, Українська Центральна Рада, станемо твердо на тому, щоб мир було встановлено як найшвидче. **Для того ми вживаємо рішучих заходів, щоб через Центральне Правительство примусити і союзників і ворогів негайно розпочати мирні переговори.**

Так само будемо дбати, щоб на мировому конгресі права народу українського в Росії і поза Росією не було в замиренню порушено. Але до миру кожен громадянин Республіки України, разом з громадянами усіх народів Російської Республіки повинен стояти твердо на своїх позиціях, як на фронті, так і в тилу.

Останніми часами ясні здобутки революції було затемнено відновленою карою на смерть. Оповіщаємо:

Однині на землі Республіки Української смертна кара касується.

Всім увязненим і затриманим за політичні виступи, зроблені до сього дня, як уже засудженим, так і незасудженим, а також і тим, хто ще до відповідальности не потягнений, дається повна амністія. Про се негайно буде виданий закон.

Суд на Україні повинен бути справедливий, відповідний духові народу.

З тою метою приписуємо Генеральному Секретарству Судових Справ зробити всі заходи упорядкувати судівництво і привести його до згоди з правними поняттями народу.

Генеральному Секретарству Внутрішніх Справ приписуємо:

Вжити всіх заходів до закріплення і поширення прав місцевого самоврядування, що являються органами вищої адміністративної влади на місцях, і до встановлення найтіснійшого звязку і співробітництва його з органами революційної демократії, що має бути найкращою основою вільного демократичного життя.

Так само в Українській Народній Республіці має бути забезпечено всі свободи здобуті всеросійською революцією: свободу слова, друку, віри, зібрань, союзів, страйків, недоторканности особи і мешкання, право і можливість уживання місцевих мов в зносинах з усіма установами.

Український народ, що сам довгі літа боровся за свою національну волю і нині її здобувши, буде твердо охороняти волю національного розвитку всіх народностей, на Україні сущих, тому оповіщаємо: що **народам великоруському, єврейському, польському та иншим на Україні признаємо національно-персональну автономію** для забезпечення їх права і свободи самоврядування в справах їх національного життя, та доручаємо нашому Генеральному Секретарству Національних справ подати нам в найближчому часі законопроект про національно-персональну автономію.

Справа продовольча є корінь державної сили в сей тяжкий і відповідальний час. Українська Народня Республіка повинна напружити всі свої сили і рятувати як себе, так і фронт і ті частини Російської Республіки, які потребують нашої допомоги.

Громадяне! Іменем Народньої Української Республіки в федеративній Росії ми, Українська Центральна Рада, кличемо всіх до рішучої боротьби з усяким безладдям і руйнництвом, та до дружнього великого будівництва нових державних форм, які дадуть великій і знеможеній Республіці Росії здоровя, силу і нову будучність. Вироблення тих форм має бути проведено на Українських і Всеросійських Установчих Зборах.

Днем виборів до Українських Установчих Зборів призначено 27 грудня (декабря) 1917 року, а днем скликання їх 9 січня (января) 1918 року.

Про порядок скликання Українських Установчих Зборів—негайно видано буде закон.

Українська Центральна Рада.

У Київі 7 листопаду року 1917.

Универсалъ Украинской Центральной Рады.

Народъ украинскій и всѣ народы Украины. Тяжелое и трудное время переживаетъ Россійская республика. На сѣверѣ въ столицахъ идетъ междоусобная и кровавая борьба. Центральнаго Правительства нѣтъ. И по всему государству растетъ безвластіе, анархія и разруха.

Нашъ край также въ опасности. Безъ власти сильной, единой, народной Украина также будетъ повергнута въ бездну кровавой междоусобицы и полнаго упадка.

Народъ украинскій, ты вмѣстѣ съ братскими народами Украины поставилъ насъ блюсти права, добытыя борьбою, творить порядокъ и творить будущее нашей земли. И мы, Украинская Центральная Рада, творя твою волю, во имя установленія порядка въ нашемъ краѣ, во имя спасенія всей Россіи объявляемъ.

Отнынѣ Украина становится Украинской Народной Республикою.

Не отдѣляясь отъ республики Россійской и сохраняя единство ея, мы твердо станемъ на нашей землѣ, чтобы силами нашими оказать помощь всей Россіи, чтобы вся Россійская республика стала федераціею равныхъ и вольныхъ народовъ.

До созыва учредительнаго собранія Украины вся власть творить порядокъ на земляхъ нашихъ, устанавливать законы и править принадлежитъ намъ, Украинской Центральной Радѣ, и правительству нашему—Генеральному Секретаріату Украины.

Имѣя силу и власть на родной землѣ, мы станемъ на стражѣ права и революціи не только у себя, но и во всей Россіи.

И потому объявляемъ:

Къ территоріи Украинской Народной Республики принадлежатъ земли, заселенныя въ большинствѣ Украинцами: Кіевщина, Подолія, Волынь, Черниговщина, Полтавщина, Харьковщина, Екатеринославщина, Херсонщина, Таврія (безъ Крыма). Окончательное установленіе границъ Украинской Народной Республики, какъ относительно присоединенія населенныхъ въ большинствѣ Украинцами частей Курщины, Воронежчины, Холмщины, такъ и другихъ смежныхъ губерній, должно послѣдовать въ соглашеніи съ организованною волею народовъ.

Всѣмъ гражданамъ этихъ земель объявляемъ:

Отнынѣ существующее на территоріи Украинской Народной Республики право собственности на земли помѣщичьи и на иныя земли нетрудовыхъ хозяйствъ сельско-хозяйственнаго значенія, а также на земли удѣльныя, монастырскія, кабинетскія и церковныя уничтожается. Признавая, что земли эти составляютъ собственность трудового народа и должны перейти къ нему безъ выкупа, Украинская Центральная Рада поручаетъ Генеральному Секретарю по земельнымъ дѣламъ немедленно выработать законъ о порядкѣ распоряженія земельными комитетами, избранными народомъ, этими землями до украинскаго учредительнаго собранія.

Трудъ рабочихъ въ Украинской Республикѣ имѣетъ быть немедленно урегулированъ. Теперь же объявляемъ: **на территоріи Народной Украинской Республики устанавливается во всѣхъ предпріятіяхъ восьмичасовый рабочій день.**

Тяжелый и грозный часъ, какой переживаетъ вся Россія, а съ ней и наша Украина, требуетъ упорядоченія производства, равномѣрнаго распредѣленія продуктовъ потребленія и лучшей организаціи труда. Поэтому предписываемъ Генеральному Секретарству труда съ настоящаго дня вмѣстѣ съ представительствомъ отъ рабочихъ установить государственный контроль надъ производствомъ на Украинѣ, соблюдая интересы какъ Украины, такъ и цѣлой Россіи.

Четвертый годъ на фронтахъ льется кровь и напрасно тратятся силы всѣхъ народовъ міра. Волею и именемъ Украинской Республики мы, Украинская Центральная Рада, станемъ твердо на томъ, чтобы возможно скорѣе былъ заключенъ миръ. **Для этого мы предпримемъ рѣшительныя мѣры, чтобы черезъ Центральное Правительство заставить и союзниковъ и враговъ немедленно начать переговоры о мирѣ.**

Точно также будемъ заботиться, чтобы на мирномъ конгрессѣ права украинскаго народа въ Россіи не были нарушены при заключеніи мира. Но до заключенія мира каждый гражданинъ Республики Украины долженъ вмѣстѣ съ гражданами всѣхъ народовъ Россійской Республики стоять твердо на своихъ позиціяхъ, какъ на фронтѣ, такъ и въ тылу.

Въ послѣднее время свѣтлыя пріобрѣтенія революціи были затемнены возстановленіемъ смертной казни. Объявляемъ:

Отнынѣ на землѣ Украинской Республики смертная казнь уничтожается.

Всѣмъ заключеннымъ и арестованнымъ за политическія выступленія, совершенныя до настоящаго дня, какъ уже осужденнымъ, а также и тѣмъ, кто еще не привлеченъ къ отвѣтственности, дается полная амнистія. Объ этомъ будетъ немедленно изданъ законъ.

Судъ на Украинѣ долженъ быть справедливый, соотвѣтствующій духу народа. Съ этой цѣлью предписываемъ Генеральному Секретарству по судебнымъ дѣламъ принять всѣ мѣры къ упорядоченію судопроизводства и къ приведенію его въ соотвѣтствіе съ народными понятіями о правѣ.

Генеральному Секретарству внутреннихъ дѣлъ предписываемъ **принять всѣ мѣры къ закрѣпленію и расширенію правъ мѣстнаго самоуправленія**, которое является органомъ высшей административной власти на мѣстахъ, **къ установленію самой тѣсной связи и сотрудничества его съ органами революціонной демократіи**, что и будетъ наилучшей основой свободной демократической жизни.

Точно также въ Украинской Народной Республикѣ будутъ обезпечены всѣ свободы, добытыя всероссійской революціей: свобода слова, печати, вѣры, собраній, союзовъ, стачекъ, неприкосновенность личности и жилища, право и возможность употребленія мѣстныхъ языковъ въ сношеніяхъ со всѣми учрежденіями.

Украинскій народъ, самъ долгіе годы боровшійся за свою національную свободу и теперь ее получившій, будетъ твердо охранять свободу національнаго развитія всѣхъ народностей, живущихъ на Украинѣ, а потому объявляемъ: что **за народами великорусскимъ, еврейскимъ, польскимъ и другими на Украинѣ признаемъ право на національно-персональную автономію** для обезпеченія имъ права и свободы самоуправленія въ дѣлахъ ихъ національной жизни.

Поручаемъ нашему Генеральному Секретарству національныхъ дѣлъ представить намъ въ ближайшемъ времени законопроектъ національно-персональной автономіи.

Дѣло продовольствія—корень государственной силы въ этотъ тяжелый и отвѣтственный часъ.

Украинская Народная Республика должна напречь всѣ свои силы и спасать какъ себя, такъ и фронтъ, и тѣ части Россійской Республики, которыя нуждаются въ нашей помощи.

Граждане! Именемъ Народной Украинской Республики въ федеративной Россіи мы, Украинская Центральная Рада, призываемъ всѣхъ къ рѣшительной борьбѣ со всякими безпорядками и разрушеніями и къ дружному великому строительству новыхъ государственныхъ формъ, которыя дадутъ великой и обезсиленной Республикѣ Россіи здоровье, силу и новую мощность. Выработка этихъ формъ имѣетъ быть совершена на Украинскомъ и Всероссійскомъ Учредительныхъ Собраніяхъ.

Днемъ выборовъ въ Украинское Учредительное Собраніе назначаемъ 27 декабря 1917 г., а днемъ созыва его—9 января 1918 г.

О порядкѣ созыва Украинскаго Учредительнаго Собранія немедленно будетъ изданъ законъ.

Украинская Центральная Рада.

Кіевъ. 7 ноября 1917 года.

Third Universal of the Central Rada, Broadside, November 7, 1917 (old style) (left half: Ukrainian and Russian columns)

Reproduced with the permission of the General Archival Collection, Reference Library of the Harvard Ukrainian Research Institute

Uniwersał Ukraińskiej Rady Centralnej.

Narodzie ukraiński i wszystkie narody Ukrainy!

Ciężka i trudna nastała chwila na ziemi Republiki rosyjskiej. Na północy w stolicach toczy się bratobójcza i krwawa walka. Rządu Centralnego niema, a w państwie brak władzy i szerzy się bezład i ruina.

Kraj nasz również jest w niebezpieczeństwie. Bez władzy, silnej, jednolitej, ludowej— Ukraina może też wpaść w otchłań walki bratobójczej, rzezi, upadku.

Narodzie ukraiński! Tyś razem z bratnimi narodami Ukrainy postawił nas na straży swoich praw, zdobytych walką, byśmy tworzyli ład i budowali pełne życie na naszej ziemi. I my, Ukraińska Rada Centralna, z woli twojej, w imię zaprowadzenia porządku, w imię ocalenia całej Rosji—ogłaszamy:

Od dzisiej Ukraina zostaje Ukraińską Republiką Ludową.

Nie odłączając się od Republiki rosyjskiej i dbając o całość jej, staniemy mocno na ziemi naszej, by pomódz całej Rosji, by cała Republika rosyjska stała się związkiem wolnych i równych narodów.

Do czasu zwołania Konstytuanty Ukraińskiej pełne prawo tworzenia władzy na ziemiach naszych, wydawania praw i rządzenia, należy do nas, Ukraińskiej Rady Centralnej i rządu naszego — Sekretarjatu Generalnego Ukrainy.

Mając siłę i władzę na ziemi ojczystej, my przy pomocy tej siły i władzy staniemy na straży praw i rewolucji nietylko ziemi naszej, ale i całej Rosji.

I oto ogłaszamy:

Do terytorjum Ukraińskiej Republiki Ludowej należą ziemie, zamieszkane w większości przez ukraińców: Kijowszczyzna, Podole, Wołyń, Czernihowszczyzna, Połtawszyzna, Charkowszczyzna, Ekaterynosławszczyzna, Chersońszczyzna i Taurvda (bez Krymu).

Ostateczne określenie granic Ukraińskiej Republiki Ludowej co do przyłączenia części gubernji kurskiej, chełmskiej, woroneskiej i innych ziem sąsiednich, gdzie większość ludności jest ukraińska, ma być ustalona za zgodą zorganizowanej woli narodów.

Wszystkim obywatelom tych ziem oznajmiamy:

Od dziś na terytoryum Ukraińskiej Republiki Ludowej istniejące prawo własności do gruntów ziemiańskich i innych gruntów, nie uprawianych własnoręcznie, mających znaczenie gospodarczo-rolne oraz do gruntów apanażowych, monasterskich, gabinetowych i cerkiewnych zostaje skasowane. Uznając, że grunty te stanowią własność całego ludu pracującego i mają przejść do niego bez wykupu, Ukraińska Rada Centralna poleca sekretarzowi generalnemu do spraw rolnych niezwłocznie opracować prawo, jak mają Komitety rolne, obrane przez lud, zarządzać tymi gruntami do czasu zwołania Konstytuanty ukraińskiej.

Sprawa pracy robotników w Ukraińskiej Republice Ludowej ma być niebawem unormowana. Obecnie zaś oznajmiamy: Na terytoryum Ukraińskiej Republiki Ludowej od dnia dzisiejszego ustanawia się we wszystkich przedsiębiorstwach **ośmiogodzinny dzień pracy.**

Ciężka i groźna chwila, którą przeżywa Rosja, a z nią i nasza Ukraina, wymaga sprawiedliwego i korzystnego użycia sił robotniczych, równomiernego podziału produktów spożywczych i lepszej organizacji pracy. I dlatego polecamy Sekretarjatowi Generalnemu pracy, wspólnie z przedstawicielami robotników, od dnia dzisiejszego ustanowić kontrolę państwową nad produkcją Ukrainy, pilnując interesów zarówno Ukrainy, jak i całej Rosji.

Czwarty rok na frontach leje się krew i giną marnie siły wszystkich narodów świata. Z woli i w imieniu Republiki Ukraińskiej, my, Ukraińska Rada Centralna, staniemy na stanowisku niezłomnem, by pokój został jak najprędzej zawarty. Dlatego dołożymy stanowczych starań, by za pośrednictwem Rządu Centralnego zmusić sprzymierzeńców i wrogów do natychmiastowego rozpoczęcia pertraktacji pokojowych.

Również dbać będziemy, by na kongresie pokojowym prawa narodu ukraińskiego w Rosji i po za Rosją nie zostały naruszone przy zawarciu pokoju. Lecz do chwili zawarcia pokoju każdy obywatel Republiki Ukraińskiej powinien razem z obywatelami wszystkich narodów Republiki rosyjskiej, stać twardo na swych stanowiskach, tak na froncie, jak i na tyłach armji.

W ostatnich czasach świetlane zdobycze Rewolucji zostały zaćmione wznowieniem kary śmierci. Ogłaszamy: Od dzisiaj na ziemi Republiki Ukraińskiej **kara śmierci zostaje zniesiona.** Dla wszystkich już uwięzionych i aresztowanych za przestępstwa polityczne, dla już osądzonych i jeszcze nie osądzonych, jak również dla tych, którzy do odpowiedzialności nie zostali pociągnięci, ogłasza się **zupełną amnestję.** Odpowiednie prawo będzie wydane niezwłocznie.

Sąd na Ukrainie powinien być sprawiedliwy, odpowiadający duchowi narodu. W tym celu polecamy Sekretarjatowi generalnemu do spraw sądowych poczynienie wszelkich starań celem uporządkowania sądownictwa i doprowadzenia go do zgody z pojęciami prawnemi narodu.

Sekretarjatowi generalnemu spraw wewnętrznych polecamy: dołożyć wszystkich starań w celu utrwalenia i rozszerzenia praw samorządu miejscowego, będącego organem wyższej władzy administracyjnej miejscowej i do ustanowienia najściślejszego związku i współpracy jego z organami demokracji rewolucyjnej, co powinno być najlepszą podstawą wolnego życia demokratycznego.

Również w Ukraińskiej Republice Ludowej mają być zabezpieczone wszystkie wolności, zdobyte przez rewolucję wszechrosyjską: wolność mowy, wiary, zebrań, stowarzyszeń, strajków, nietykalności osobistej, mieszkań, jak również prawo i możność używania języków miejscowych w stosunkach z władzami. Naród ukraiński, który sam przez długie lata walczył o swą wolność narodową i obecnie, osiągnąwszy ją, będzie mocno ochraniać wolność rozwoju wszystkich narodowości, będących na Ukrainie; a przeto ogłaszamy: że narodom wielkorosyjskiemu, żydowskiemu, polskiemu i innym na Ukrainie przyznajemy autonomję narodowo-personalną dla zabezpieczenia im prawa i wolności samorządu w sprawach ich życia narodowego i polecamy naszemu sekretarzowi generalnemu do spraw narodowościowych w czasie jak najbliższym złożyć nam projekt prawa o autonomji narodowo-personalnej.

Sprawa aprowizacyjna jest podstawą siły państwowej w tej ciężkiej i odpowiedzialnej chwili. Ukraińska Republika Ludowa powinna wytężyć wszystkie swoje siły i ratować tak siebie, jak front i te części Republiki rosyjskiej, które wymagają naszej pomocy.

Obywatele! W imieniu Ukraińskiej Republiki Ludowej w Rosji federacyjnej my, Ukraińska Rada Centralna, wzywamy wszystkich do stanowczej walki z wszelkiemi objawami bezładu i zniszczenia, oraz do zgodnego wielkiego budownictwa nowych form państwowych, które dadzą wielkiej i osłabionej Republice rosyjskiej zdrowie, siłę i nową przyszłość. Opracowanie tych form ma być przeprowadzone na Konstytuancie ukraińskiej i wszechrosyjskiej.

Dniem wyborów do Konstytuanty Ukraińskiej jest 27 grudnia 1917 r., a dniem zwołania jej 9 stycznia 1918 r.

O porządku zwołania Konstytuanty Ukraińskiej będzie wydane niezwłocznie prawo.

Ukraińska Rada Centralna.

w Kijowie, dn. 7 listopada 1917 r.

אוניווערסאל

פון דער אוקראאינער צענטראלער ראדע.

אוקראאינער צענטראלער ראדע.

Third Universal of the Central Rada, Broadside, November 7, 1917 (old style)
(right half: Polish and Yiddish columns)

Reproduced with the permission of the General Archival Collection, Reference Library of the Harvard Ukrainian Research Institute

faith," may sign the *kadaster*. Since Jewish nationality, unlike Polish or Russian, was fundamentally a religious identity (regardless of whether or not one currently held those beliefs), it is entirely possible that non-Jews might have joined the Jewish nationality register if they chose to identify themselves as Jews. Furthermore, what was there to stop a Russian-speaking Ukrainian from signing the Russian nationality register, or a Jewish Polonophile from signing the Polish? Depending on the advantages of membership, such as differences in taxation or exemption from work on Saturday, the Jewish Sabbath, and so on, it is conceivable that a person could switch nationalities at will.[77] Even presuming that membership in a given nationality is after all based solely on personal inclination (excluding other factors such as birth, birthplace, religion, language, and so on), it is obvious that this vague definition could lead to bureaucratic chaos. The law's general principles seemed flawed in ways that would present insuperable legal difficulties.

Articles 5 and 6 allowed the Nationality Union a share of the state budget proportionate to the size of the *kadaster* and granted it the right to tax its own members.[78] The remainder of the law dealt with the operating organs of the Nationality Union: a Constituent Nationality Assembly based on a statewide vote of all members of the Nationality Union, and the Nationality Council, its executive organ, although it merely outlined the structure and function of these organs. It is interesting to note that the position of Minister of Jewish Affairs is nowhere mentioned in the document, leaving open the large question of the relationship between the Minister and the duly elected bodies of the nationality.

Article 7 outlined the method by which conflicts between the Nationality Union and other bodies were to be solved. Although a mechanism involving conciliatory committees was stipulated, the final word in any conflict rested with the Central Rada. This met with some opposition, particularly among the Zionists, who argued that it necessarily implied a conflict of interest, as the Central Rada could not be expected to judge impartially in a conflict between itself and a Nationality Union.[79]

A final article originally approved by the Mala Rada, which allowed the Nationality Unions of Ukraine to "unite" with similar bodies in the hoped-for Russian Federated Republic, was dropped at the last minute before the law was passed. The Bolshevik revolution rendered it impossible, and the article was abandoned.[80] Debate on the Law of National-Personal Autonomy was heated and delayed the vote two days. On January 24, however, it passed with no abstentions or opposition.[81] Moshe Zilberfarb was appointed the Minister of Jewish Affairs.

This is not to say that these momentous decisions were reached in a spirit of mutual respect and tolerance. As Joseph Schechtman, a Zionist participant in the debates, recalled, when "this legislation was introduced, the relationship of the Ukrainian parties to the national minorities, and especially the Jewish minority, was substantially deteriorating. The atmosphere of benevolence that had predominated during the first few postrevolutionary months was succeeded by an obvious or scarcely veiled mistrust and ill-will."[82] The Red Army, meanwhile, invaded Ukraine from the north and the east, placing intolerable pressure on the Rada, which issued its Fourth and final Universal. Although the text was dated January 9 (old style, January 22 new style), the vote was not held until 12:20 A.M. on January 25 due to the delay caused by the debates on the Law of National-Personal Autonomy.[83] The Fourth Universal was far more assertive than the previous three, declaring Ukrainian independence: "...from this day forth, the Ukrainian National Republic becomes independent, subject to no one, a free, sovereign state of the Ukrainian people."[84]

When the Jewish parties did not support the Fourth Universal, the resultant uproar was so great that Hrushevs'kyi was forced to clear the hall of spectators.[85] With the exception of the Poles, all the nationality parties voted against the Fourth Universal.[86] In light of the Soviet-Ukrainian war, the Rada had abandoned the possibility of participation in a federated Russian state, thus undermining one of the key pillars of Jewish support for the government. On these grounds the Bund voted against the Universal, while the Fareynikte, Poale-Tsion, and Folkspartey abstained. The Zionists, who were not present for the vote, later issued a statement indicating their abstention.[87]

Solomon Goldelman, who was present at the debate on behalf of the Poale-Tsion, reflected in his memoirs on the clamor in the Rada when the Jewish parties failed to support the Ukrainian declaration of independence. Their opposition was received with particular bitterness, since the Rada had just passed the historic Law of National-Personal Autonomy: "...the Ukrainians were convinced that by this act they had won at least the moral right to a solemn and unanimous vote for the Universal of the Central Rada, including all its members, Ukrainians and non-Ukrainians."[88] The military and political situation in Ukraine worsened day by day. On January 29, 1918, Vynnychenko and his entire cabinet, including Moshe Zilberfarb, the Minister of Jewish Affairs, who had held office for only five days, resigned.[89] Zilberfarb's resignation was a matter of parliamentary etiquette, since the ministers were expected to resign along with their prime minister.[90] Shortly thereafter, on February 7, the Ukrainian National Republic evacuated Kyiv in the face of the Bolshevik advance.

"When our love was strong," recounts the Talmudic sage Shmuel, "we made our beds on the edge of a lance. Now that our love is not strong, a bed sixty cubits wide will not suffice" (*Sanhedrin* 7a). In a similar fashion, the political *rapprochement* between Jews and Ukrainians attained unprecedented heights of mutual cooperation in the months following the collapse of the tsar: the Ukrainian leadership extended an offer of autonomy, while the Jewish political leadership shifted from a traditional Russocentric to a more Ukrainophile position. For Ukrainians, an alliance with the Jews meant valuable support in the urban sector. At the same time, by granting extraterritorial autonomy to their minorities, the Ukrainians took the high moral ground in their negotiations with the Provisional Government over greater territorial autonomy for Ukraine as a whole. For Jews, autonomy promised the benefits of self-government, with assurances of the maintenance of a *Rechtsstaat* and the inclusion of Ukraine within a federated, democratic Russian Republic. For both, the utopian dream of harmonious relations between traditionally antagonistic communities were shattered with the Bolshevik putsch in November 1917. When Jewish political leaders balked at voting for the Fourth Universal proclaiming Ukraine an independent state, the brief honeymoon period between the two nationalities was over.

Chapter Three

Autonomism in Practice

With the passing of the Law of National-Personal Autonomy in January 1918, Moshe Zilberfarb took his position as the head of the Ministry of Jewish Affairs, the first such institution to be created in a modern nation-state.[1] His ministry was heir to the original Vice-Secretariat for Jewish Affairs and subordinate to the Secretariat of Inter-nationality Affairs (June to November 1917). With the Third Universal, the office was made an equal member of the General Secretariat, and Zilberfarb's title changed from Vice-Secretary for Jewish Affairs to Secretary for Jewish Affairs. (For the sake of clarity only the title "Minister for Jewish Affairs," which was applicable after January 1918, will be used.)

The real activity of the Ministry, limited though it was, began in October 1917, when the Central Rada confirmed the rights and powers of the Ministry and the Nationality Council convened its first meeting. To mark the occasion Zilberfarb issued a moving declaration to the Jewish people of Ukraine:

> In the days of war which pitted the peoples of the world one against the other, the great Russian Revolution raised the flag of liberation of the peoples of Russia, the flag of their fraternal coexistence. It not only firmly established full equal rights of all citizens without difference of nation; but its striving to give each national community, be it large or small, territorial or extraterritorial, the equal opportunity to independently organize its national life without any external coercion—for only therein lies the full guarantee of amicable and fraternal association of peoples—shows up all the more outstandingly…
>
> In all areas of Jewish life great tasks await us. The liberated people with its democracy at the head should apply itself with all its forces to create new forms of national life. The work of creation, however, should not for one moment blind us to the danger on the part of the

> black and counter-revolutionary powers, which lurk around the Jewish street and wait only for an opportune moment to carry out their criminal plans. It is a deep offense to our national feelings that at a moment when the principles of freedom and brotherhood of nations are proclaimed so loftily, we must still in all senses retain this accursed inheritance of dead generations…
>
> As an agent of the Jewish revolutionary democracy, which has placed him in his responsible position, the Vice-Secretary hopes for active support on the part of all living forces of the people and calls the Jewish people in Ukraine to energetically set out to build our national life, in order to enter, revived and renewed, into the great family of equally entitled peoples, for whom the victory of the great Russian Republic bears peace and fraternal coexistence.[2]

Zilberfarb divided his Ministry into three sections, doling out the departments equally among the larger socialist parties.[3] Education was under Avraham Strashun (Bund), Community Administration under Avraham Revutsky (Poale-Tsion), and General Affairs under Y. Khurgin (Fareynikte). According to a budget drawn up in the spring of

Moshe Zilberfarb
From: Shalom [Solomon] Goldelman, "Di Yidishe Natsionale Oitonomie in Ukrayne (1917–1920)," in *Yidn in Ukrayne*, 2 vols., New York: Shulsinger Bros., 1961, vol. 1, p. 133.

Avraham Revutsky
From: Shalom [Solomon] Goldelman, "Di Yidishe Natsionale Oitonomie in Ukrayne (1917–1920)," in *Yidn in Ukrayne*, 2 vols., New York: Shulsinger Bros., 1961, vol. 1, p. 155.

1918, 604,200 *karbovantsi* of state funds, roughly 10 percent, were to be devoted to the Ministry, representing a surprisingly large amount of projected state expenditures.[4] The Education Department received 40.2 percent of Ministry funds, with a staff of fifty. General Affairs, with a staff of forty-one, took 32.6 percent of the funds, and Community Administration the remaining 27.2 percent to maintain thirty-four staff members.[5] A further amount of 550,000 was approved in the form of a loan to the Education Department, but the Rada fell before the transaction could be realized.[6]

During the brief period of its existence, Zilberfarb's Ministry was concerned primarily with preparing legislation to develop the infrastructure of Jewish autonomy in Ukraine, and dealing with requests for assistance from the public. The latter provide an interesting glimpse of popular opinion. Judging from the limited number of petitions preserved in the archives, which may of course be only a fraction of the total, it does not seem that the Ministry had a tremendous impact on the lives of ordinary Jews in Ukraine. The letters typically consist of appeals for assistance with personal financial matters often related to the changes in local government since the revolution. Zilberfarb reflected upon this in his memoirs:

> The general public did not understand quite clearly what exactly the Jewish Vice-Secretariat was and for what it was created. It clearly sensed that it was a kind of Jewish institution, moreover a democratic one, to which one could come to 'pour out one's heart' in 'simple Yiddish' and even to submit a 'request' in the 'mother-tongue.'[7]

Bliume Bagahmaline of Ladyzhyn, Podolia, for example, wrote to the Ministry in the spring of 1918 regarding her local mail service.[8] It seems that her father used to pick up the mail and distribute it to the residents, presumably for some sort of remuneration, and later she married the man who used to help her father with this. When she became a widow, she took over this small business, until a petty bureaucrat (*nachal'nyk*) refused to turn over the mail to her. In her opinion, this was done "with the motive that a Jew has no right to follow this kind of work."[9] Mrs. Bagahmaline appended a petition signed by forty-four persons (forty-three of whom signed in Yiddish) requesting that she be allowed to deliver their mail to them.

As with all the requests preserved in the archives, the Minister was diligent in passing the matter along to the appropriate authorities. A Ukrainian translation of Mrs. Bagahmaline's letter was prepared and sent off to the Minister of Post and Telegraph, with a covering letter supporting her request: "Such behavior of the local post officer is completely unlawful, as in Ukraine no restrictions based on nationality are tolerated."[10] Unfortunately, the archives do not contain any further documentation of this affair. It is likely, given the chaotic atmosphere of foreign occupation, revolution, and civil war, that Mrs. Bagahmaline's complaint was lost in the general tumult.

Several of the letters complain to the Minister about inconsistencies in Ukrainian language policy. Yiddish was an official language of the state, but it proved difficult for the young state to develop the necessary administrative infrastructure to support this policy. A Jewish club in Kaniv, Kyiv province, complained to Zilberfarb in August 1917 that they were unable to speak in Yiddish on the telephone to government officials.[11] Zilberfarb wrote to the Kyiv Provincial Commissar requesting that staff be hired to provide Yiddish telephone service.[12] The Commissar wrote back, apologizing that he was unable to support this as he was too busy maintaining order in the province.[13] Several such requests dealing specifically with Yiddish on the telephone were sent to the Ministry, yet little progress was made. One complaint in May 1918 indicated that the phone service did not even have a Yiddish-speaking operator: the caller was asked to use either Ukrainian or Russian.[14]

Several of the appeals deal with monetary damages as a result of the war and often involve violence. Friede Briskin of Kyiv wrote to the Ministry in early 1918. On the way home from Petrograd, she reported, her husband was removed from the train at Vorozhba station by Bolshevik troops. Ten thousand roubles were stolen from him, and he was then shot.[15] Others appealed for remuneration for damage related to the movement of troops, and several calculated damages and submitted invoices.[16] Entire budgets of homes for the aged and soup kitchens found their way to the Ministry of Jewish Affairs.[17] The local Chamber of Commerce of Uman' even wrote to Zilberfarb in January 1918 on behalf of one of their members, who had worked for a Kyiv doctor for two months and was owed back wages.[18]

In some cases, the Jewish Ministry was very successful in protecting the rights of Jewish citizens. When martial law was declared in Kyiv in connection with the Bolshevik attack, the Ukrainian military issued a decree expelling all inhabitants who had not been registered before January 1, 1915. This would have had a major impact on the Jewish population, some three-quarters of whom were unregistered. Zilberfarb, however, was able to prevail on the military to rescind this order.[19]

One of the duties of the Ministry of Jewish Affairs was to protect Jewish religious rights, yet in general it was seldom called upon to do so. In one of the few examples, dated November 1917, well in advance of the spring festival of Passover, the Ministry sent out a letter to the Minister of Supplies to allow one Rabbi Gleizer permission to cross boundaries to secure the unleavened bread required for the holiday.[20] On another occasion, the Minister issued a letter authorizing Jewish storekeepers to open on Sundays and other Christian holidays.[21]

In general, the appeals indicate the basic presumption on the part of the Jewish public that the Ministry of Jewish Affairs was primarily an institution for *shtadlones*, or "intercession."[22] This traditional form of Jewish political activity consisted of directing public appeals to a Jewish figure of influence, usually wealthy and possessing personal charisma, who could sway the gentile authorities to grant the Jewish petition. By and large, Jews regarded themselves as essentially outside the political process, possessing few rights but some fortunate privileges. An illustration of this attitude may be found in the traditional prayer that concludes the reading of Psalms: "Nullify all harsh and evil decrees that threaten to harm us…Let a benign spirit sway the hearts of the government regarding us, that they may decree favourable laws upon us."[23] This view was fundamentally different from the conception of citizenship espoused by the Central Rada. Complaints about war reparations should have gone to the Ministry of Defense or the Ministry of the Interior, not to the Ministry of Jewish Affairs, since the nationality of the damaged party should have no effect on the decision. And while questions regarding the language used on the telephone might have had some relevance for the Ministry of Jewish Affairs, certainly the initial complaint should have been handled by the Ministry of Post and Telegraph. The Jews of Ukraine, however, were conditioned by centuries of *shtadlones*, and the Jewish Ministry did not effectively communicate its new and unique service to the general Jewish population.[24]

Until the pogroms of 1919, the controversy between Zionists and socialists was not about whether or not to take part in the Ukrainian government but rather on what basis Jewish representatives would be chosen. This controversy raged on during the period under discussion, and thus serves as an introduction to the complex political history of the era. Jewish parties were represented on all three levels of the Ukrainian government. At the cabinet level, a Vice-Secretary for Jewish Affairs served in the General Secretariat for Inter-nationality Affairs (later this position was upgraded to General Secretary for Jewish Affairs and finally Minister of Jewish Affairs); at the parliamentary level, Jews took 25 percent (fifty seats) of the Mala Rada, or Smaller Council, and in the larger Central Rada, which met infrequently, approximately 7 percent.[25] In the absence of democratic elections, these representatives were not chosen by popular vote; rather, they were appointed as delegates from recognized Jewish political parties and organizations. The allotment of seats in the various bodies therefore easily became a bone of contention.

The most bitter controversy arose over the representation of the various political parties in the Nationality Council (in Yiddish, *Natsional-Rat*), an organ formed under the Vice-Secretary for Jewish Affairs.[26] As no election had been held and the relative popularity of the Jewish parties thus could not be established, this Nationality Council was convened according to "revolutionary democracy": each political party would be given equal representation. Ideally, this would be limited to "democratic elements" (meaning socialist parties), but the large Zionist party was simply too significant to be ignored, and was invited into the Nationality Council as well. This was not the case with the religious party Akhdes Yisroel, which petitioned the Nationality Council, only to have its case summarily rejected.[27] The Council began deliberations on October 1, 1917, with equal representation of four members from each of five parties: Bund, Poale-Tsion, Fareynikte, Folkspartey, and Zionists. Later this was increased to ten delegates from each of the five parties.[28]

During the opening session of the Nationality Council, the Zionists registered a serious protest. Whereas their allies Tseire Tsion and Akhdes Yisroel were not represented in the Council, the grouping of the three socialist parties together with their ally the Folkspartey meant that the Zionists were essentially outnumbered by a ratio of four to one. The Zionist delegate A. Kaplan announced that the Zionists would refuse to participate in the one-sided deliberations of the Nationality Council. Denouncing it as merely a "commission" of the Ukrainian government and unrepresentative of the true democratic wishes of Ukrainian Jewry, Kaplan informed the Nationality Council that the Zionists would send a representative only "for information purposes."[29] The socialists were deeply insulted by the Zionist gesture. Ber Borochov of the Poale-Tsion argued that in the chaotic political moment it was impossible to adhere to the "613 commandments of democracy."[30] The Zionists were unmoved, and sent a delegate to the socialist-dominated organ only occasionally.[31]

The major task of the diminished Nationality Council was to prepare the groundwork for the future organs of Jewish autonomy in Ukraine. Although the idea of a socialist hegemony was appealing, it had to be moderated with a less "revolutionary" democracy, and so plans were laid for a projected Provisional Jewish National Assembly (*Tsaytvaylike Idishe Natsionaler Farzamlung*), also known as the Pre-parliament (*Forparlament*). This assembly was to be established with a total of 125 members: 75 members democratically elected by the municipal Jewish communities *(kehiles)* as defined by a law passed in December 1917, and 10 members each from the Bund, Poale-Tsion, Fareynikte, Folkspartey, and Zionists.[32]

There was a basic philosophical difference between the socialist and the Zionist conception of the nature of Jewish autonomy. The socialist parties, while differing over specific issues, were generally eager to increase and expand the power and responsibility of the Jewish representatives in the Ukrainian government. The Zionists, on the other hand, wished to limit the responsibility of the Jewish delegate to the state, and proposed that a lower-ranking official called a "State Secretary" (*Shtats-sekretar*) represent the Jewish population rather than a Minister of Jewish Affairs.

Three issues shaped the Zionist position: First, the Zionists contended that a Minister for Jewish Affairs, such as the socialists desired, would be responsible to the particular government that sponsored his appointment. A State Secretary, however, appointed by the Jewish Parliament and having debating but not voting rights, would be immune to the political upheavals that characterized the Central Rada. The rapid changes of ruling parties, for example, prematurely ended the tenure of the first Minister of Jewish Affairs after less than five days in office. Second, the Zionists contended that a Minister of Jewish Affairs would be forced to "dance at two weddings." Responsible to both the policies of the State and the mandate of the Jewish community, the Minister would be embroiled in conflicts of interest, and would serve neither institution properly.[33] Perhaps most significant, however, was an inner contradiction posed by the conflict of Autonomism and the Zionist agenda. The Zionists pursued the maintenance of Jewish rights in the Diaspora, but their fundamental sense that the land of Israel was the only true homeland of the Jews precluded the integral participation of the Jewish community in a state of "exile" (*galut*). A State Secretary, therefore, would satisfy the basic needs of the Jewish community without cementing the Jewish presence in Ukraine.[34]

The local *kehiles*, as the bases for autonomy, were also a subject of considerable dispute between the socialists and the Zionists. While all parties agreed that they were to be the fundamental building blocks of Jewish self-government, there were questions about their constituency and competency. The Bund, for example, in consonance with its leftist agenda, wished to limit the competency of the *kehiles* essentially to matters of language, education, and culture. The development of a nonsocialist Jewish national consciousness was to be avoided, even to the degree of excluding organs of communal self-help.[35] The *kehiles* were to be restricted to activities that were ideologically harmonious with the development of a class rather than a national consciousness among the Jewish proletariat.[36] In one proposal, the Bund suggested that the Ministry exercise its influence through the *kehiles* only in schools, taking over charity, medicine, sanitation, and similar concerns if there were no private organizations to operate them.[37] These limitations were hotly disputed, even by nonpolitical organizations such as local Jewish soldiers' groups.[38] The Akhdes Yisroel argued for religious activities in the *kehiles*, and the Zionists accepted their concerns while also promoting involvement in education, health, and communal self-help.[39] The socialist parties were generally antagonistic to traditional Judaism and attempted to undermine it whenever possible. On one occasion they attempted to take over powers traditionally held by the Rabbinate by reorganizing the financial structure of the *kehiles*, hoping thereby to liquidate "the role of the bourgeois-clerical (*gvirish-klerikale*) elements and give over Jewish nationality life into the hands of the Jewish masses themselves."[40] The Zionists objected bitterly, quashing the proposal.[41]

Membership in the *kehiles* was also a matter of dispute. The most antireligious of the socialist parties, the Bund, argued that all those who declared themselves Jewish were eligible for membership. The other socialist parties adopted similar broad, flexible definitions of Jewish identity. The Zionists, on the other hand, probably influenced by their Orthodox allies, excluded people belonging to non-Jewish religions.[42] The question of membership was important in the context of issues such as marriage and divorce law. The socialists opposed the traditional Talmudic law administered by the Rabbinate, and the Zionists, again no doubt influenced by their Orthodox allies, did not favor the institution of civil procedures in marriage and divorce.[43]

The final contentious issue that plagued socialist-Zionist relations was language. Like many other stateless peoples in Europe, the Jews used several. They had to choose between the ancient Hebrew language, with impeccable qualifications as the historic Jewish language yet vestigial as a means of oral communication, and the relatively newer Yiddish language, with a much younger literary tradition yet claiming authenticity as the vernacular of 97 percent of the Jewry of the Russian Empire.[44] The socialist parties promoted the development of Yiddish as the true language of the Jewish proletariat, while the Zionists considered Yiddish a language of exile, and encouraged the re-adoption of Hebrew as the Jewish vernacular. The socialists enjoyed some success, and Yiddish was made an official state language. Ukrainian currency printed in late 1917 bore Yiddish inscriptions, and some Yiddish street signs were erected in Kyiv. Printing money was one thing, however, and running state institutions in Yiddish was another.

Obverse of UNR 100 *karbovanets'* note (designed by Hryhorii Narbut, 1917) The serial number has been cut out of bill. The Yiddish inscription at the lower center reads "hundert karbovantses." The Russian (upper left-hand corner) and Polish (upper right-hand corner) also translate the denomination. The face of the bill contains the denomination in Ukrainian.

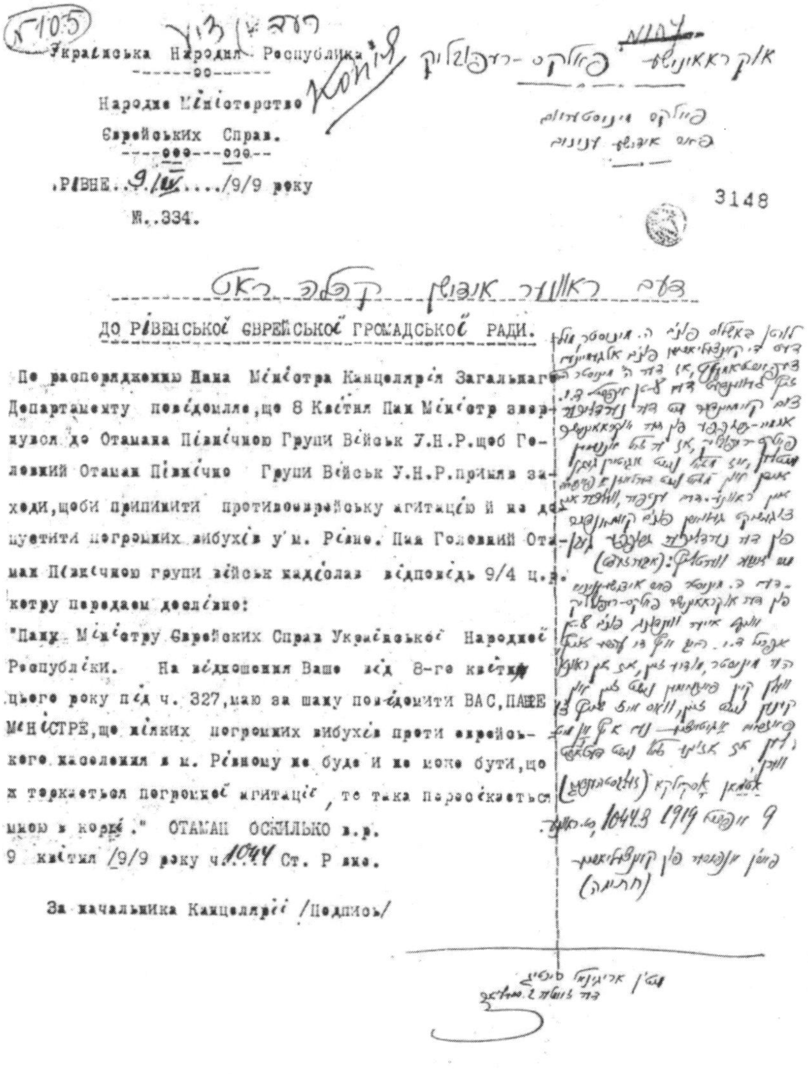

Українська Народня Республика
------оо------

Народне Міністерство
Єврейських Справ.
----ооо---ооо--

.РІВНЕ..9/IV..../9/9 року

№..334.

3148

ДО РІВЕНСЬКОЇ ЄВРЕЙСЬКОЇ ГРОМАДСЬКОЇ РАДИ.

По распорядженню Пана Міністра Канцелярія Загального Департаменту повідомляє, що 8 Квітня Пан Міністр звернувся до Отамана Північною Групи Військ У.Н.Р. щоб Головний Отаман Північно Групи Військ У.Н.Р. прийняв заходи, щоби припинити противоєврейську агітацію й на допустити погромних вибухів у м. Рівно. Пан Головний Отаман Північною групи військ надіслав відповідь 9/4 ц.р. котру передаем дословно:

"Пану Міністру Єврейских Справ Української Народної Республіки. На відношения Ваше від 8-го квітня цього року під ч. 327, маю за шану повідомити ВАС, ПАНЕ МІНІСТРЕ, що ніяких погромних вибухів проти єврейського населения в м. Рівному не буде и не може бути, що ж торкається погромної агітації, то така пересікається мною в корні." ОТАМАН ОСКІЛЬКО в.р.

9 квітня /9/9 року ч.1044 Ст. Рівне.

За начальника Канцелярії /Подпись/

Copy of Ministry of Jewish Affairs Correspondence (April 9, 1919).

It proved too difficult for the young Ukrainian state, and these policies were later abandoned.[45]

The Zionists faced a problem in their promotion of Hebrew, namely, that few Jews were able to speak it with fluency, and so some compromise had to be reached. The official correspondence of the Nationality Secretariat reflects this rather absurd situation: letterhead was often printed in three languages (Hebrew, Yiddish, and Ukrainian) with a line running down the middle to separate the Yiddish and Hebrew texts of the given letter.[46] At the same time, the Zionists had to resort to Yiddish to communicate with their supporters; their platform, which called for the establishment of a Hebrew school system, was published in Yiddish;[47] and even their magnum opus on the revolutionary period, *Di idishe avtonomie un der Natsionaler Sekretariat in Ukrayne*, was published in that language. The projected Hebrew translation never appeared.[48]

The Zionists attempted to deal with these language issues by following a policy of neutrality. This drew the ire of the socialists, who called it a "nonprogram." In his unpublished memoirs, Gergel recalls the impression that "this principle [was] simply a program of not to work, not to create,...and 'thou shalt not,'" a policy that represented "two peoples with two languages."[49] It threw the education system into utter chaos. The socialists, who envisioned plans for a Jewish university,[50] considered this Hebrew language policy utterly artificial, requiring large and unprofitable expenditures of intellectual energy and financial resources.[51]

While the Zionists and Jewish socialists bickered over ideological minutiae, a small but disturbing number of reports of anti-Jewish pogroms in western regions began to arrive. Distracted by their partisan feuding, Jewish activists failed to take sufficient note of these danger signs to abandon their disputes and address this issue of communal violence. Ultimately, the failure of both Jewish and Ukrainian leaders to control these attacks led to the fundamental dissolution of the *rapprochement* that united them in the first place.

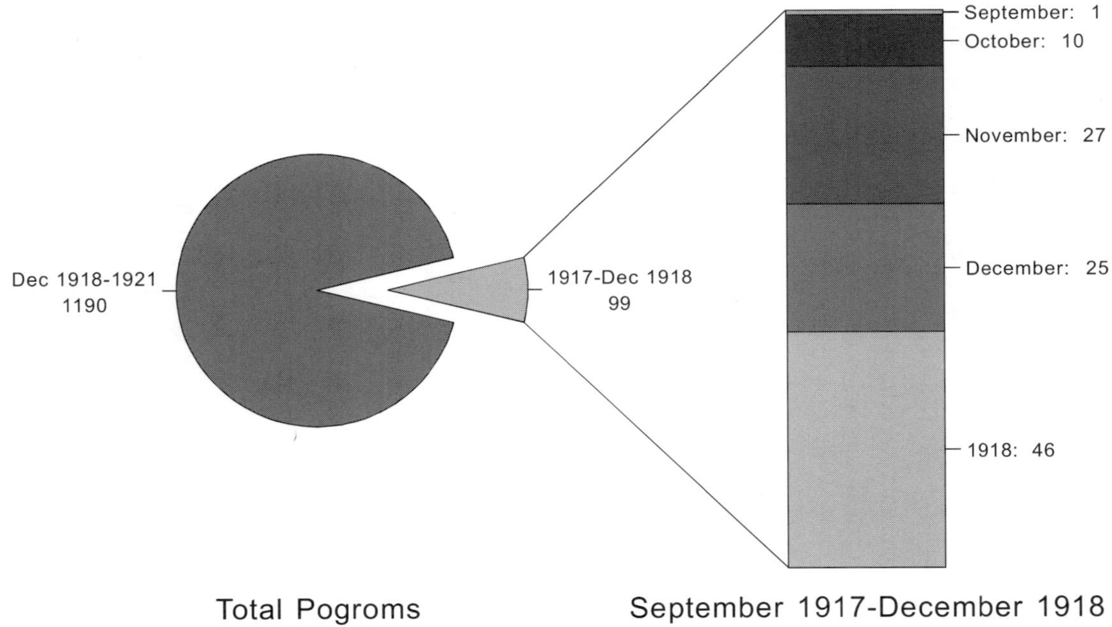

Figure 3.1. Recorded Pogroms, 1917–1921
Source: Tcherikower, *Antisemitizm*, pp. 197–98; Gergel, "Pogroms," p. 240.

A large body of scholarship has been published on the brutal pogroms of the Civil War era, certainly the most-studied example of anti-Jewish violence in the twentieth century before the Nazi Holocaust. The conflict between the Zionist and socialist bloc over the issue of self-defense has remained as a bitter and tragic legacy of this period. In the wake of the Paris trial of Symon Petliura's assassin in 1926–1927, popular understanding viewed the pogroms as an overwhelmingly Ukrainian phenomenon and believed that the vast majority of pogroms were perpetrated by Petliura's Directory troops.[52] The most comprehensive statistical analysis of the pogroms, however, estimated the Directory share to be closer to 40 percent of anti-Jewish attacks.[53] Since the bulk of them occurred in the summer and late fall of 1919, after all the Jewish parties had abandoned the possibility of cooperating with the Directory, these pogroms will be discussed in detail in Chapter 4.

Compared to the greater devastation of late 1918 and 1919, the pogroms of 1917 were limited in both number and scope. The Ministry of Jewish Affairs recorded over sixty, the bulk of them occurring in November and December 1917 (see Figure 3.1, previous page).[54] The violence was confined to the region of the front lines in the West, where anarchy and a culture of violence prevailed. There had been pogroms earlier in 1917, including a brief resurgence of the infamous "blood libel," in which a Jewish farmer in Kyiv province was accused of murdering a Christian girl to use her blood for ritual purposes.[55] Volodymyr Vynnychenko, then General Secretary for Internal Affairs, issued a circular to all provincial and municipal Commissars on October 20, condemning the disorder and warning pogromists that they would be subject to prosecution.[56]

Vynnychenko's circular was accompanied by a similar appeal from O. Shul'hyn, the Minister for Nationality Affairs and at that time Zilberfarb's immediate supervisor:

> From various locations in Ukraine comes the disturbing news that with the robberies, vandalism, and other acts that are happening, agitation for anti-Jewish pogroms and theft of Jewish goods is being conducted. This pogrom agitation is the product of national hatred, and is not representative of the broad masses…all the decent peoples

> of Ukraine must assist with all their strength the work of the General Secretariat and the local administrations in their struggle with the pogroms, which are an inheritance of tsarism...We have issued decrees [to the effect] that every Ukrainian should consider our freedom insecure until we are free of national hatred and anti-Jewish pogroms, a black spot on our faces, which makes the entire world consider us a people who are still enslaved.[57]

Zilberfarb also called for calm, promising that he would do his utmost to protect Jewish interests.[58] One further appeal, this time from Symon Petliura, in charge of Military Affairs, appeared later that month:

> I, as General Secretary for Military Affairs in the Ukrainian People's Republic, call upon all of you, my comrades and friends, to work in unity during this difficult time. Be organized and unified, one for all and all for one. Our army is young, it is just standing on its feet, but it will live up to the reputation of our ancestors.
>
> All must unite for the Central Rada and its General Secretariat. Do not tolerate any pogroms or disorderly behavior, because tolerating such activity will bring shame on the name of the Ukrainian army. No pogroms must occur on our land. I have already called upon Ukrainian troops to protect the order in Ukraine.
>
> Be ready throughout all of Ukraine, particularly on the railroads, to put a stop to any pogrom activity...This responsibility I can place only on your shoulders, and I will have trust in you, Ukrainian soldiers.[59]

The pogroms did not become a serious concern until the Bolshevik revolution in November. Under increasing Bolshevik agitation, the hungry and disenchanted soldiers of the former Provisional Government began to desert their posts on the Western front, some engaging in pogrom activity. On November 6, on the eve of the Bolshevik revolution, a Polish representative demanded in a formal session of the Mala Rada that the Ukrainian government take steps to control the burgeoning pogrom wave.[60] The first Jewish demand for more aggressive measures came in December, when Joseph Schechtman of the Zionists delivered a long speech detailing the nature of the pogroms and the Jewish predicament:

> Notwithstanding the appeal made twice already by the General Secretariat to the people of Ukraine to abstain from pogrom crimes,

> which are a slur on the revolution and on free Ukraine, notwithstanding the warning that all such crimes will be ruthlessly punished, the pogrom wave in Ukraine not only has not abated, but has increased in volume, and is threatening anarchy and utter ruin to the towns and townships of Ukraine.
>
> From more than thirty places, in the provinces of Podolia, of Volhynia, and of Kiev, we receive telegrams daily from the Jewish communities imploring protection from the pogroms that are under way or threatening.
>
> The telegrams disclose the tragic position of the defenseless Jewish population, entirely at the mercy of drunken pogrom bands. Towns are set aflame, shops are looted, household effects are destroyed; the last possessions of the terrorized Jewish working masses are being destroyed without reason or mercy by a mad crowd. The lives of large numbers of defenseless persons are at stake. The local authorities are powerless.
>
> There is no protection whatsoever. The fact that the pogroms are on the increase, notwithstanding the measures taken by the General Secretariat, is conclusive evidence that the local militias and the army detachments detailed to assist them are incapable of fulfilling their task.
>
> The horror of the situation is intensified by the absence of all adult and able-bodied Jews away on military service. There is no one left to check the assailants. There are only the old men and the women, whose lives and honor are in great danger.

Schechtman concluded with a concrete proposal to remedy the situation:

> The Jewish soldiers know this, and their feelings may be imagined. They cannot remain quietly in their units, passive onlookers of the crimes that are being perpetrated. We receive from all sides insistent demands from Jewish soldiers asking to be allowed to organize special voluntary defense units to protect their fathers, mothers, and sisters. They naturally regard it as their right and their duty to defend their helpless families.
>
> Without raising the wider principle as to whether separate national units of non-Ukrainian soldiers should be formed, we are of the opinion that the Jewish soldiers cannot be refused the right to form defense units for the special purpose of protecting the Jewish inhabitants from pogroms.
>
> It goes without saying that on all military matters these Jewish units would act entirely under the orders of the General Secretariat for Military Affairs.

> We are sure that the General Secretariat will do everything in its power to put an end to these devastating crimes, and that the Jewish units, in cooperation with the other disciplined units of the Ukrainian revolutionary army, will give the General Secretariat efficient support.[61]

The issue of Jewish self-defense proved highly contentious. The Jewish socialist parties in the Rada were inclined to form investigative committees to examine all the particulars, and were not warm to the idea of self-defense.[62] The Central Rada, and in particular Symon Petliura as General Secretary for Military Affairs, however, considered it a reasonable suggestion. The minutes of the session record his initial response to Schechtman's proposal:

> Petliura, the General Secretary for Military Affairs, confirmed that the pogroms have become quite severe and that the measures taken so far have been insufficient. He was sympathetic to the idea of a separate unit of Jewish soldiers and a special military unit for pogrom defense. He also declared that the [General] Secretariat [for Military Affairs] would take the strongest measures against the pogroms, and in the areas where the pogrom activity is the worst, he will send special military units which may be relied upon.[63]

The infrastructure for Jewish self-defense units was already well in place. A Jewish Military Union (JMU) was formed and held its first conference in Kyiv in October. The decorated tsarist officer Iosyf [Joseph] V. Trumpeldor (1880–1920) returned from Palestine to attend.[64] Although the JMU was primarily a self-defense organization, its platform included cultural issues and even publishing ventures.[65] The JMU was also staunchly in favor of the Kyiv Central Rada, as it indicated in a telegram to the government in October:

> The Congress of the Jewish Soldiers' Special Army greets the young democracy of the Ukrainian republic and its authoritative leadership, the Ukrainian Central Rada, which, we believe, will steadfastly uphold its principles with deep guarantees for citizens and nationalities. Standing on guard for freedom, fighting for the Russian revolution, we Jewish soldiers, cut off from our relatives and dear ones, hope that in this progressive epoch of Free Ukraine, anarchistic attacks on the lives and property of our brothers behind the front line will not be tolerated.[66]

Officially, the organization kept aloof from formally affiliating with any party, and sent invitations to the socialist parties to participate in its several congresses.[67] Unofficially, however, the JMU supported the Zionists. For their part, the socialist parties actively fought the influence of organizations such as the Jewish Military Union. In one internal propaganda bulletin, the Fareynikte urged supporters to be particularly energetic in recruiting soldiers, as they were especially drawn to the Zionist camp.[68]

In early December 1917, a representative of the JMU went to the Nationality Council to gain support for the creation of Jewish military units, only to be met with condemnation. Moshe Rafes of the Bund claimed that Jewish military units would only instigate further pogroms, and Maks Shats-Anin of the Fareynikte denounced the idea as being "against the interests and the will of the people."[69] The socialists were generally opposed to the establishment of distinct army units based on nationality alone. Ukrainians in the former tsarist army had been breaking from their units to establish all-Ukrainian formations as early as March 1917. The Jewish socialists hoped to halt this centrifugal phenomenon, in part because it represented a movement toward separation from the proposed federated Russian republic. There were also real fears that Jewish military units might antagonize the solely Ukrainian units and exacerbate the existing tension. Behind the scenes, the socialists succeeded in arriving at a compromise with the Central Rada. With the exception of the Khmel'nyts'kyi and Polubotok regiments, the Ukrainian army was to admit recruits and officers of any nationality. Despite incentives, however, "Jews were not pounding at the gates of the Ukrainian induction centers."[70] After the acceptance of this accord, the Nationality Council issued a statement opposing the formation of Jewish self-defense units.[71]

This position simply could not be maintained in the face of mounting violence. On January 28, 1918, when the Jewish Ministry finally agreed to the creation of separate Jewish military units, it was too late to form a central command in the deteriorating political climate. Independently formed units operated in scattered locations, but the absence of a central authority severely limited their effectiveness.[72] The degree to which socialist opposition actually affected the pogrom waves is uncertain. In several instances, however, pogromists were turned away by only a minimal show of force—one memoir records that organized yelling drove off pogromists—and it could be argued that the weeks of Ministry for Jewish Affairs hesitation were of critical importance.[73] Early anticipation of the coming violence and wide establishment of organized and authorized Jewish units might have stemmed the flow of blood in 1919.

Although the Central Rada was able to reassert its presence in Ukraine with the help of the Central Powers, Jewish and Ukrainian political leaders could not achieve the high level of cooperation they had experienced before the Bolshevik invasion. The socialist-dominated Central Rada was overthrown within months by the more conservative regime known as the Hetmanate, and the Law of National-Personal Autonomy was abolished. Within the Jewish political community, Zionists and socialists squabbled over issues minor and major, leaving them ill-prepared to deal with the conflagration that would envelop Ukraine in 1919.

The Bolshevik presence in Ukraine in 1917 and early 1918 was minimal and centered in the heavily russified industrial regions of the east, where an estimated four to five thousand members were active. Moreover, the Ukrainian ethnic element was underrepresented in the party; the Bolshevik strategy emphasized activism among the proletariat, which was more Russian and Jewish than Ukrainian. Among the population at large, the membership in other parties was much more significant. The Ukrainian Socialist Revolutionaries, for example, claimed over 300,000 members.[74] Despite their small numbers, the Bolsheviks had some influence in the cities, and were therefore a force to be reckoned with.

The Bolsheviks had hoped that the All-Ukrainian Congress of Soviets held in December in Kyiv would give them added weight in governing the region. Only some 80 of the 2,500 delegates were pro-Bolshevik, however, and so it was decided to transfer their center of operations to the more sympathetic eastern city of Kharkiv.[75] At another Congress of Soviets held on December 25, Ukraine was officially declared to be a Republic of Soviets with strong ties with the Russian Soviet Republic, this despite the presence of the Ukrainian Central Rada in Kyiv.[76] On January 29, 1918, the Bolsheviks attempted to take Kyiv, and fighting was fierce as insurgents overran several key areas of the city.[77] The rebellion was contained only on

February 4. The Rada had little time to relax, however, since Soviet forces invading from the north and east took Kyiv within days. The Rada was forced to withdraw to Zhytomyr in the west.

The Bolshevik policy on nationalism represented an attempt to harness the raw energy of a national movement and direct it to goals of a more socialist nature. It tolerated minor differences between nationalities but stressed the essential unity of the world proletariat. In this manner, the Communists (as the Bolsheviks called themselves after 1918) encouraged the trappings of Ukrainian statehood only in so far as this was in harmony with the world socialist movement. The Ukrainian language, for example, as an authentic expression of the peasants and workers, was an acceptable medium for the conveyance of Communist propaganda. However, any attempt to deviate from the unity of the world proletariat—by praising national distinctiveness, for example—was a form of nationalism and thus to be condemned.[78] As one scholar described this strategy, the Bolsheviks had a "utopian belief that national consciousness had to be fully developed before it could vanish."[79]

The Ukrainians possessed a common territory and common language, which the Communists considered prerequisites for national existence. Jews, on the other hand, were minorities everywhere and spoke a language (Yiddish) many considered to be a mere dialect of medieval German. Religious ties alone were not sufficient to establish a group as a distinct nationality. Lenin was faced with the reality of having millions of Jews in his territory who lacked these theoretical requisites but very much considered themselves members of a distinct nationality, an opinion shared by their neighbors. The Communists therefore relented and recognized the Jews as a distinct nationality, and a section of the Communist party was set up to propagandize them in Yiddish.[80]

The "Yevsektsiia," as the Jewish Section of the Communist Party was called, was initially very unpopular among Jews, so much so that the Communists were unable to appoint a Commissar for Jewish Affairs in Kyiv.[81] The Yevsektsiia raided the office of the Ministry of Jewish Affairs and confiscated its files, hoping to take charge of propagandizing the Jewish community.[82] Although the Communists had officially espoused a doctrine that eschewed antisemitism,[83] it persisted at high levels of the invading Red Army. A poster issued by the

Kyiv Military Commissar betrays the overriding concern that the Communist movement was dominated by Jews: "In the Soviets there are some Jews [*zhidy*], but to raise them to high office is absurd. Thus, Piatakov is no Jew, but a Ukrainian and a gentleman [*ukrainets i chelovek*]...Skrypnik is no Jew, also a gentleman...Zatonskii, obviously, is neither a Jew nor a Lett, but rather a Ukrainian as well. Bubnov, too."[84]

With the exception of segments of the Jewish proletariat, the general Jewish population had little sympathy for the Bolshevik occupation. It was also manifestly evident, however, that individual Jews were prominent among the Soviet leadership in Ukraine, particularly in the cities. In Kyiv, the Commissars for Finance, Press, Army, and even the City Commissar serve as examples.[85] On the other hand, the Jewish political parties were unanimous in their condemnation of the Bolshevik regime. Rafes, leader of the left-wing Bund, wrote in its organ *Folkstsaytung*: "a foreign power has entered Kyiv. An occupying army has arrived. They have driven out all democracy, and have taken all law into their own hands—and they wish to lord over us."[86] The Fareynikte wrote that the Bolsheviks "bring, in truth, only destruction and death [*khurbanos un korbanos*]."[87] Conversely, the Jewish parties were unanimous in their support of the Ukrainian Central Rada.[88]

Nevertheless, considerable tension existed between the Central Rada and the Jewish representatives over the issue of support for the beleaguered government. Most serious was the Ukrainian charge that the Jews refused to flee Kyiv with the rest of the government, effectively abandoning the cause by not accompanying the Rada to Zhytomyr. This charge implied that the Jews were "neutral" in the struggle with the Soviets, a position that for Ukrainians was untenable. Solomon Goldelman of the Poale-Tsion addressed the question in his memoirs:

> In respect to this I must say that I, who during the whole time of the existence of the Central Rada was one of the representatives of the Jewish parties in the little [Mala] Rada, had received no indication of the intention of the Government and the Rada to leave Kiev. Exactly on the day of departure from Kiev I met on the street...the current Head of the new Government. On this occasion we discussed events—Bolshevik bombers flying overhead—and we then parted, each on his own way, without the Head of the government giving so much [as a] hint that at night he was abandoning Kiev along with his

> Government, the Rada, and the Army. No notice of his retreat was sent to me from the office of the Rada either, although hitherto and afterwards there were many occasions, even at nighttime, when I was called to a meeting when I was needed. At this time, quite evidently the ruling circles did not consider me, or any other [Jewish] representative, as essential in the mutual activity and co-operation, and responsible for the fate of the state in this grave moment of its existence.[89]

Meanwhile, the Ukrainian delegation was meeting with the Central Powers in Brest-Litovsk and on February 9, a treaty was concluded between them in which the Ukrainians agreed to provide a supply of foodstuffs and raw material.[90] Although the Brest-Litovsk treaty did not formally stipulate that the Central Powers would aid Ukraine in the event of a foreign invasion, the Germans were nevertheless quick to protect their eastern investment and advanced on Soviet forces on February 18.[91] Within two weeks Kyiv was recaptured, and the Central Rada back in power.

With the exception of the Bund, all the Jewish parties were in favor of a separate peace with the Central Powers. The positive impression this might have made on the Ukrainians, however, was minimized in the eyes of Ukrainian ethno-nationalist extremists by the fact that speakers who opposed the treaty were ethnically Jewish, representing the Bund, the Mensheviks, and the Russian Socialist Revolutionary Party.[92] Members of the right-wing Ukrainian Socialist-Independentist Party (UPSI) were the most vocal in their criticism of the minority representatives, demanding that the entire Ministry of Jewish Affairs be abandoned "as a penalty for the 'bad conduct' of the national minorities."[93] The Ministry was maintained despite right-wing pressure, but two changes were introduced into the Law of National-Personal Autonomy. The article allowing Nationality Unions to unite with other Nationality Unions in the proposed federated Russian republic was removed, and Ukrainian currency was henceforth to be printed only in Ukrainian. The former seemed impractical for the moment, since the Federated Russian Republic did not exist, and the change in currency was defended on the grounds of the technical difficulties involved in multilingual printing.[94]

Adding to the tensions created by this course of events was the fact that Ukrainian troops under the command of Symon Petliura were proving susceptible to the virus of antisemitism. During the initial Bolshevik invasion of Kyiv, the army had already attacked many Jews and "suspicious non-Ukrainian elements," executing them without trial.[95] With the resurgence of the Central Rada, Ukrainian military formations committed acts of violence against Jews, particularly those traveling by road or rail between Korosten' and Kyiv. In Borodianka, for example, Jews donned their prayer shawls and phylacteries and gathered all the Torah scrolls in the town to make a formal oath to the Ukrainian troops, but a pogrom took place nevertheless.[96] In Brusyliv, Kyiv province, the inhabitants complained to the Minister of Jewish Affairs that a local Ukrainian commander had entered the town and demanded 50,000 roubles from the Jewish population. To back up his claim, he said that he had been authorized by the Central Rada "to…beat, shoot, and otherwise kill to establish order."[97] Of course, pogroms were not committed solely by the Ukrainian troops. In one cruel episode, Red Army troops running wild killed three sons in front of their mother, and then said to her, "Tomorrow we will return to you for lunch—prepare it." And return they did.[98]

The most serious of these sporadic attacks was the pogrom in Kyiv upon the return of the Ukrainian military. After meeting with a Jewish delegation, Petliura attempted to avoid the possibility by having his troops skirt the Podil neighborhood, which had a large Jewish population. This proved to no avail, however, for violence against Jews erupted spontaneously on the streets of Kyiv. With cries of "Jewish Commissars" (*Zhyds'ki komisari*), Jews were beaten in broad daylight. One of the military formations known as a "Death Batallion" (*Kurin' smerty*) set up its headquarters in the Mikhailovs'kyi monastery, turning the site into a major center for torturing and murdering Jews; many corpses were later found floating in the river.[99]

In contrast to the Ukrainian military, the local authorities were aghast at the anti-Jewish violence, and issued several appeals to the soldiers. Typical was an appeal published on March 3 in *Kievskaia mysl'*:

> I beg you, in the name of the future of the Ukrainian National Republic, desist from the murders, which have taken place without any justice whatsoever; desist from the meaningless arrests of innocent citizens…understand that the Cossacks should refrain from attacking Jews based only on the assumption that among the Bolshe-

> viks there were Jews. Jews were among and are among those who fight the Bolsheviks, and also there were Ukrainians among the Bolsheviks...I ask you, stop this bloody vengeance."[100]

The Jewish *kehile* authorities sent the Prime Minister of the Central Rada a memorandum pointing out that the pogrom agitation was couched in nationalist terms, as if violence against Jews was a service to the Ukrainian movement. The delegation was assured that the policies of the Central Rada toward minorities remained the same as before the Bolshevik occupation. This satisfied the Jewish delegation, and shortly thereafter the Jewish municipal community (*kehile*) published a proclamation to this effect, publicly absolving the Central Rada of blame.[101] Pogroms perpetrated by Ukrainian troops continued sporadically throughout the spring of 1918, however, provoking hostile debates in the Rada.[102]

Zilberfarb had resigned from the post of Minister of Jewish Affairs in mid-January, but the Ministry continued to function under the temporary leadership of his deputy, Y. Khurgin.[103] Khurgin's administration faced two pressing tasks: convening a Jewish parliament based on democratic elections in the *kehiles*, and, in the interim, consolidating the Jewish Ministry. A law passed in December established the basis for the legal existence of the *kehiles*,[104] and elections of representatives had been steadily taking place throughout Ukraine. At the beginning of 1918, only 21 *kehiles* had registered, but the idea became increasingly popular, and by July 9 a further 165 had joined them. Despite the administrative and military chaos of the period, this number eventually increased to 202 Jewish communities, representing roughly one-third of all potential *kehiles*.[105] Needless to say, most were financially weak and lacked coherence.[106]

While the Jewish parties set about organizing representative bodies, the Central Rada was losing its allies, the Central Powers. German support was based on the efficient transfer of Ukrainian foodstuffs, which was becoming increasingly difficult due to peasant resistance. The German occupying forces had grown tired of the fractious and inefficient Ukrainian government, which was unable to guarantee delivery of grain, and began to court possible candidates to lead an administration more to their tastes. On April 28 the Central Rada met to debate, among other things, a proposed constitution of the Ukrainian Repubic. The Jewish delegates had brought forward two bills, but before these could be debated, the Rada was shut down by a German-sponsored coup. Zilberfarb recalled the event in his memoirs, which were published not long afterward:

> In an oppressive atmosphere the Rada adopted the chapters of the constitution one after the other; the eighth chapter, which reiterated word for word the law of January 9 [National-Personal Autonomy], was also soon adopted...and then the chairman declared a recess...the recess hitherto has still not ended, and the draft law regarding the Pre-parliament and the Jewish Constituent Assembly still waits for the Jewish democracy to return to its work.[107]

The coup was led by General Pavlo Skoropads'kyi (1873–1945), a former tsarist officer of Ukrainian ancestry and one of the region's important landowners.[108] Taking the historic title of *hetman*, Skoropads'kyi dissolved the Rada and proclaimed the creation of the State of Ukraine (*Ukraïns'ka Derzhava*). Although Ukrainianization proceeded apace under the Hetman, in general, the government's policies represented a return to the bourgeois culture that had predated the revolution.[109]

The Jewish response to the coup was generally skeptical. While the bourgeoisie was happy with the idea of increased order under a regime more closely supervised by the Germans, there were some doubts about how friendly a right-wing government would be to Jewish interests.[110] Protests came from the socialist parties, including a letter from the Fareynikte to the President of the Central Rada, Mykhailo Hrushevs'kyi.[111] Individual Jews (including the Finance Minister) were present in the Hetman's government, yet official policy was cool to Jews. Freedom of worship was proclaimed, for example, but Orthodox Christianity was declared the official religion of the state.[112] More seriously, the dissolution of the Central Rada destroyed the legal basis for Jewish National Autonomy.[113] The actual organs were not disbanded by the Hetman (in fact, the Law of National-Personal Autonomy was not officially repudiated until July), but the Ministry was cut off from the government, becoming "a Ministry without a Minister."[114]

In the weeks leading up to the abolition of the Law of National-Personal Autonomy, negotiations were held to bring the Zionists back into the Nationality Council. Their bargaining position was strong. The Hetmanate government, through reactionary decrees, clearly intended to remove the last vestiges of the Ministry of Jewish Affairs.

Furthermore, incoming election results revealed the greater popularity of the Zionists and the religious parties, and it was obvious that the Nationality Council had to appear more democratic if it were to enjoy even limited support from the Jewish population.[115]

In return for rejoining the Nationality Council, the Zionists insisted on several conditions, which together were intended to make the organs of Jewish Autonomy more democratic (and the fact that increasing democratization would only add to Zionist strength was not lost on the socialists). The Nationality Council would have to be reconstituted to reflect more closely the political opinions of the Jewish population. First, the Zionists proposed that they get 40 percent of the reconstructed Nationality Council and their allies, the Akhdes Yisroel, another 10 percent. Second, they insisted that the proportion of delegates in the proposed Pre-parliament would be determined only by this reconstructed Nationality Assembly and that its competency would be decided by the body itself, not by the Nationality Council. Finally, they proposed that the Nationality Council could not recall the Pre-parliament without the assent of the Kyiv *kehile*.[116]

The Zionist pressure was effective. The size of the Nationality Council was increased to sixty members: the Zionists were given twenty-four seats and Akhdes Yisroel another six. The remaining thirty went to the socialist parties,[117] the Bund receiving the largest share (ten), followed by the Fareynikte with eight and the Poale-Tsion with seven. The Folkspartey received only five seats. This settled, the Zionists and Akhdes Yisroel rejoined the Nationality Council in May.[118] Debate concerning the Pre-parliament was heated. The socialists originally wanted 50 of the 125 delegates to be representatives from the old Nationality Council, thereby guaranteeing that at least forty seats (ten each from the Bund, Poale-Tsion, Fareynikte, and the Folkspartey) would go to the socialist bloc.[119] The Zionist argument that the Pre-parliament should consist solely of elected representatives was eventually accepted. It was also decided, against socialist opposition, that the constitution of the Pre-parliament could only be changed with a two-thirds majority in that body.[120]

By mid-May the Nationality Council had begun to regard itself as an "institution of struggle" (*kamf-organ*). The tenor of government politics clearly indicated that the Jewish Ministry, as a holdover from the leftist Central Rada, would no longer be tolerated by the

Hetmanate. It was obvious that the position of Minister for Jewish Affairs could not be left vacant for long, adding fuel to the arguments for the total dissolution of the Ministry. Previously, while the Ministry was temporarily maintained by Zilberfarb's deputy, Khurgin, the Jewish parties could not come to any agreement on a candidate. The socialist parties refused to consider a Zionist candidate yet did not submit one of their own because they disapproved of the overall government in power.[121] One of the major stumbling blocks in the debate was the Zionist policy of "neutralism" on the language question. The Zionist movement wished to further the use of the ancient Hebrew language but realized that immediate legislation encouraging this goal was impractical, since the vast majority of Jews spoke Yiddish. The Zionists therefore held that no language was to be officially sponsored by the Jewish Ministry, blocking the strongly pro-Yiddish policies of the socialists. This deadlock in the Nationality Council was broken when the Folkspartey struck a bargain with the Zionists, agreeing to support the Zionist language policy in return for Zionist support in choosing a Folkspartey member for the post of Minister.[122]

The pact having been made, in April Yakov Ze'ev Wolf Latsky-Bertholdi, known simply as Wolf Latsky, was appointed Minister of Jewish Affairs.[123] A compromise candidate, his major task was to manage the Ministry until the elections to the Pre-parliament could be held. One political activist of the day remarked that "the Nationality Council debated two months to choose a representative without a program."[124] The comment was something of an exaggeration, as Latsky did undertake some legislative projects.[125]

Meanwhile, plans for the convening of the Pre-parliament proceeded apace. Although the Hetmanate had officially declared the Ministry of Jewish Affairs dissolved, a delegation to the government argued that the elections to the Pre-parliament should be held. The Pre-parliament, it was argued, would act as a central organ of the Jewish community, thus facilitating its administration by the state. After some negotiation, the Hetmanate government eventually agreed, but with the condition that the Pre-parliament confine its deliberations solely to the internal life of the Jewish community and not discuss general political issues.[126]

The parties prepared for a heated battle, as one Fareynikte leaflet indicates:

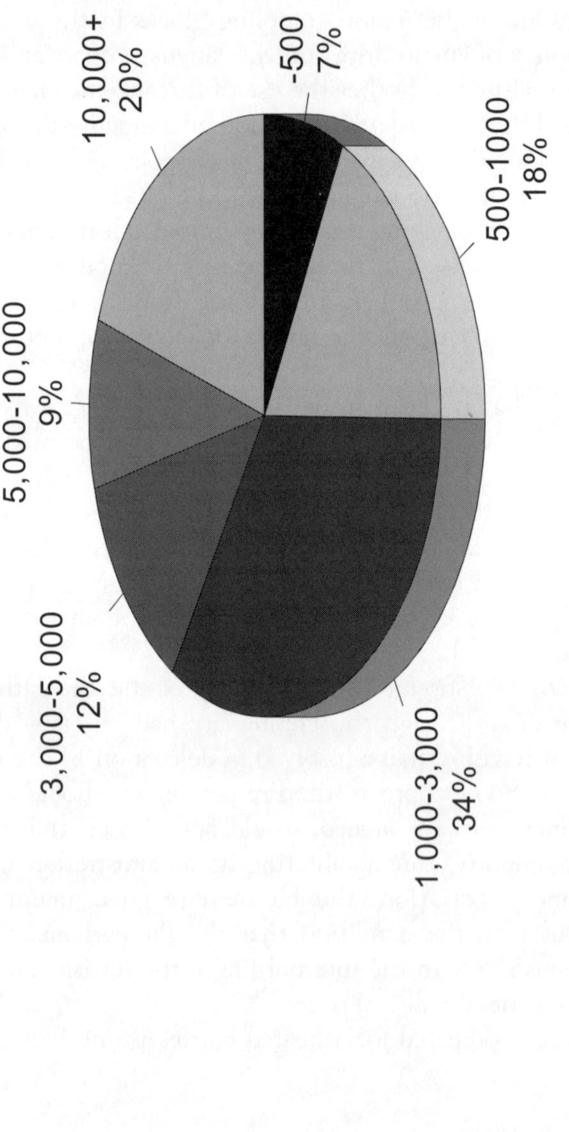

Figure 3.2. Votes to the Pre-parliament by size of *kehile*
Source: Avtonomie, pp. 204–206.

> Jews, Protect Yourselves!
>
> They are trying to mislead us, our "fat cats" [*gvirim*]!
>
> They want respect—and you elect them into office!
>
> They are far from Jewishness—and speak of the World to Come!
>
> They care only about their pockets—and say that they are socialists; do you hear? Don't you get the feeling, folks, that you're being driven into the ground?!
>
> A great shame will fall upon us Jews if these people are elected to office by our votes.
>
> Jews should elect those, who are ashamed of their Jewish names, of the Yiddish language?! No, that should not be. Therefore all Jewish votes should go to the socialist ticket number 3.[127]

Elections were held in some 200 communities, but by the end of October results had been ratified in only 161.[128] The majority of votes for the Jewish constitutent assembly came from the smaller urban localities (*shtetlakh*). Fifty-nine *kehiles* with one to three thousand voters represented 34 percent of the 270,000 votes cast, and another 25 percent of the votes came from *shtetlakh* with less than a thousand voters (see Figure 3.2, previous page).[129] Thirty-five hundred elected *kehile* leaders in turn cast votes for the delegates to the Pre-parliament. The voter turnout was roughly proportional to the Jewish population in each province, indicating a relatively equal level of popularity among Jews throughout Ukraine (see Figure 3.3). Voter turnout was much higher in the smaller communities, with large cities like Kyiv and Odesa having roughly 25 percent turnout (see Figure 3.4).

The election results provide a profile of Jewish political consciousness in Ukraine. First, only a minority of Ukrainian Jewry cast ballots. Although a total of some 270,000 votes were registered, this figure represented less than 10 percent of the electorate. This must be placed in context, however, since only one-third of the *kehiles* were sufficiently organized and motivated to hold elections. Scattered information from later rounds of elections indicates a voter turnout of approximately 40 percent, a more respectable figure in a time of chaos.[130] Second, a significant portion of those voting (19 percent) chose not to support political parties at all, favoring instead local women's groups, youth clubs, and so on. In one case, a pallbearer's society was elected to office.[131]

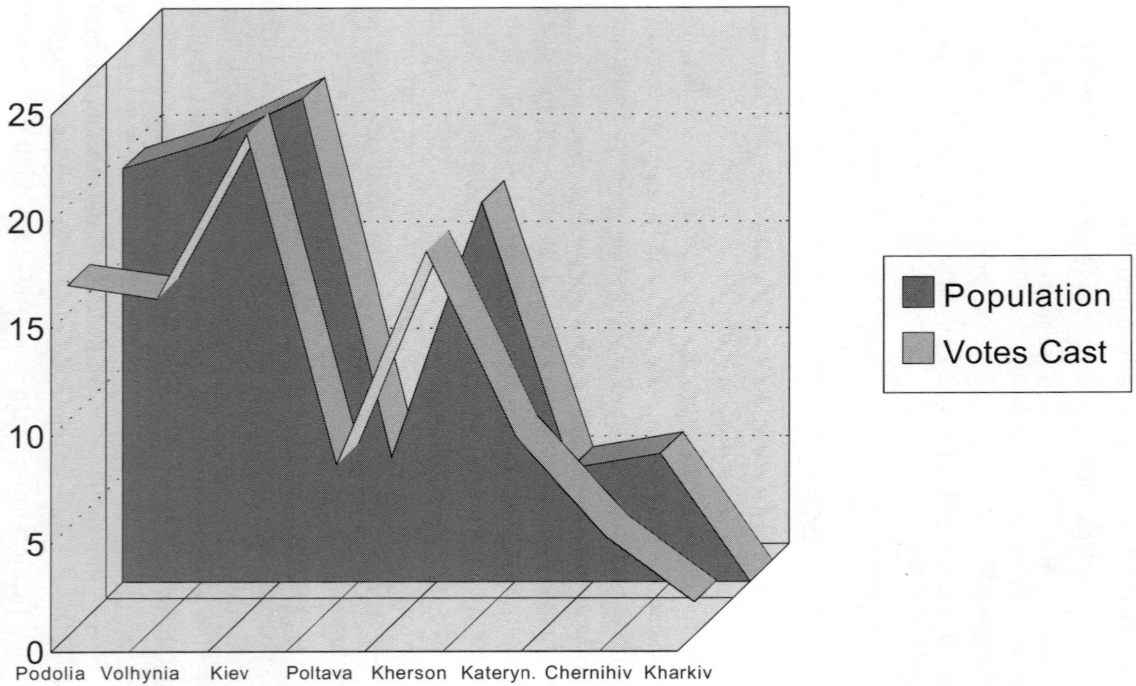

Figure 3.3. Distribution of Jewish Votes to the Pre-parliament (percent)
Source: Avtonomie, p. 207 ; *Perepis'*.

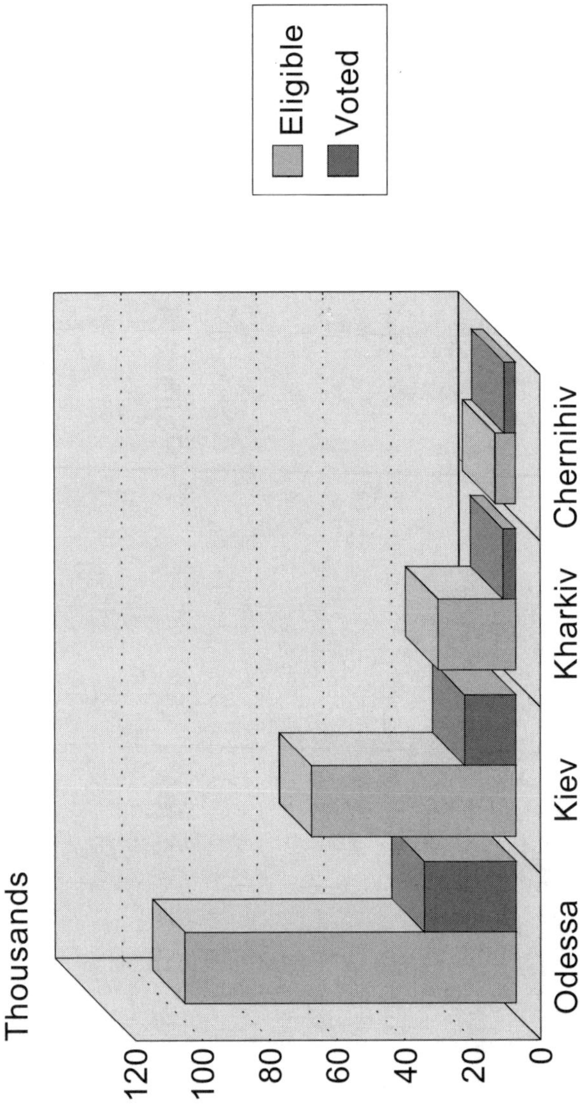

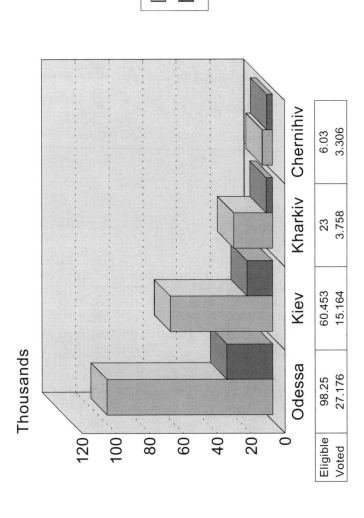

	Odessa	Kiev	Kharkiv	Chernihiv
Eligible	98.25	60.453	23	6.03
Voted	27.176	15.164	3.758	3.306

Figure 3.4. Voter Turnout in Large Cities (thousands)
Source: *Avtonomie*, p. 213.

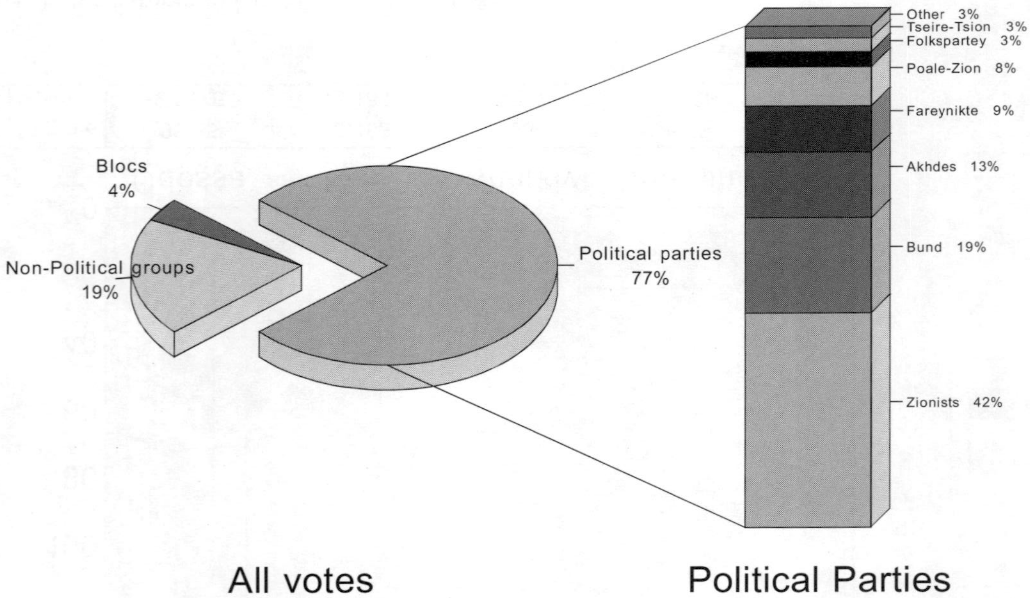

Figure 3.5. Results of Elections to the Pre-parliament
Source: Avtonomie, pp. 210–13.

Of the 77 percent of voters that supported Jewish political parties, the politically conscious Jewish population was clearly Zionist-clerical in orientation, much to the dismay of the socialists (see Figure 3.5). The Zionists claimed 42 percent of the vote, and their religious ally Akhdes Yisroel another 13 percent. Together with 3 percent of Tseire Tsion, the youth wing, the Zionist-religious bloc commanded 58 percent of the popular vote. The Bund fared the best of all the socialist parties, taking 19 percent of the vote, with the Fareynikte, Poale-Tsion, and Folkspartey splitting 20 percent among them. The elections had confirmed the socialists' worst fears: mobilized Jewish political opinion in Ukraine was Zionist and clerical, and the Zionist bloc with their Orthodox allies had taken nearly 60 percent of the seats in the Pre-parliament.

The Pre-parliament was convened in November 1918. A twenty-five member Committee and a twelve-member Executive, known as the Nationality Secretariat, sat at its head. Despite the democratic character of the assembly, it failed to heal the rift between the socialists and the Zionists. The Zionists, now demonstrably representing the most popular political position in Ukraine, invited the socialists to work together with them in the new Pre-parliament.[132] At the very first meeting, however, the socialists chose to boycott the executive organs of the Pre-parliament, claiming that "the majority does not consider the minority."[133] They argued that the Pre-parliament was insufficiently democratic, as the elections took place in extremely difficult times and in a convoluted three-stage process that disenfranchised large sections of the Jewish population.

While the Jewish political parties sparred with each other, Ukraine was once again about to be plunged into the maelstrom. Hetman Skoropads'kyi had never had much success at controlling peasant unrest in the countryside, which was further aggravated by the German grain confiscations. German and Austrian garrisons, spread far apart and with few resources, were prone to attack by armed peasant bands, and violence increased. By July, some 30,000 peasants had organized themselves into eighteen battalions to fight the Germans. These units armed themselves by raiding German bases and by purchasing weapons from troops eager to desert. Occasionally soldiers even murdered their commanders and fled west.[134]

The German military regarded the Jewish community with considerable hostility, in part because of the increase of speculation in the countryside, which had become a mainstay of the Jewish war economy.[135] A form letter was sent out to the Jewish communities warning them to keep speculation under control or the entire Jewish population would suffer the consequences. The military specifically warned the Rabbinate that they were not above suspicion, as "religion has nothing to do with this matter."[136]

More seriously, the German and Austrian authorities were not above directing peasant anger toward the Jews when possible, and issued proclamations that blamed the Jews for Ukrainian misfortune in very harsh language. In one, they stated:

> The Commmandant has been informed that a large part of the Jewish population, especially the Jewish merchants, in the markets and in their travels, are agitating against the Ukrainian government and its German allies, saying that the Germans intend to take provisions without payment.
>
> *That is a terrible infamous lie!* On the contrary, the German forces are dedicated to maintaining the peace and prosperity of all agriculturalists, enabling them to continue their honest labor. When requisitions are made, farmers will be *paid punctually with money*. The German troops wish peace, order, and above all to maintain security, in order to allow all to continue in their professions.
>
> The German Commandant is displeased with this Jewish disruption of the general peace. He will prosecute these individuals without mercy, and will make it widely recognized that these persons, who endanger the public safety, will be severely punished, if through their subversive activity they seek to interrupt the free peasantry from performing their orderly activities.
>
> Local authorities should urgently make enquiries, to immediately collect the names of shameful elements, in order that the strongest prosecution may be brought against them.
>
> Whoever of these Jewish merchants agitates against the Ukrainian State and the German troops situated in Ukraine endangers the food supply and the orderly free work of the Ukrainian people![137]

And in another proclamation:

> From various sources it has come to my attention that despite my Announcement of 6 October 1918, which made the dissemination of

> rumors a punishable offence, leaders of bands and rumor mongers are spreading [the rumor] that the German troops are going to leave Ukraine.
>
> *Above all, it is always Jews who drag these rumors among the people.*
>
> Through these rumors, bandits provoke and endanger peaceable and hardworking citizens and farmers, who have trust in the orderly and lawful development of the land and the establishment of a citizens' society.
>
> *These rumors are based on untruth and lies.*
>
> Whoever spreads such rumors is a shameless liar and is guilty of promoting banditry, which brings misfortune on Ukrainian cities and villages, often destroyed in smoke and flames.
>
> I therefore request the following:
>
> Whoever spreads the rumor that the German troops are leaving Ukraine or are abandoning Ukraine will be fined 3000 Marks or will be jailed, and in extreme cases will be imprisoned or shot to death.[138]

On one occasion, a Jewish delegation approached a local commandant to complain about an antisemitic proclamation; the commandant received them in a hostile manner and asserted that the Jews were in fact the worst instigators against the German military, and that this opposition was most intense in the religious study halls [*batei midrash*].[139] The German position served to increase anti-Jewish attitudes in the general population, and thus bears some responsibility for the violence that followed the German retreat.

❀

For the Jewish political leadership of revolutionary Ukraine, the possibility of realizing national-personal autonomy was quite new and unexpected. In many ways, they made poor use of it. Rather than deal with the pressing concerns of state-building, they became bogged down in polemics and undermined partisan attempts to create an effective organ of Jewish representation to the Ukrainian government. Their infighting had serious consequences, since they proved incapable of taking concrete steps to control the burgeoning pogrom wave that would overwhelm the region. The times, however, were not auspicious for the implementation of national-personal autonomy. The Central Rada was soon embroiled in a war with Soviet Russia. After signing a separate peace with the Central Powers, the Rada quickly secured its territory, only to be overthrown by a German-sponsored coup shortly thereafter.

During the period in which they were active in the Ukrainian government, the Jewish political parties wasted precious time in ideological feuding. With the exception of some interesting legislation, which has now become merely an object of curiosity, the parties failed to make any lasting impression on Ukrainian Jewry. They engaged in fruitless power struggles, often sabotaging efforts to make a positive contribution to the Jewish community. They agreed on only the most skeletal of plans and differed on virtually every detail of significance. Most seriously, they were unable to come to terms enough to take measures against the impending violence. Early intervention might well have been very effective.

By November it was patently obvious that the Hetman's days as leader of Ukraine were numbered, particularly after the revolution in Germany and the subsequent armistice. On the night of November 13, a resurgent Central Rada, operating under an executive government called the Directory, stepped forward to take the reins of power, unprepared for the chaos that awaited them.

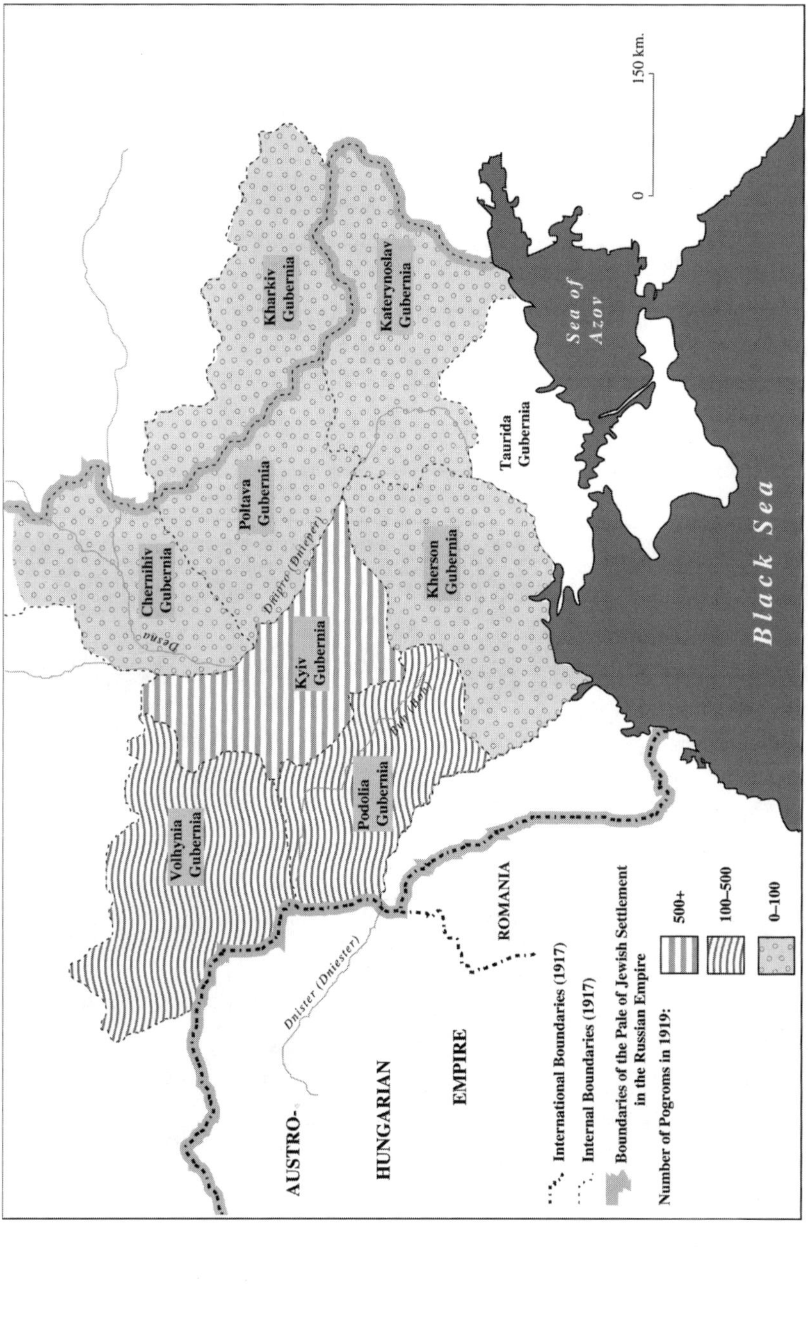

Map 2. Recorded Pogroms on Territory Claimed by the UNR, 1919 (by gubernia)

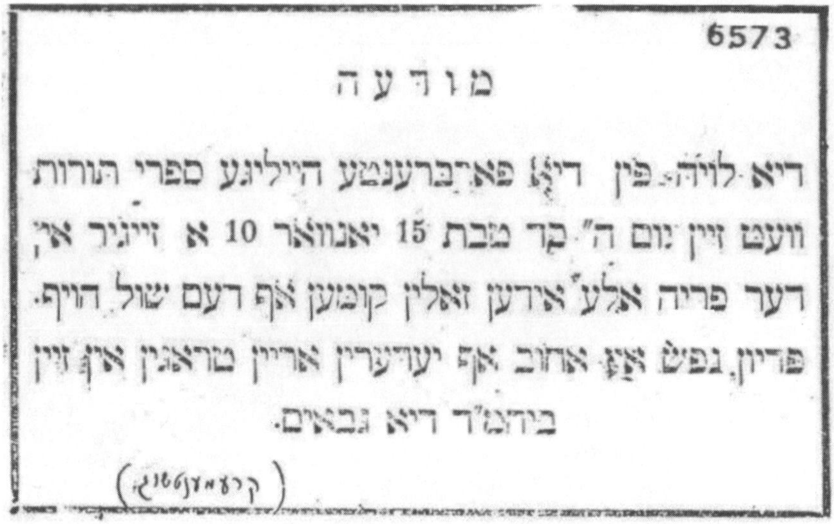
6573

מודעה

דיא לויה פון דיא פארברענטע הייליגע ספרי תורות
וועט זיין יום ה״ כד טבת 15 יאנוואר 10 א זייגער אין
דער פריה אלע אידען זאלין קומען אף דעם שול הויף.
פדיון נפש איז ארוב אף יעדערין אריין טראגין און זיין
בידמ״ד דיא גבאים.

(קרעמענטשוג)

Top: Announcement of the Burial of Desecrated Torah Scrolls and Appeal for Money to Rescue Captive Jews, Kremenchuk. *Bottom:* Desecrated Torah Scroll.
Source: (both) Archives of the YIVO Institute for Jewish Research. *Reproduced with permission.*

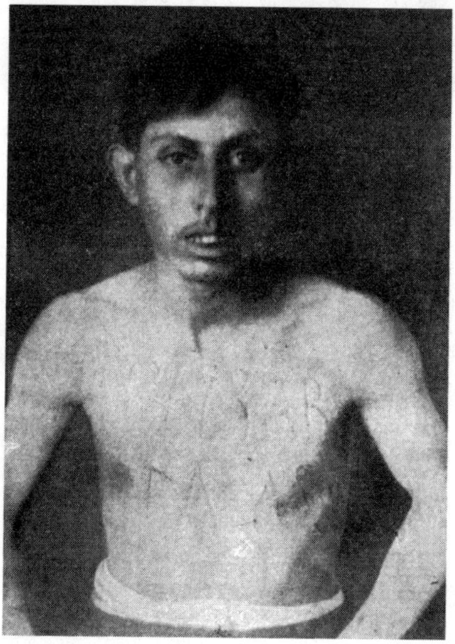

Pogrom Victims. *Top:* A young woman with child. *Bottom:* Victim with the phrase "A *haidamaka* carved this" cut into his chest.
Source: (top) Archives of the YIVO Institute for Jewish Research. *Reproduced with permission.* (bottom) *Evreiskie pogromy*, p. 40.

Top and *bottom:* Victims of the Proskuriv pogrom (see pp. 122ff, below).
Source: Evreiskie pogromy, pp. 32–33.

Cover of Eliyohu Gumener, *A kapitl Ukrayne* (Vilnius, 1921); see p. 174 below.

Top: Ukrainian and Russian workers killed by White Army forces at Iasynivka and Makiïvka in December 1917. *Bottom:* Gravesite of mineworkers at Iuzivka (now Donets'k) killed by White forces in 1919.
Source: Hiroaki Kuromiya, from the Central State Cinematographic, Photographic, and Phonographic Archives in Kyiv, od. zb. 2-28891 and od. zb. 0-53773. *Reproduced with permission.*

Chapter Four

The Pogroms of 1919

The etymological roots of the term *pogrom* are unclear, although it seems to be derived from the Slavic word for "thunder(bolt)" (Russian: *grom*, Ukrainian: *hrim*).[1] The first syllable, *po-*, is a prefix indicating "means" or "target." The word therefore seems to imply a sudden burst of energy (thunderbolt) directed at a specific target. A pogrom is generally thought of as a cross between a popular riot and a military atrocity, where an unarmed civilian, often urban, population is attacked by either an army unit or peasants from surrounding villages, or a combination of the two. Early instances of this phenomenon in the Russian Empire were described using various terms (here in Russian): *demonstratsii*, *gonenie*, *draky*, *besporiadki* (demonstrations, persecution, fights, riots).[2] Pogrom, however, has been the most effective in entering European languages, perhaps through Yiddish usage. Jews have not been the only group to suffer under this phenomenon, but historically Jews have been frequent victims of such violence. In mainstream usage the word has come to imply an act of antisemitism.

Comparison of the violence of the revolutionary era to earlier pogroms reveals elements of both continuity and discontinuity. In the context of the former Russian Empire as a whole, the geographic location of the pogroms followed a traditional pattern, that is, the majority of attacks took place in Ukrainian ethnolinguistic territory (see Map 2, p. 103).[3] It should be noted that the pattern of pogroms roughly conformed to the density of Jewish settlement—the more Jews, the more pogroms. These statistics do not, however, reveal anything about the pogroms perpetrated against other minorities. Mennonites, for example, suffered horribly during the revolutionary years. Pogromists were aware of their religious doctrine of pacifism, and would take brutal advantage of it, moving into their homes and repeatedly raping and murdering without fear of reprisal. Violence against Mennonites and other minorities has not yet been statistically evaluated, however, and comparisons are only possible using isolated memoirs.[4] Although the pogroms were concentrated in Ukrainian ethnolinguistic territory, it would also be inappropriate to compare the carnage of Ukrainian Jewry to the experience of Jews in neighboring Poland and Lithuania. These areas were secured behind German lines and did not undergo the anarchic experience of protracted civil war after the armistice.

The elements of discontinuity are perhaps more striking than the elements of continuity. The scale of the pogroms of 1919 dwarfed previous violence. While reasonable estimates of those massacred in the 1881–1884 pogroms are numbered in the tens and low hundreds, and those of the 1903–1906 wave in the low thousands, estimates of 1917–1921 run in the tens and even hundreds of thousands. The chaotic nature of the times, particularly the mass migrations that accompanied and followed the civil war, make the collection of accurate statistics extremely difficult. The most authoritative study by far, using both primary materials collected by the "East-Jewish Historical Archive" and carefully evaluated Soviet and Western secondary sources, was prepared by Nakhum Gergel and published in 1928. Several smaller statistical studies of the pogroms have appeared, most of them published shortly after the revolution, but they are handicapped by having only partial data and in general failing to document the witness reports carefully.[5] Gergel's analysis, on the other hand, is distinguished in its exhaustive catalogue of the "East-Jewish Historical Archive" materials, held now in the Tcherikower Archive in New York City (see below, p. 175). It is also worth noting that Gergel's estimate of the total number of Jewish dead is very conservative in comparison to less well-documented studies. Had Gergel wished to inflate his estimate of 50,000 and 60,000 by doubling or even tripling that number, he would have found much support in the more apologetic Jewish scholarship of the day, and the fact that he refrained from doing so also lends credibility to his work.[6] His first-hand participation in the autonomy organs also distinguishes his research, and in general, even a cursory comparison of the available historiography will immediately demonstrate the superiority of his analysis.

The pogroms must also be put into context. Anti-Jewish violence was often related to political upheavals—the pogroms of 1648–1649,

1768, and 1905–1906 were secondary phenomena of larger social rebellions, and the attacks on Jews of 1881–1884 followed the assassination of Alexander II. With the possible exception of the Khmel'nyts'kyi rebellion, however, none of these upheavals came close to the chaos of 1917–1920. The revolutionary era was characterized by a prolonged absence of central authority, which encouraged anarchic and violent behavior. It is also worth noting that preceding these three years of revolution and civil war were three years of struggle with the Central Powers in World War I, which ravaged the western regions of Ukraine in particular.

The violence of 1917 was an explosion "of mass discontent—elemental, unpremeditated, and unorganized."[7] Unfortunately, little is known about the social and economic background of the pogromists themselves. Anecdotal evidence indicates that, at least in the initial period of the major pogrom wave (late 1918–early 1919), the instigators were from various socioeconomic backgrounds.[8] The available biographic data are too scattered and anecdotal to posit any recognizable patterns.[9] The very fact that little is known about most pogromists, however, might indicate that they preferred to terrorize villages where they would not be recognized—a practical reinforcement of the principled tendency to attack minorities.[10]

It can be argued that simple bloodlust was the common element behind all pogroms, regardless of perpetrator and, indeed, of victim. As all people like to appear righteous in their own eyes, however, some more honorable pretext was usually fabricated. Throughout the late nineteenth century in Western Europe, the concept of "Anti-Semitism" gained considerable popularity and even respectability; politicians ran as "Anti-Semitic Candidates" and in many cases won elections, notably in France and Austria. The term itself was coined by Wilhelm Marr to replace the term "Jew-hatred" (*Judenhass* or *Judenfeinde*), which was regarded as uncouth and boorish. Borrowing the term "semitic" from the language family that includes Hebrew and Arabic, Marr and others succeeded in making the ideological opposition to Jews frighteningly popular at the end of the century. After the Holocaust, the term regained its negative connotations and is properly spelled "antisemitism," since there is no such thing as "Semitism."[11]

It would be a mistake, however, to regard Ukrainian antagonism to Jews as a form of this highly developed antisemitic ideology.[12] Ukrainians were in fact so unfamiliar with the term that contemporary usage was rare. One pamphlet referring to antisemitism defined the term in parentheses as "anti-Jewish."[13] Motivated by greed, lust, and the simple craving for blood, Directory troops commonly phrased their anti-Jewish proclamations in almost exclusively *political* terms.[14]

The most common charge against Jews was that they were allied with the Bolsheviks,[15] and the phrase "Jew-Bolshevik" was used as a construct in several proclamations of Directory military leaders.[16] A synonymous term was "Jew-Commissar," referring to the Bolshevik predilection for the term Commissar, or more explicit phrases, such as "Soviet power in the Jew's hands."[17] One proclamation asked, "Why do our little Jews [*nashi zhydky*] wait so for the Bolsheviks [to come to the] towns and townlets, and why do they agitate for the Russian Bolsheviks?" and answered that Bolshevism "gives the Jews lordship [*panuvannia*] over our peasants and workers."[18] Some proclamations refer to Jews as "capitalists," but this phenomenon is less pronounced.[19] Seldom is any other charge, such as religious antipathy, brought against the Jews, and this is often conflated with other slurs: "the anti-Christian Muscovite Jews…who kill [our] brothers, fathers and sons."[20]

As discussed in Chapter 1 (see Figure 1.7, p. 29), a small minority of Bolsheviks were Jews and an even smaller minority of Jews were Bolsheviks. History, however, is better understood as the unfolding of events based on perceptions rather than as the linear progression of facts. Jews were perceived as the driving force behind the Bolshevik movement, and it was not difficult to identify significant examples. In 1917 roughly 30 percent of the Central Committee members were Jewish.[21] Jews joked that the abbreviation of the Central Committee (VTsIK) really stood for the Yiddish phrase *vu tsen idn komandeven*, 'where ten Jews are in command.'[22] The most visible Bolshevik after Lenin himself was Leon Trotsky, leader of the Red Army attacking Ukraine. Perhaps because of their urbanization and greater literacy, Jews who joined the Bolsheviks rose to leadership positions at a rate disproportionate to their membership in the party as a whole. This phenomenon gained so much notoriety that Bolshevism was popularly understood as a Jewish movement.[23] No doubt the sudden appearance of Jews in prominent positions of authority exacerbated this negative impression.[24] The Bolshevik canard, however, seemed to function best as a sort of justification for simple plunder and mayhem. The motivation behind most pogroms seems to have been of the most basic variety: "to steal from the rich, to drink one's fill of vodka, to savor the wild pleasures of rape and murder."[25]

Pogroms erupted as soon as the Germans began to evacuate Kyiv, and it was the regular Directory troops that committed most of the early acts of violence (see Figure 4.1). This trend continued until spring and then suddenly dropped off. Until July, the Directory's affiliates increasingly committed pogroms. The sudden rise in violence in May was due to the activity of the local warlord Hryhoriïv (Grigoriev), while Denikin's troops were responsible for most of the violence later in the summer. By late 1919, as the Red Army consolidated its control over much of Ukrainian territory, the pogrom wave faded, with the exception of the slight increase in December that accompanied Denikin's retreat.[26]

Non-Jewish communities suffered many of the early attacks and indeed, it has been argued that Jews faired slightly better during this period. More accustomed to the pogrom phenomenon, they were better prepared to deal with local warlords and spontaneously offered "contributions" to avoid violence.[27] In terms of geography, the great majority (80 percent of some thirteen hundred recorded pogroms) occurred in the right-bank provinces of Kyiv, Podolia, and Volhynia, where roughly 80 percent of the Jewish population lived (see Map 2, p. 103).[28] Just over half (51.4 percent) of the communities were attacked more than once, and two were terrorized eleven times.[29]

Virtually all regular and irregular forces operating on Ukrainian territory were responsible for pogroms,[30] but the largest number recorded, 40 percent of the total, were perpetrated by the Directory and its allies under Symon Petliura (see Figure 4.2). The Directory's army consisted of roughly 100,000 troops who joined the cause of the Ukrainian revolution when the Germans retreated in December:

> In reality, however, the peasants and Cossacks who poured into Petliura's formations had little or no comprehension of the Directory's political and social programs. They knew only that they were sick of the Germans and of Skoropadskyi's police. They rose to seize the lands Skoropadskyi had forced them to return to the big landowners, to rid themselves of armed food collectors, to attack and plunder withdrawing German units, to rob stores in the cities—in sum, to profit in any way possible from the chaos.[31]

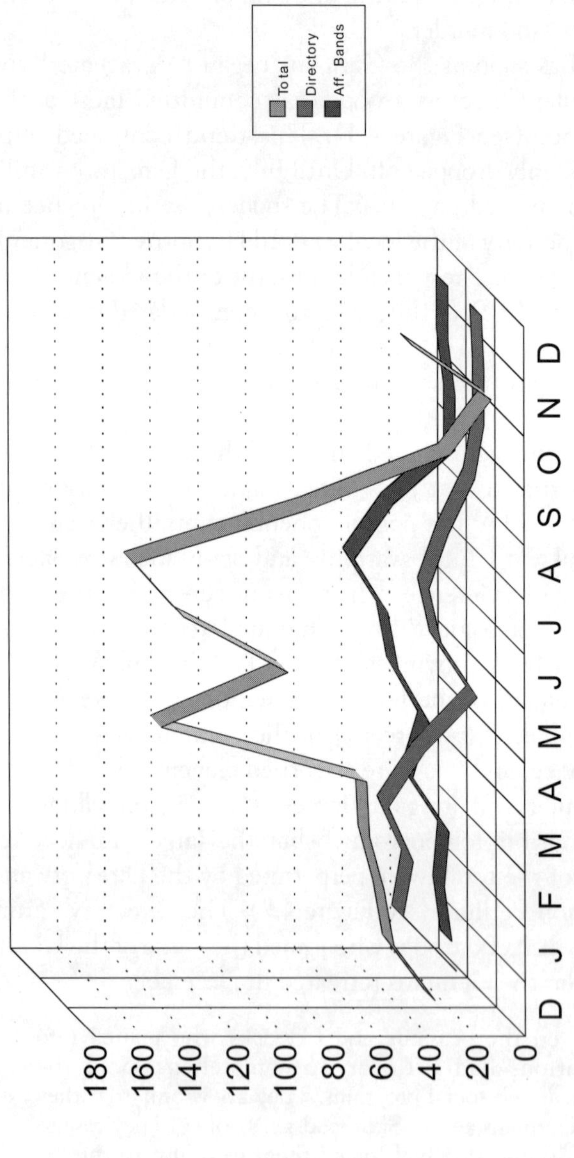

	D	J	F	M	A	M	J	J	A	S	O	N	D
Total	34	51	55	61	62	148	95	138	159	85	27	10	43
Directory	13	35	31	41	26	4	19	24	16	5	1	1	2
Aff. Bands	3	6	4	19	12	25	29	43	27	1	1	4	4

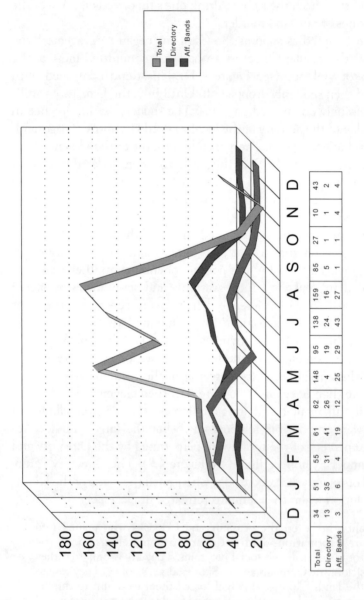

Figure 4.1. Pogroms in Ukraine, December 1918–December 1919
Source: TA35371-35392; Gergel, "Pogroms," p. 240 from 12 December 1918.

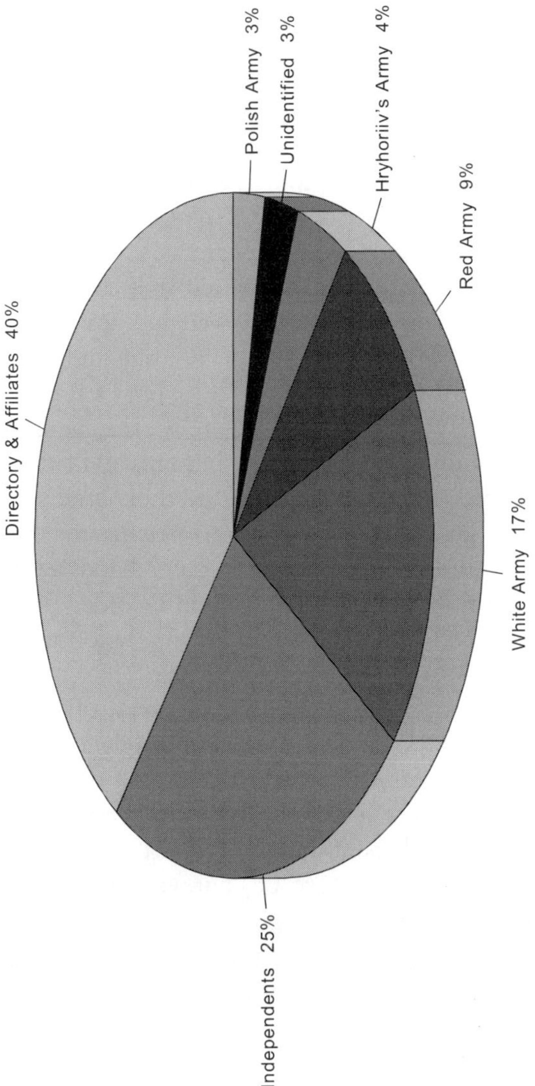

Figure 4.2. Perpetrators of Recorded Anti-Jewish Pogroms
Source: Gergel, "Pogroms," p. 245.

Besides these ragtag soldiers, many local warlords declared themselves allies of the Directory, although they were more motivated by personal gain than by patriotism. Highly opportunistic, these independent warlords sometimes switched allegiances as the tides of war changed.[32] Many of them, like one Lazniuk, the self-proclaimed Commandant of the Chornobyl region, and his comrade Struk, the self-styled "*polkovnyk*" ('colonel,' the designation for a regional military leader in the Cossack State) of the Hornostaipol' area, declared allegiance to the Directory but refused to leave their areas, preferring to terrorize Jews and demand "contributions." Indeed, failure to produce protection money was a major cause of pogroms.[33] The Directory was unable to supply its ragtag army, and some felt that the burden of "financing" the war effort fell on the Jews, who were less active participants in the armed forces.[34] The Nationality Secretariat studied these brutal warlords, whose favorite method of murdering Jews was to throw them into the Dnipro River and "send them to the Directory" downriver in Kyiv. According to their report, Lazniuk and Struk extorted over 800,000 rubles from communities in their area.[35] Such bands accounted for 31 percent of the pogroms perpetrated by the Directory (see Figure 4.3). In addition to the Directory, bands acting in its name, and combinations of the two, 3 percent of recorded pogroms were perpetrated by the Sich Riflemen, a unit originally formed from Ukrainian citizens in the Austrian province of Galicia.

Some distinctions may be made regarding the type of violence perpetrated by each army. Nykyfor (Matvii) Hryhoriïv's forces were responsible for only fifty-two of the recorded pogroms, but they were by far the bloodiest, murdering 3,471 Jews, or sixty-seven per pogrom (see Figure 4.4). The Directory and its affiliates were responsible for the greatest number of confirmed deaths (16,706) but were somewhat less brutal, murdering thirty-eight Jews per pogrom. The Whites were responsible for twenty-five murders per pogrom, while independent troops, the Red Army, and the Polish army accounted for fifteen, seven, and four respectively (see also Figure 4.5).

Bohuslave, a regional center in the province of Kyiv, attracted thousands of refugees from pogroms. Their experiences were recorded by the Jewish Pogrom Relief Committee of the Kyiv Region (*Evobshchestkom, Idgezkom*), and the statistics gathered from this information shed light on the nature of pogrom violence. Figure 4.6

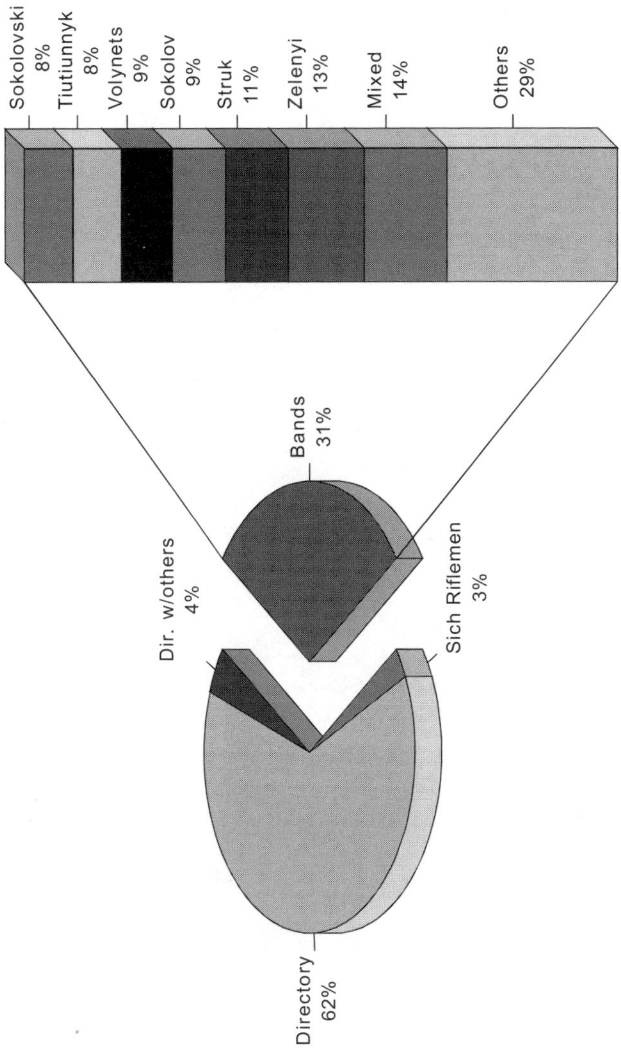

Figure 4.3. Recorded Pogroms Perpetrated by Directory and Affiliated Troops
Source: TA 35371-35392

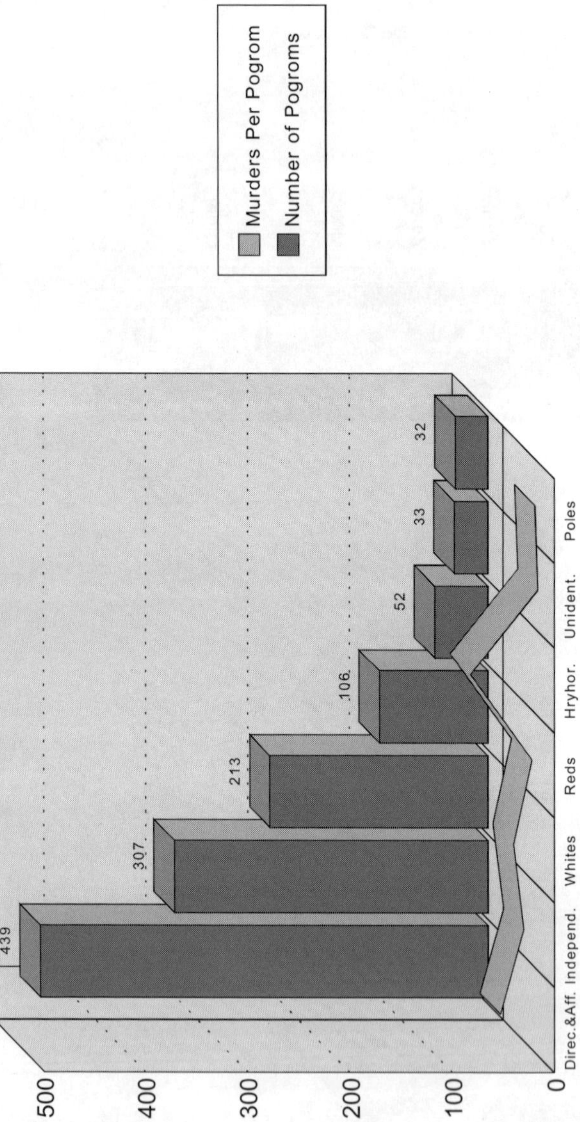

	Direc.&Aff.	Independ.	Whites	Reds	Hryhor.	Unident.	Poles
Murders Per Pogrom	38	15	25	7	67	1	4
Number of Pogroms	439	307	213	106	52	33	32

Figure 4.4. Murders per Recorded Pogrom by Perpetrator
Source: Gergel, "Pogroms," pp. 245, 248. Ukrainian territory only.

provides some insight into why residents fled to Bohuslave in the first place. A total of 59 percent of the refugees were forcibly evicted from their homes. Of those, the homes of 56 percent were destroyed by fire or other means, while another 2 percent were confiscated, and 1 percent "requisitioned." This indicates a high degree of destructive violence that was probably related to robbery and looting. On the other hand, 39 percent of the refugees managed to leave before suffering this fate: one-third had time to sell their homes, 5 percent abandoned them intact, and 1 percent even managed to rent them. It seems therefore that while destruction was rampant, there was often sufficient time to avoid the danger with advance planning. The life lived by Jews during this period was likely not one of constant persecution, but rather of relative normality (within the context of a civil war, of course) punctuated by sudden, violent attacks. It should also be noted that while pogroms were the principal reason Jews left their homes, it was certainly not the only one in such chaotic times.[36] The very fact of ending up in a refugee camp, however, indicates that these people left their homes under duress.

The rate of murders per pogrom varied widely, depending for the most part on the identity of the perpetrators. Of the refugee families in Bohuslave who had experienced pogroms, 19 percent had lost at least one family member in the violence: 14 percent had lost one member, 4 percent—two members, and 1 percent—three members (see Figure 4.7). Eighty-one percent of the families were fortunate enough to survive pogroms intact. Surprisingly, far fewer families experienced wounds: in 93 percent of families who escaped intact, not a single member was wounded, perhaps, because they fled in anticipation of a pogrom. These figures might imply that only a small percentage of the Jewish population was physically attacked in a pogrom, but once attacked, a person was somewhat more likely to be murdered than simply wounded.

Relatively few pogroms, however, were free of murder, and only 12 percent can be so counted. The most common number of deaths was between one and ten (36 percent of recorded pogroms); 88 percent claimed fewer than one hundred lives (see Figure 4.8). The age of the victims reveals some pattern, although no one was exempt: 333 persons, or 3.4 percent of the recorded murders for which there are such data, were children under the age of seven; forty-five were infants

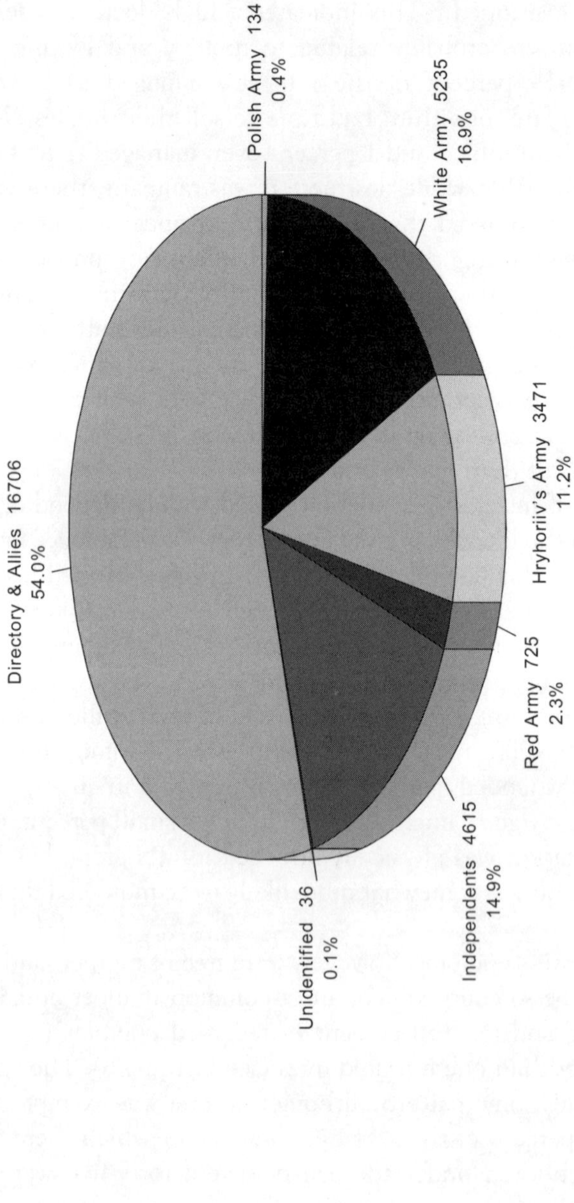

Figure 4.5. Murders in Recorded Pogroms
Source: Gergel, "Pogroms," pp. 245, 248. Ukrainian territory only.

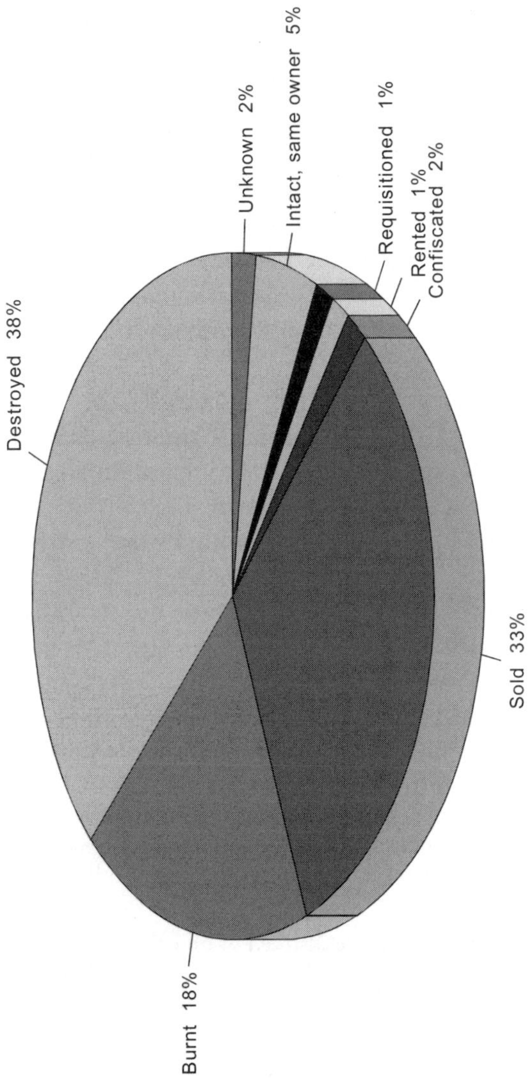

Figure 4.6. Status of Homes of Pogrom Refugees (Based on Homeless in Bohuslave, Kyiv Guberniia)
Source: Statistik, p. 12. Of those sold: 4% to Jews, 6% to Ukrainians, 90% to others.

under one year of age. The age group most affected comprised those over fifty-one (26 percent). Perhaps this is because older Jews, who were more established and wealthier, had homes that were more attractive to looters. At the same time, because they tended to be weaker and in poorer health than other age groups, they were less likely to survive an attack (see Figure 4.9). Although pogrom survivors often speak of rape as a common occurrence during pogroms, no reliable statistical data exist because of the hesitancy of victims and their families to talk about the experience.

If a single pogrom stands out in the collective Jewish memory, it is that of February 15 to 18 in Proskuriv.[37] It was not the bloodiest pogrom, but it was one of the earliest to be characterized by a high degree of murder, and became in the minds of many Jews "the symbol of those terrible years."[38]

Early in February 1919, Otaman Semesenko, commander of the Petliura brigade of the Zaporozhian Cossacks, 3rd Haidamak Regiment, entered the town with orders to maintain a garrison and allow his soldiers some rest.[39] Little is known about this former farmer in his twenties who had risen to a command position in the Directory, although soon after his arrival he summoned a doctor to examine him and was diagnosed with a severe case of venereal disease.[40] On the sixth of the month, he issued a decree putting the town under martial law. A 7:00 P.M. curfew was imposed, and strikes and meetings were forbidden. The decree also called for all storefront signs to be changed to Ukrainian "so that I might not see a single Muscovite sign." Most ominously, under point 6 the decree proclaimed:

> I call upon the population to cease its anarchist demonstrations, for I am sufficiently strong to fight you. I especially warn the Jews [*zhydam*] of that.
>
> Know that you are a people disliked by all nations, yet you cause such trouble to Christian people. Do you not want to live? Have you no pity on your own people?
>
> So long as you are not attacked keep quiet. Wretched nation, troubling poor people.[41]

For all his antisemitic bluster, Semesenko was at least correct in presuming that there was some anti-Directory activity in town, although it was only minimally connected with the Jewish community.

(text continues on p. 126)

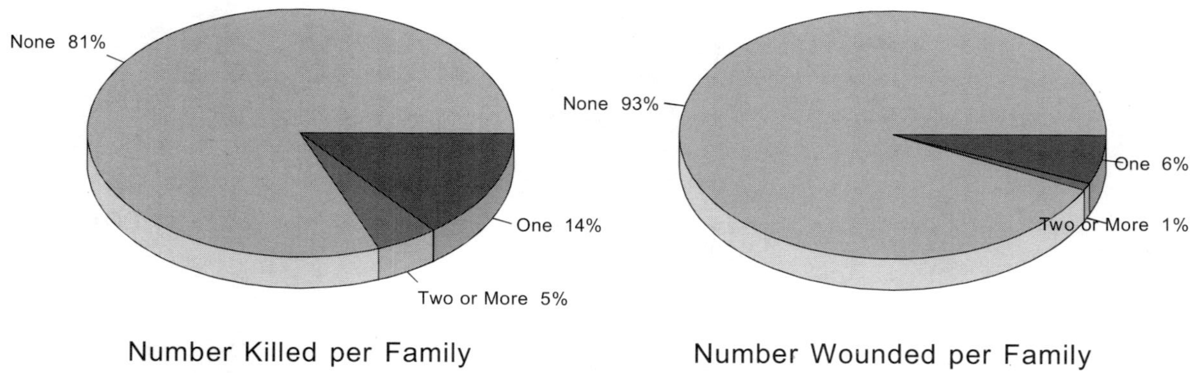

Figure 4.7. Number Wounded and Killed during Pogroms per Family (Based on Homeless Pogrom Victims Taking Refuge in Bohuslave, Kyiv Guberniia)
Source: Statistik, p. 12.

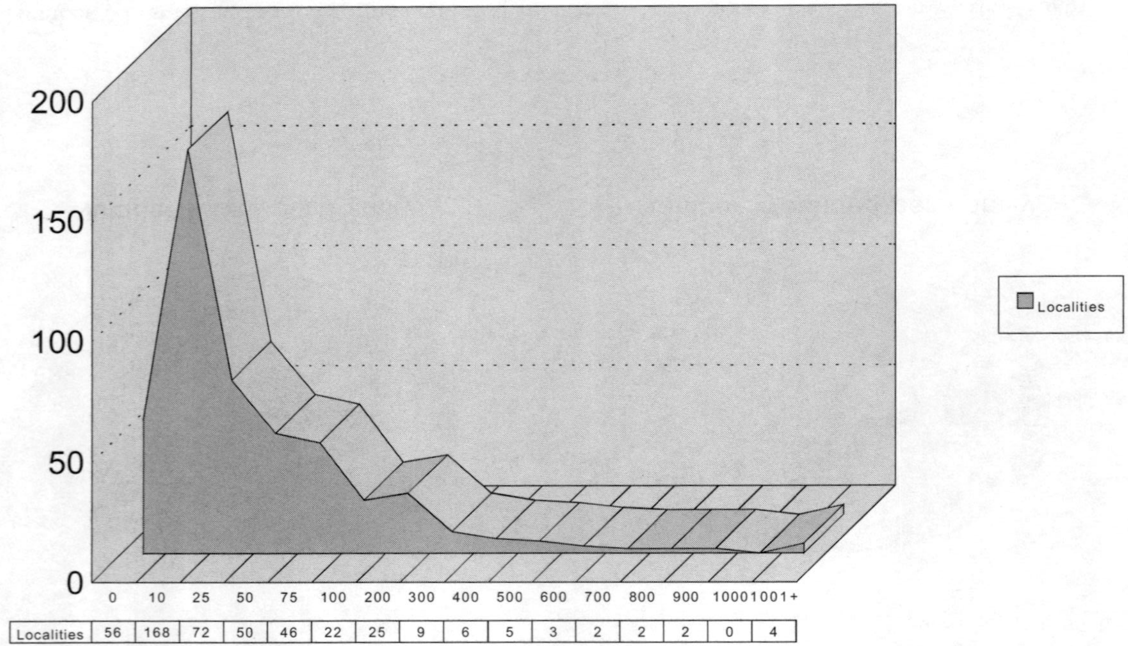

Figure 4.8. Number of Murders per Locality
Source: Gergel, "Pogroms," p. 251. Towns without estimates not included.

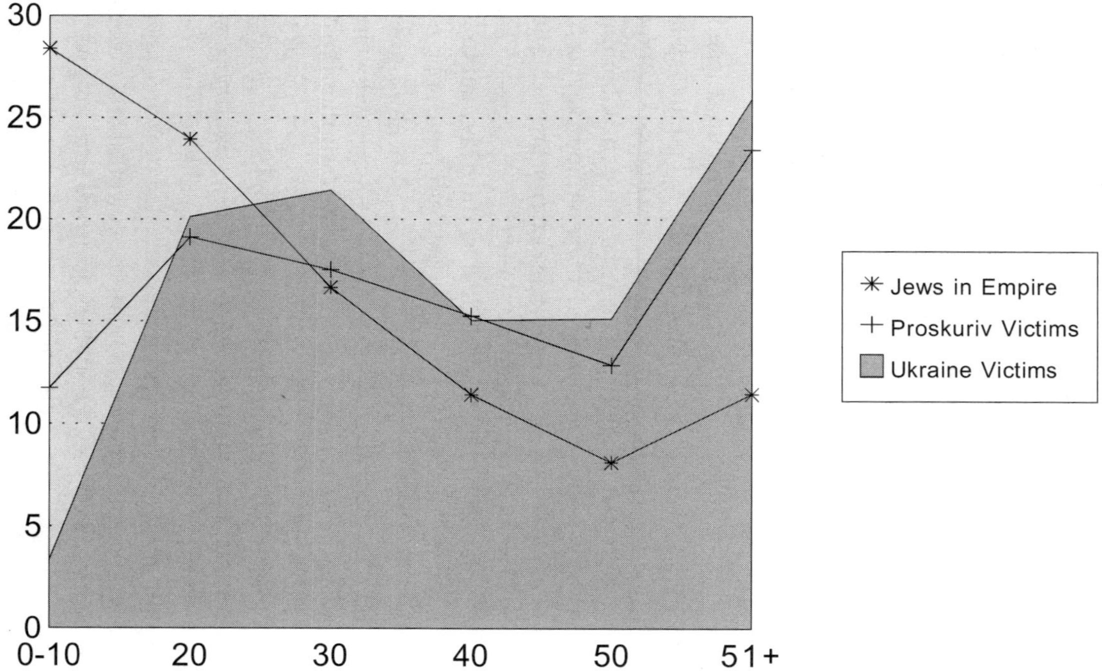

Figure 4.9. Age of Recorded Pogrom Victims in Ukraine and in Proskuriv (percent) vs. Age Distribution of Jews in Russian Empire, 1897
Source: Gergel, "Pogroms," p. 251 (Ages 8–10=10+); *Khurbn Proskurov*, pp. 77–104; Bauer, *Nationalitäten*, vol. 2, p. 82.

Proskuriv was chosen by the provincial Communist organization to carry out the initial uprising of a provincewide rebellion.[42] Despite the would-be leader of the uprising's complaint that there were too few workers in the town of 20,000 to carry it off, plans were laid for an uprising in the early hours of February 15, a Saturday. The other Socialist parties learned of it only on the thirteenth, and called an emergency meeting, fearing that such an uprising would result in a pogrom, but the Communists were not to be deterred, insisting that the uprising was to take all of Podolia at once.[43] It is likely that Semesenko was apprised of all these developments, since rumor had been rife in the town well before the uprising, and the military parade that marched through seemed to be a warning of the battle-readiness of his troops.[44]

Sometime after midnight on February 14/15, Communist insurgents successfully convinced the 15th Belhorod and 8th Podolia regiments to rebel and attack the rest of the troops stationed in a series of railway cars near the station. But the uprising turned against the Communists, and loyal Directory troops easily routed the mutinous soldiers. The reinforcements expected by the Communists never arrived, and the entire rebellion was put down within two hours.[45]

The local population had been awakened by the heavy gunfire, and as one memoir put it, "the night of the holy Sabbath came upon us like a terrible dream."[46] The following day, however, brought a beautiful morning, and the fact that the violence had not spread to the city was taken as a good sign. A rumor spread through the town that Proskuriv was once blessed by a Hasidic rabbi, protecting it from any pogrom.[47]

Semesenko organized an impromptu celebration for his troops, and thereafter exhorted them to murder the local Jewish population, whom he saw as responsible for the rebellion. He assembled the soldiers together in military formation and marched a few hundred men on horseback down the main thoroughfare of the town, a band preceding them.[48] At precisely 2:00 P.M. the soldiers dispersed searching for Jews, and the pogrom began. For their part, the Jewish victims were completely unprepared. As it was the Sabbath, many of them were at home asleep after the heavy midday meal. The massacre that followed was absolutely horrific:

> The witness Shenkman gave evidence that the Cossacks killed his younger brother in the street near his house, then entered the house

> and cut open his mother's head. Other members of the family tried to hide under beds, but when a small brother of his saw his mother dead, he got out from under the bed and kissed the dead body. Thereupon the old father also came out from his hiding and was shot dead...
>
> In the house of Blechman six persons were killed; one of them had his head broken in two halves. A girl was wounded in her buttocks, her dress having been lifted up for the purpose.
>
> The house of Krotchak was visited by eight men, who began breaking all the window-panes. Five men entered the house while three remained outside. Those in the house seized the old man Krotchak by his beard, dragged him to the window of the kitchen and threw him out of the window to the other three who killed him. Then they killed the old woman and her two daughters. A young woman who was visiting in the house was dragged by her long hair into another room, then thrown out of the window into the street and there killed. After that the Cossacks re-entered the house and inflicted several wounds on a boy aged 13, who became deaf in consequence. His elder brother received nine wounds in his stomach and in his side, having first been placed on his mother's dead body.[49]

Some Ukrainians attempted to stop the carnage. A man named Kocherovs'kyi ran into the street and took hold of a fleeing child, shouting to the pogromists, "Christians, what are you doing?" He and the child were killed on the spot.[50] Among the pogromists was a Jew, who had changed his name from Rakhman to the Ukrainian-sounding Rakhmanenko to better fit in with his new comrades-in-arms.[51] Later, Semesenko's troops attacked nearby Felshtin, where some of the mutinous soldiers had fled, and perpetrated another horrible atrocity. Eva Sochin was thirteen at the time of the pogrom:

> The first intimation that I had that anything was amiss was that three soldiers burst into our home at about 9:30 A.M. on a Monday morning. At the time, our family, with the exception of my father, who had not come home the previous night, were all at home. I distinctly remember this because the *samovar* was prepared for tea at the time. On the entry of the soldiers, the family dispersed in fright, running in different directions. I ran into the room of our tenant and hid in a wardrobe in his room. I heard a voice calling me to come out, and stepping out, was seized by a soldier who dragged me into the dining-room and began questioning me roughly. This soldier I remember as being tall and red-haired, with a forage-cap with a red center-piece extending down one side of the head. The soldier then

> asked me whether I was Christian or Jewish. I replied that I was a Christian and the tenant's daughter. This the tenant denied, whereupon the soldier demanded I make the sign of the cross, saying that he would release me if I were a Christian child but would kill me if I were Jewish. In terror, I kissed his hand and called him "brother" and begged him to release me, but the soldier replied using the Russian slang term "a goose and a pig have no relationship" (*gus' svine ne tovarishch*). He then shouted, "Lie down!", but this I refused to do. He again demanded that I lie down, and on my again refusing, struck me down with a blow on the head. After receiving this blow I lost consciousness and only remember regaining it for a few moments when I found myself on the floor.
>
> In hospital I discovered that in addition to the wound in the head, my arm had been amputated to just below the elbow, [I had] a deep gash in the neck and several wounds on my body which had been stitched together. I also then discovered that my father had been killed the previous night in the street and his body thrown into a cellar where it was afterwards found. Also, that the soldiers that had entered our house had killed my mother, my brother aged 28 years, my brother aged 15 years and my sister aged 8 years, and that my sister Dvorah was wounded whilst hiding in an adjoining cellar as a result of a bomb being thrown in and having exploded. This bomb also killed our neighbor, his wife, and their child, and wounded another child. Another child was also wounded and died afterwards as a result of [those] wounds.[52]

The pogrom at Proskuriv stopped some three hours later when a telegram arrived from the Directory headquarters at Kam'ianets'-Podil's'kyi, which had been informed of the local atrocities by a Ukrainian official named Taranovych. Presented with the telegram, Semesenko ordered a bugle blast to be sounded as a signal for the pogrom to end, after which he organized a second large celebration of the troops' "victory."[53] Looting continued after nightfall.[54]

The local commandant, one Kiverchuk, was also implicated in the pogrom. Not only was he responsible for disbanding the student militia, which was comprised primarily of Jewish adolescents, he also received a share of the stolen goods, some of which were collected by the above-mentioned Rakhmanenko.[55] The Danish Red Cross report of the massacre indicates that he had ordered some sixty empty peasants' carts brought to town from the environs, presumably to cart away loot.[56] On February 17 he cynically issued a call for the restoration of order.[57]

Isolated murders took place on Sunday morning. A rumor was circulating that the full-scale pogrom was to begin again in the afternoon. Alarmed, the local town council called Semesenko to an emergency meeting, demanding that the atrocities cease. Semesenko agreed, but issued another threatening proclamation:

> In the night of February 14/15, some irresponsible men without honor or conscience attempted an armed rising against the authorities of the district and of the town, men who, according to precise information that has reached me, are of the Jewish nation, wanted to seize power, bring confusion into the services of the State and lead our Ukraine, which has already suffered so much, into anarchy and disorder. I have taken the most decisive steps to suppress the rising they have attempted. It is quite possible that among the victims who fell by the arms of my Cossacks there were many innocent persons, but as nothing can be accomplished without making mistakes, such cases may have occurred.
>
> I pity the innocent victims, and common death has covered the town of Proskuriv, but the blood of these innocent victims will be a curse upon the heads of those who have acted as provocateurs and as adventurers, or, which is the same thing, leaders of the rising that failed.
>
> I call the whole population of the town and district to keep the peace and to attend to their daily avocations, and I give warning that if anybody should attempt again to bring discord into the lives of the peaceful inhabitants and to incite them against the lawful authorities, I shall stop at nothing, and that what has happened should be a "memento" to all those who would try more experiments.[58]

Proskuriv Jewry turned to the task of burying its dead, which numbered in the neighborhood of 1,500, some 10 percent of the town's Jewish population. Five mass graves and numerous private graves were dug, and the burial of all victims was not completed until 4:00 A.M. on Tuesday morning. Looters had also come to collect what they could from the corpses; several women were buried without fingers, which had been cut off in order to remove their rings.[59]

In some ways the violence in Proskuriv was atypical. For one thing, it was exceptionally bloody, with a very high murder rate; only three other recorded pogroms were as bloody (see Figure 4.8). It also had a slightly higher incidence of murder of children than other pogroms (see Figure 4.9). The Proskuriv pogrom was also marked by its "disciplined" military execution, with a formation of soldiers acting within a specific time frame and under clear orders from superiors. A further atypical element is Semesenko's initial insistence that his troops refrain from robbery to dedicate themselves solely to the task of murdering Jews. Several accounts record how his troops tore up offered bribes before they murdered Jews, although Semesenko himself later accepted the sum of 600,000 rubles from the Jewish community "for the difficult life of the soldiers."[60] It was more common for such exactions to take place before the pogrom, often averting violence. Occasionally receipts would be issued for such "voluntary contributions."[61]

Semesenko continued to hold the population in terror for several weeks. On February 27 he issued yet another threatening declaration:

> JEWS [*ZHYDY*], it has become known to me that yesterday you wanted to hold a gathering in Oleksandrovs'kyi Street to discuss taking power into your own hands, and that in four days you will carry out an insurrection, just as you did on the 14–15th of this year. I warn you that at present I have under my command 10,000 reliable men of the Ukrainian artillery and sufficient machine guns to strangle this uprising with my bare hands.[62]

Semesenko's syphilis had obviously passed into the tertiary stage when he was finally recalled from Proskuriv by the Directory military command. At this point he was so weakened by the disease that he was required to travel in a carriage attended by a nurse.[63] The pious Jewish

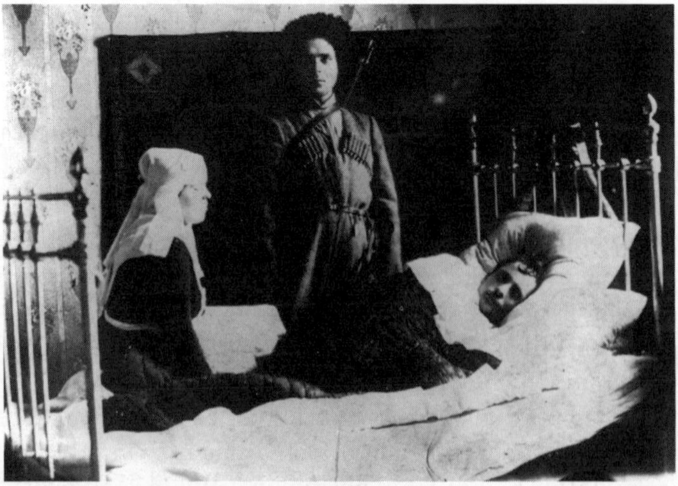

Semesenko Bedridden with Syphilis.
Source: Archives of the YIVO Institute for Jewish Research. *Reproduced with permission*.

population of the town circulated another fantastic legend that Semesenko was visited in his dreams every night by a Rabbi in blood-stained funereal garb, pointing a finger at him and shouting, "Get out of Proskuriv!" According to the legend, Semesenko would wake screaming every night with the image of the Rabbi before him until he finally fled the town.[64]

One of the central paradoxes of the pogroms is the large-scale participation by troops loyal to or acting in the name of the Ukrainian National Republic. At the very moment a Minister of Jewish Affairs sat in a government that was providing pogrom relief funds to victims of attacks, military and paramilitary troops were committing atrocities in the name of that same government. Clearly there were elements in the government who were actively working against the liberal policies it officially espoused. Historiographic debate continues to focus on the level at which this antisemitism existed. As an illustration, a delegation of Jewish local officials met with Vynnychenko, then Prime Minister of the government, to ask about who was responsible for the pogrom in Zhytomyr. Vynnychenko, who was himself a philosemite, answered testily: "What's the use of you speaking to me about this? You shouldn't be 'convincing' me. You would do better to speak to the other members of the Directory."[65]

Did the Directory pursue two policies, one of developing Jewish national autonomy and another of wreaking pogroms on Jewish citizens? It must be remembered that the Directory was not a stable parliamentary government with normal checks and balances and an established judiciary but a ragtag group of individuals, most of whom were inexperienced in government and who found themselves in the midst of a brutal civil war. At one point, the Directory was actually reduced to governing from a few train cars, which could be evacuated from place to place as the battle raged. Even during the Kam'ianets'-Podil's'kyi period, when the Directory was reduced to controlling only a small portion of the right bank, pogroms continued to be a problem.[66] More important, a huge gulf loomed between the intellectual leaders in Kyiv and the general population. While the former were caught up in issues of factional dispute, the latter were concerned with securing a loaf of bread for their family in times of great instability. As

Taras Hunczak put it, "indeed, this preoccupation with ideology separated the Ukrainian leadership from the vast majority of the politically inarticulate Ukrainian population, for whom more tangible social, economic, and ethnic considerations were more understandable and therefore more acceptable."[67] The commitment to nationality rights was only one of the many policies the UNR was unable to implement, or even communicate, to the population at large.

The question of *responsibility* must be more adequately defined. At one level, the word implies agency: Did the Directory, or some of its members, order pogroms? At another level, the question of responsibility involves accountability: To what degree does the Directory have to be held accountable for the actions of its troops? To use a concrete example: a window is broken in a schoolyard. If a father threw the baseball, then he would certainly be responsible in terms of agency and would have to pay for the repairs. If his child threw the baseball, then he would not be *responsible* as an agent. Since the child is his charge, however, he would be held *accountable* for the child's actions and would similarly have to pay for the window. This is true even if the father had warned the child repeatedly not to throw baseballs at windows.

In terms of agency, then, did the Directory order its troops to commit pogroms? Leaving Symon Petliura aside, since his case will be dealt with in greater detail, was there any explicit or implicit order from the Directory calling for pogroms? No such document has been preserved. On the other hand, there was a tendency in some circles, even in official bulletins, to issue inflammatory statements that may have acted as incitements. This was particularly true of the military and its publications.[68] Typical is this statement from *Ukraïns'ka stavka* (January 19): "In whose hands are Ukrainian lands, rivers, factories and so on? In the hands of wealthy Russians, Jews, and Poles. Who always argues against an independent Ukrainian National Republic? Russians, Jews, and Poles."[69] Besides the military, even the official organ of the Directory, the "Information Bureau of the Ukrainian National Republic," published inflammatory statements,[70] which must be contrasted with other articles published by the very same organs condemning pogroms.[71] *Ukraïns'ka stavka* also printed antipogrom articles and other pro-Jewish materials, such as the lengthy and sympathetic discussion of "Jewish Democracy at the Present Moment" (December 29, 1918).[72] Furthermore, the Directory earmarked funds and maintained commissions of inquiry into the violence.[73]

Such contradictions indicate varying policies within the Directory. If there was a political will for pogroms, however, the most likely candidate seems to be Opanas (Panas) Andriievs'kyi (1878–1955), representing the fiercely nationalist Socialist-Independentist party (UPSI) and a member of the Directory.[74] Reputed to be an alcoholic,[75] Andriievs'kyi was nevertheless regarded as one of the principal holders of power in the Directory.[76] He was the immediate supervisor of Colonel Paliienko, leader of the infamous Battalions of Death (*Kurin' smerty*), the executive arm of the *Verkhovna slidcha komisiia* designed to root out Bolshevik agents active in Ukrainian territory.[77] Paliienko and his underling Mykhailo Kovenko were responsible for the first organized pogroms perpetrated against Jews after the retreat of the Germans.[78] Other members of the Directory, Vynnychenko and Volodymyr Chekhivs'kyi in particular, attempted to shut down this operation, but Andriievs'kyi consistently blocked these efforts, despite the fact that Paliienko's guilt was evident.[79] Vynnychenko and Chekhivs'kyi's pressure was sufficient to secure Paliienko's arrest, but he was released shortly thereafter, given possession of the documents of the prosecution against him, and asked only to respond to Petliura concerning these charges.[80]

It is difficult to blame the Directory as a whole with *agency* in the pogrom waves. Nonetheless, the question of *accountability* must be considered. For the Directory to be absolved of the charge of accountability, it would have to be shown that it took energetic and decisive action against the pogroms, arresting perpetrators and issuing strongly worded condemnations of the violence. Although it is true that several such condemnations were issued, actions taken against the perpetrators were insufficient. Paliienko's "arrest" is a case in point, and even the fate of the notorious Semesenko is in dispute. While the sources indicate that he was indeed arrested several months after the massacre, the reasons are unclear, as is his final punishment. Some sources indicate that he was freed, others that he was executed.[81]

This lack of decisive action is especially disturbing in terms of the trends in the pogrom wave. During the first few months after the departure of the Germans, the pogroms were a phenomenon strongly associated with regular Directory troops. Between December 1918 and

April 1919 alone, nearly 60 percent were perpetrated by these soldiers. If the affiliated bands were slow to pick up on this trend, by May they had overtaken the Directory in number of pogroms committed, and this remained the pattern for the rest of the period (see Figure 4.1, p. 114 above). What this seems to indicate is that while the Directory was able to exercise greater control over its own troops in the late spring of 1919, the local warlords who had declared themselves on the side of the UNR were influenced by the earlier behavior of the regular troops, and proceeded to attack Jewish communities at will.

The actions taken by the Directory to control pogroms will be discussed in greater detail in the next chapter, since this topic is intrinsically linked with internal Jewish politics. The initial declarations and sanctions against pogroms, satisfactory in many ways, were not followed up with consistent measures. Had the Directory acted with greater resolve, perhaps the local warlords would not have committed atrocities to the same degree. Had they seen regular troops consistently punished for their attacks on civilians as well as repeated declarations from the Directory condemning pogroms, perhaps the destruction would not have been so severe. These measures would have been difficult to achieve in times of such chaos, but these are the types of measures required to absolve the Directory of the charge of accountability.

Much of the debate over responsibility has focused on one man: Symon Petliura. He occupies a tragic place in Ukrainian-Jewish historiography, revered by Ukrainians as a fearless national leader and hated by Jews as a vicious antisemite. In this capacity, Jewish historical memory links the name of Petliura with those of Bohdan Khmel'nyts'kyi, leader of the 1648 rebellion, and Ivan Gonta of the 1768 Haidamak uprising. Although the issue of Petliura himself is somewhat more narrow than the otherwise broader focus of this study, the sheer amount of debate on this question requires some treatment of what Ukrainians sometimes call the "Petliura era" (*Petliurivshchyna*).

It would seem that Petliura, as head of state, could have implemented orders to eliminate the pogroms. This, however, was far from the truth. While it is true that Petliura's name acted as a rallying point for patriotic Ukrainians, his government was bereft of effective power,

Volodymyr Vynnychenko
From the Bohdan Krawciw Collection at the Research Library of the Harvard Ukrainian Research Institute.

Symon Petliura
From the Bohdan Krawciw Collection at the Research Library of the Harvard Ukrainian Research Institute.

with no communication network to speak of and very little energy to enforce such discipline on its troops. Desertion was rampant, and troops often switched loyalties over what was most profitable at the moment.[82] Perhaps the clearest indication of Petliura's tenuous control over his troops is their rapid abandonment of the UNR. Petliura succeeded in drawing some one hundred thousand troops to his cause in December 1918, but, faced with the Red Army's invasion, by the end of January 1919 only 21,000 had not deserted.[83] The Red Army, by way of comparison, lost about 50 percent of its army to desertion, but this still left some three million troops over the entire period of the civil war. According to Trotsky, of these, some five to six hundred thousand were useful in combat: "This hastily improvised, poorly structured, and socially fluid force would hardly have been a match for a regular European army…[b]ut it was enough to fend off the equally improvised, less ideologically motivated, and even more fluid White armies" and even more so the Directory troops.[84]

Several pieces of anecdotal testimony, usually provided in the context of the emotionally charged 1926–1927 trial of his assassin, Samuel Schwartzbard, tend to ascribe antisemitic views to Petliura. In his memoirs, Vynnychenko referred to Petliura's resentment of Jews for their low level of participation in the army—a fairly widespread sentiment.[85] As another example of Petliura's reported antisemitism, one Israel Dines of Buenos Aires testified that when Petliura passed through a certain town, the Jews asked him to protect them from pogroms. Petliura replied, "Well, this is nothing, the soldiers must amuse themselves."[86] Other anecdotal evidence contradicts this image of an antisemitic Petliura. One Alexander Dotzenko, for example, claims he heard Petliura publicly say things like, "I have decided to have my entire army shot if it is going to drown the nascent Ukrainian Republic in Jewish blood."[87] Such conflicting testimony, of which there is an ample supply, is at best inconclusive and at worst completely unreliable.

There is no conclusive evidence to prove that Petliura himself held antisemitic views. On the contrary, all the documentation indicates that he was relatively friendly to Jews well before the revolution.[88] In 1907, for example, he wrote the foreword to a Ukrainian translation of Evgenii Chirikov's play *The Jews*:

> The suffering of Nakhman [a Jewish character] in Chirikov's *The Jews* will arouse deep sympathy from all, even those who do not belong to that nationality, who have suffered historically and have been forced to carry a heavy cross of oppression and persecution... This play has much significance in that it evokes in the hearts of the members of the audience deep love and sympathy for that oppressed man, while inspiring hatred and contempt for the regime, under which it is possible for such rapacious tortures [*khyzhats'ki znushchannia*] of innocent victims to occur.[89]

In another publication, Petliura criticized Jewish colonial agents for attracting Ukrainian emigration to America, but he also spoke out against antisemitic tendencies in the European press.[90] Petliura even defended the Jewish population against charges that they were, as a whole, pro-Communist. Individual Jewish Communists, he wrote, were branded with the "mark of Cain" by their own communities for abandoning Jewish traditions.[91] Articles signed by Petliura well after the revolution reinforce this interpretation of his personal views.[92] More convincing is the support Petliura gave to Jewish self-defense groups, even when the Jewish socialists disapproved (see Chapter 3). The evidence seems to indicate that Petliura himself would have disapproved of pogroms on ethical grounds.

Some scholars cite a mysterious telegram to Semesenko that is attributed to Petliura, which implies that he was the hidden hand behind the brutal Proskuriv pogrom. Certainly this would be the most damning piece of evidence against Petliura, and if reliable, much of the preceding discussion would be unnecessary. Yet the history of this telegram and the scholarship based on it is as mysterious as the telegram itself. Tsvi Tseker, a Jewish Communist, claims to have discovered the telegram after the Directory abandoned Proskuriv. When Directory troops advanced on the town again in June, Tseker gave it for safekeeping to a friend, who subsequently destroyed it in a fire, fearing its discovery. Thus, the telegram itself no longer exists. Tseker's political background should be borne in mind at this point, since it may have colored his recollection of the contents of the alleged telegram, reducing its value essentially to that of anecdotal evidence. The thesis that Petliura acted secretly to organize pogroms rests on the assumption that he was a committed antisemite. Given Petliura's consistent published record against pogroms, the account of the telegram has limited credibility.[93] Writing in the context of the Schwartzbard trial, Avraham Revutsky, the former Minister of Jewish Affairs, wrote that "they search, therefore, for public calls to pogrom violence [*pogrom-oifrufen*] signed and authorized by Petliura, but such decrees will not be found, and this work is in vain."[94]

It has been shown that troops nominally under Petliura's supervision, including the notorious Semesenko, committed pogroms.[95] It should be remembered, however, that little control could be exercised over the military, including Chevkhivs'kyi's attempt to shut down the *Kurin' smerty*, which provoked a prime ministerial resignation. On the other hand, precious little was done to punish pogromists, and many offenders were allowed to remain at their posts even after the most brutal pogroms.[96] Why did Petliura tolerate these offenders? The most obvious answer is that Petliura was hesitant to take such action, despite his conscience, because he was afraid of desertions in the army.[97] We have seen how fragile his control over the troops was, and the punishment of popular leaders might have resulted in mutiny.

There was a crucial period in the pogrom wave when Petliura did not act decisively, with either condemnation or other measures. This period was between January 1919, when Vynnychenko issued his condemnation, and April 1919, when Martos issued his.[98] With hindsight, it is possible to see that this gap, between January and April, represented a turning point in the pogrom wave. Several of the most brutal, particularly the Proskuriv-Felshtin massacres, occurred without eliciting a response from the Directory. As has been argued above, the lack of response sent a signal to the myriad warlords across Ukraine indicating that pogroms could be committed with impunity.[99] Why did Petliura not act?

Recalling the context of the war, one must remember that the Directory was in retreat throughout much of January and lost Kyiv to the Bolsheviks on February 4. The Directory had been actively seeking military aid from the French, who had landed in Odesa, but without success. Vynnychenko resigned on February 1, and the Directory was forced to board a train, "fleeing from station to station and having the appearance of a gypsy band rather than that of a government."[100] With all this turmoil, and the constant threat of desertion from his rapidly shrinking army, Petliura chose not to antagonize his troops by taking measures against the pogroms. Arnold Margolin, a Jewish participant in the Ukrainian movement, wrote in 1926:

> A careful study of all the available data leads one to the conclusion that the Directory during the first three months of its rule failed to show sufficient determination in combating Jewish pogroms. In its enthusiasm for the main object of the struggle—for national self-determination and independence—the Directory was bent primarily on the formation of a powerful army, without any restrictions as to the type of recruits. The result was that there were found in the ranks of that army, side by side with genuine, fine Ukrainian patriots, quite a few elements of the most undesirable Black Hundred type and even criminal and other dangerous characters.[101]

It is worth noting, however, that the declarations against pogroms did have some impact, at least on those perpetrated by regular Directory troops. The January condemnation, which decried violence but simultaneously reinforced the notion of "Jewish Bolshevism," was inappropriate and therefore had only a small effect (see Chapter 5). The April proclamation, however, seems to have had a strong impact: recorded pogroms dropped by 37 percent in April and by 85 percent in May (see Figure 4.1, p. 114 above). The pogroms slowly picked up again until the August declarations, which were followed by a 56 percent decrease. The proclamations seem to have been of use in stopping the violence, unlike similar proclamations issued by the White Army.[102] The failure to issue them more consistently and forcefully adds to Petliura's guilt.

In conclusion, then, what can be said about Petliura's personal responsibility? It cannot be proved that he had the responsibility of *agency*; indeed, all available evidence indicates that he was in no way the "architect" of the pogroms. On the other hand, as head of state he must be held *accountable* for the actions of his army, despite his relative lack of control over them. Petliura failed to chastise his troops adequately, particularly in the critical period between January and April 1919, when it might have had some impact on the independent warlords. Furthermore, he maintained relations with known pogromists and punished few. This behavior can be attributed to his fear of losing the loyalty of his disintegrating army—his inexperience in governing led him foolishly to accept compromises that were at odds with his personal political leanings, and for this he bears responsibility.[103] The

Jews, Mennonites, and other minorities bore the brunt of his hesitation. As Revutsky wrote years later:

> So this is the historical truth. And this truth makes it clear for us the guilt of those persons, such as Petliura, even if they did not directly execute pogroms. As human beings, with pretensions to socialism and national heroism, they should have utilized all their strength to ensure that the murder and slaughter of innocent people would not occur. Yet this they did not do, and they directly or indirectly built their political careers on allowing themselves to let the pogrom instinct of the wild masses run its course. In our eyes they are guilty.[104]

Chapter Five

The End of Autonomy

Shortly after the Directory took power in December 1918, measures were put in place to re-establish links with the Jewish community through national-personal autonomy.[1] The first proclamation included the following passage, as recalled by Avraham Revutsky in his memoirs:

> Jews are our friends. They are our fellow travellers. No agitation against them is permitted and anyone guilty of such agitation will be considered a counter-revolutionary, trying to create confusion in people's minds in order to reestablish the power of landlords and capitalists.[2]

On December 10, a temporary Ministry was set up under Solomon Goldelman of the Poale-Tsion, and on January 24 the Law of National-Personal Autonomy was officially reinstated.[3] Russians and Poles, however, were no longer included in the provisions of the Law, because, according to Revutsky, of Polish and Russian hostility to the Ukrainian movement.[4] Goldelman recalls a conversation with Vynnychenko on this topic:

> "We will immediately renew autonomy," Vynnychenko then said to me, "we shall invite into government a Minister for affairs of the Jewish minority, but the representation by the...Russians and Poles can wait. This is because the experience of a former period has shown that the...Russians in Ukraine consider themselves the natural representatives of Russian state interest, and not ordinary and loyal citizens of our own state. As regards the Poles, we should learn beforehand if the rights of the Ukrainian minority in an independent Poland shall be regulated...The case of the Jews is different: no foreign power stands up for the Jewish minority in Ukraine, none of her neighbors consider themselves obligated to protect the Ukrainian Jews and stand up for their troubles. Thus there remains to

> them one possible solution: orientation on the Ukrainian state, in which there must be a Jewish minister, who must represent them in all their national matters."[5]

Vynnychenko was somewhat optimistic in his logic, given the rapid decline in relations that followed as more and more Directory troops were implicated in pogrom activity. In the first few weeks, however, the Jewish community was relatively open to the Ukrainian proposal, and the isolated pogroms that did occur were considered tragic yet unavoidable in the atmosphere of war and anarchy.[6] The Fareynikte and the Bund officially welcomed the return of the Directory (the Poale-Tsion was already working in it),[7] and even the Zionist-clerical Nationality Secretariat greeted the Directory with much enthusiasm:

> The historic fate, which placed the Ukrainian people with the Jewish, dictates an earnest attempt at working together with all our strength and from all sides, together, both peoples, in the building of the state and its economy, for the betterment of all Ukraine. The full realization of national-personal autonomy is the best guarantee of continuing friendly coexistence of the peoples of the Ukrainian republic.[8]

The Zionists immediately entered into negotiations with the Directory on the issue of the post of Minister of Jewish Affairs, which they hoped to fill as a State Secretary. As the democratically elected representatives of the Jewish population, they felt entitled to take the post, and requested that it be turned over to them along with all records of the Ministry of Jewish Affairs.[9] The Directory, however, clearly preferred a socialist candidate. In a meeting with the Fareynikte, Vynnychenko related his earlier conversation with the Zionist delegation: "Our [the Directory's] program is the merciless struggle with the bourgeoisie, nationalizing the rail system, sugar and banking industry, state control and so on—do you have a candidate with this program?"[10] Vynnychenko knew full well that the more conservative Zionists could never sanction such upheaval. His preference was for a candidate approved by the Jewish socialist parties.[11]

Solomon Goldelman was chosen as acting Minister, primarily because of his prior involvement with the Directory in the Ministry of Labor.[12] Although the Directory would have been happy to make him the Minister of Jewish Affairs, he did not wish to take the post without the explicit approval of the Central Committee of his party, the Poale-

Tsion, nor did he feel that his Jewish ethnicity alone made him particularly competent in the area of Jewish matters; he preferred to remain in the fields where he had some expertise. He also had personal difficulties with Vynnychenko's leftist political views. Goldelman promoted instead the candidacy of Avraham Revutsky, who had a much higher position in the Poale-Tsion.[13]

Among the Socialist parties, there was considerable conflict over who should lead the Ministry. The Bund was rapidly losing confidence in the Directory. While still in favor of participating in the government, the Bund argued that the Ministry should be managed by a committee consisting of two Bundists, one Fareynikte member, and one Poale-Tsion member, rather than a Minister. The Fareynikte was against this proposal, and although they initially indicated that they would support a Poale-Tsion candidate, they secretly entered into negotiations with the Directory for a candidate of their own.[14] The Poale-Tsion party had the least internal dissention over the issue, and given Goldelman's position in the Directory, Vynnychenko eventually decided on the candidacy of Revutsky as the third Minister of Jewish Affairs.[15] The Nationality Secretariat protested the decision as a breach of democracy.[16] Thus the Jewish community was represented by two parallel, rival institutions: the Zionist-dominated Nationality Secretariat, a product of the recently held elections, and the Ministry of Jewish Affairs under Revutsky, supported fully by only the Poale Tsion, yet having the sanction of the Directory.

Almost immediately after Revutsky took office, pogroms became a major issue in Ukrainian-Jewish politics.[17] Numerous Jewish delegations protested to the Directory, insisting that it take immediate steps to control the violence.[18] Symon Petliura had previously issued orders to the army to maintain discipline but did not specifically refer to violence against Jews.[19] The Nationality Secretariat, despite their objections to Revutsky's Ministry, nevertheless took the Directory at its word and issued a proclamation saying that "the Directory has promised to take energetic measures" against the pogroms and urging for calm.[20] This confidence was inspired by the Directory's promise to issue an immediate condemnation of the pogroms, which appeared on January 11:

> In certain parts of Ukraine isolated groups of Cossacks are committing acts of violence against Jews. It has been ascertained that the

> Cossacks have been instigated to this by provocateurs—followers of the Hetman, White Army troops and persons calling themselves "Bolsheviks." This has been done in order to stain the fair name of the Ukrainian Republican Army, in order to excite hatred against the Ukrainian Cossacks among the people, in order to provoke disorder and crime, and through these methods to reinstate the old Empire of the landlords and bourgeois.
>
> Some of these provocateurs and pogrom-mongers have already been arrested and shot; others will be tried by court-martial.
>
> The Directory calls upon the Cossacks of the People's Army and upon all honest citizens to arrest any such provocateurs and all those who incite to violence and to bring them immediately before a court-martial.
>
> The Directory warns all the Hetman's counter-revolutionaries who hide under the mask of "Republicans" that anybody daring to lift his hand against the honor of the army of the Ukrainian laboring revolutionary people will be punished most severely.
>
> The Directory calls upon the whole of democratic Jewry to fight energetically those individual anarchist-Bolshevik members of the Jewish nation who behave as enemies of the working people of Ukraine and of the State. For it is these elements who enable the Hetman's men and mass of Jewry which is non-Bolshevik and who involve the Ukrainians, the true defenders of all workers, in grave misunderstandings with the Jewish democracy, which is not anarchist or Bolshevist, and is true to the Ukrainian state democracy.
>
> The President of the Directory: V. Vynnychenko
>
> The Members: Shvets, Petliura, Andriievs'kyi, Makarenko.[21]

The Directory's condemnation of pogroms was indeed strongly worded, but it was deemed highly unsatisfactory by the Nationality Secretariat. The declaration decried the pogroms as the work of enemies of the Ukrainian revolution, yet it also reinforced the notion that the Jews were closely allied with the Bolsheviks, the most common argument of the pogromists themselves. In the same breath that the Directory declared that the "mass of Jewry...is non-Bolshevik," it also demanded that the Jews "fight energetically those individual anarchist-Bolshevik members of the Jewish nation who behave as enemies of the working people of the Ukraine." Even if this formulation might have been technically correct—as there were a growing number of Jews who opposed the Ukrainian revolutionary movement—it was a political miscalculation on the part of the Directory to openly refer to a connection between Jews and Bolshevism.

Revutsky went to see Vynnychenko shortly before the proclamation was issued. When Vynnychenko showed him a copy, Revutsky was tempted to resign after reading the passage about Jews and Bolshevism, but the Prime Minister rejected the interpretation that the Directory was insinuating anything negative about Ukrainian Jewry. Revutsky asked that the passage be removed from the document. Vynnychenko refused, saying that the military demanded its inclusion, and defended the passage on the grounds that the soldiers were bombarded with antisemitic propaganda, and the issue had to be addressed in this way. Revutsky's impression was that while Vynnychenko did not feel the passage was offensive, he was unable to make significant changes in the document because of other elements in the government.[22] Revutsky's decision to resign was forestalled by the much stronger declaration issued to the military by Otaman Andrii Melnyk:

> Just as the legal organs are pursuing a distinct struggle with the internal enemies of the Ukrainian National Republic, I order all social and military organizations to fight against unauthorized house searches, arrests, and shootings, which are used as provocations by those who hate the Ukrainian National Republic.
>
> I will give [offenders] over for court-martial without mercy, that they might be punished with the most serious of penalties.
>
> The Ukrainian National Republic is engaged in a serious struggle for their independence and freedom, and therefore can deeply identify...with the freedom of other peoples. Therefore I will prosecute decisively any provocateurs who argue that it is permissible to undertake Jewish pogroms and similar agitation. They will be given over to courts-martial, all criminals of the Ukrainian National Republic.
>
> For unauthorized house searches two Cossacks have already been shot: Mykhailo Bolotnyi and Mykola Ivaniv.
>
> For pogrom-agitation [the following] were shot: Stanyslav Polians'kyi and Nikanor Savel'ev.[23]

The twenty-five-member Lesser Jewish Nationality Assembly (the parliament of which the Nationality Secretariat was the executive), however, issued the following protest:

> Having heard the report of the National Secretariat on the steps taken by it concerning the pogroms, and having heard the communication of the delegation of the Jewish Community of Berdychiv on the recent events there,
>
> And whereas acts of violence against Jews continue to be committed, notwithstanding the reassuring promises of the authorities, so that the pogrom wave is spreading and raging more violently than ever in the towns and townships inhabited by Jews,
>
> The Lesser Jewish National Assembly declares:
>
> ...That these acts [of violence] constitute a mortal danger not only to the Jewish population, but to the very existence of the young Ukrainian State...
>
> That the declaration of the Ukrainian Directory on the subject of the pogroms is absolutely unsatisfactory from the point of view of the State, and is calculated to increase and not to allay the anxiety of the Jewish population...
>
> That the Jewish population repeats its demand that the authorities take urgent and decisive steps immediately to stop the pogrom wave throughout the country...
>
> That the Jewish National Assembly calls upon the entire Ukrainian Democracy to raise its voice against the monstrous crimes committed against the Jewish population.[24]

Noteworthy in the Assembly's protest is the conviction that the Directory was not responsible for causing the pogroms, and that despite its "absolutely unsatisfactory" declaration, the government still merited appeals from the Jewish population. This attitude seems to have held sway at least until the Proskuriv-Felshtin pogroms, when Jewish opinion shifted away from the Directory as a possible source of law and order.

The Directory was rapidly losing hold of its territory, and in early February was forced to evacuate Kyiv ahead of another Bolshevik advance. What followed was a period of unparalleled chaos in Ukraine. Between the fall of the tsar in March 1917 and February 1919, for example, Kyiv had had ten different governments (the Tsar, the Provisional Government under Kerenskii, the Central Rada, the Bolsheviks, again the Rada, then the Rada with the Germans, the Hetman with the Germans, the Hetman with the Whites, the Directory, and then again the Bolsheviks).[25] The town of Proskuriv had sixteen governments between March 1917 and January 1921, eleven of them after the Germans departed (Directory, Bolsheviks, Directory, Bolsheviks, Directory with Galicians, Denikin, Poles, Ukrainians with Poles, Bolsheviks, Directory, Bolsheviks).[26] After their retreat from Kyiv in February 1919, the Directory was reduced by the end of March to working in a small region of western Podolia.[27] In the pandemonium, no serious measures were taken to control pogroms until the Directory issued another anti-pogrom decree on April 12:

> To preserve the peace and to maintain public law and order—as the first condition of a free life for all citizens of the Ukrainian National Republic—the government will fight with all its power against violations of the public order, will strike the brigands and pogrom instigators with the severest punishment and expose them publicly.
>
> Above all the Government will not tolerate any pogroms against the Jewish population in the Ukraine, and will employ every available means for the purpose of combating these abject criminals, dangerous to the State, who are disgracing the Ukrainian people in the eyes of all the civilized nations of the world.
>
> The Government of the Ukrainian National Republic is certain that the Ukrainian People—who themselves have suffered national slavery through many years and are conscious of the worth of national freedom and therefore proclaimed before all things the national-personal autonomy of the minorities in the Ukraine—will support the Ukrainian government in eliminating completely these pogroms from the dark elements of society.
>
> Boris Martos
>
> President of the Cabinet Council of the Ukrainian National Republic[28]

As in January, Melnyk also issued a strong order to troops to desist from pogrom activity, which read in part:

> Anarchy is more dangerous than the armed enemy who moves upon us from all sides. Remember, Cossacks, that through the pogroms may perish our power, for the death of innocent victims will provoke wrath against us and the numbers of our enemies will multiply. The Cossack's task is to conquer the enemy, whomsoever he may be, not to fight women, children, old men, against whom you are being incited by our enemies, in order that our people and our sovereignty may be smirched in the eyes of the world. Henceforth I command you to arrest all persons who will be discovered conducting pogrom

> agitation among the Cossacks, and to bring them before the Extraordinary Tribunal. Suppress on the spot all attempts at pogrom agitation in the military detachments.[29]

The Minister of Jewish Affairs sent out a telegram reinforcing this message.[30] Several commissions were also set up to deal with the problem of pogroms in general and in specific locations such as Proskuriv.[31] Many regarded the commissions critically. Joseph Schechtman, a Zionist, referred to this campaign as a "paper fight versus pogroms," and pointed out that one law setting up such a commission was passed on May 27, for example, but was not published in the official state journal of laws (*Visnyk derzhavnykh zakoniv*) until the middle of July.[32] On the other hand, when monies were made available, the victims were usually persuaded to accept. Proskuriv Jewry initially refused aid from the Directory, holding it responsible for the violence, but eventually relented.[33] By May the pogrom activity of Directory troops had slowed considerably, but by and large the damage was done. Jewish support had eroded beyond repair.

Revutsky's Ministry was doomed from the start, yet in the few weeks he was in office he struggled to make a positive contribution to Ukrainian Jewry.[34] Revutsky assumed the position amid considerable partisan conflict, and this contributed to the difficulties in finding adequate personnel for the Ministry. Nakhum Gergel, a former Deputy Minister, was prevented from participating by his party, the Fareynikte, which had lost its bid to have one of their own members appointed to the post.[35]

Immediately after his appointment was confirmed in early January, Revutsky was embroiled in the pogrom controversy, as news of Directory-perpetrated pogroms came in from Zhytomyr and other locations. Although Revutsky fought the pogroms actively, his abrupt resignation in early February is often erroneously thought to be a protest against the Directory's mismanagement of the situation. In his memoirs, however, Revutsky explained that his resignation was due to the foreign policy of the Directory, most specifically in its negotiations with the Entente.[36] He followed the Poale-Tsion party line, which was opposed to working with the Western powers. In a resolution dated

February 8, 1919, the Poale-Tsion protested that the Entente was imperialist, reactionary, and generally against the interests of the working class.[37]

The Jewish socialist parties and their allies disintegrated in the growing anarchy of the pogroms, much to the dissatisfaction of their Ukrainian allies.[38] The parties began to reconcile themselves more and more with the Communists, a trend that was also evident among some of the Ukrainian socialist parties.[39] The Jewish socialist parties, while in bitter rivalry with the Communists *vis à vis* their policies on Jewish nationality, looked with envy on the rapid successes of the Red Army and the seeming historical inevitability of the Communist vision. More left-leaning members of the various parties began to argue for abandoning their platforms on the Ukrainian experiment and joining the Communists, in some cases claiming that their presence would mitigate some of the more radical positions taken by the Communists on issues of Jewish nationality politics. Already in the fall of 1918 three wings had emerged in the Bund on the issue of which power the party should ally itself with; in February the party split formally, the larger portion forming the Kombund, an acronym for "Communist Bund."[40] The Kombund issued a statement on February 19:

> The social revolution has come and we have to reorient ourselves, purge ourselves of all the ideas which have grown as responses to the needs of the day, to the demands of another epoch…It was not easy for us to take the step of a military alliance with the Bolsheviks against the Directory…[41]

The Fareynikte soon followed suit, also splitting into three wings. The right wing, under Moshe Zilberfarb, the previous Minister of Jewish Affairs, was anti-Bolshevik. The left, under Mikhail Levitan and Yehuda Novakovskii, was strongly pro-Bolshevik. The center was under Moshe Litvakov, who took the position that since the Bolsheviks were going to become the new rulers, the party must find a *modus vivendi* with them, despite their opposition.[42] The Center-Left opinion was finally accepted in March. The leftist Fareynikte and Bund factions discussed uniting, which was eventually accomplished by creating the Jewish Communist Union.[43] Later this Union, some of whose members were the early champions of autonomism, explicitly and thoroughly rejected national-personal autonomy as a bourgeois institution.[44] A Communist faction developed within the Poale-Tsion, despite Revutsky's participation in the Directory.[45] As early as January elements in the Poale-Tsion publicly argued that Jews should join the Red Army. The party attempted to bridge this inconsistency by claiming that it supported the Central Rada in Ukraine and the Communists in the Russian Republic.[46]

In fact, this call was quite successful, and a groundswell of popular support for the Red Army grew in the Jewish community. In contrast to Directory pronouncements, the Communist anti-pogrom measures had been very effective.[47] The Communists mounted a comprehensive propaganda campaign aimed at discrediting the Directory by drawing attention to pogroms committed by its troops.[48] Motivated for the most part by revenge and the desire for self-protection, Jews joined the Red Army in large numbers and in many cases requested to be sent to the front lines.[49] In 1919 a recruitment section, the *Evreiskaia Voennaia Sektsiia*, or Jewish War Section, was set up to absorb them into the Communist forces. This section was specifically charged with assisting the Yiddish-speaking men (most of whom had never touched a weapon in their lives) with the task of adapting to Red Army conventions.[50] As Peter Kenez observed, "[u]ltimately the Jews realized that Soviet Rule, in spite of its economic policies and in spite of the occasional pogroms carried out by ill-disciplined troops, offered the best chance of survival."[51]

Newspaper articles appeared frequently in the Jewish press discussing the issue of Communism in general and, in particular, urging Jews to join the Red Army.[52] The Communist wing of the Fareynikte issued a circular on April 26 that was typical, arguing that "the Jewish worker has in this situation no choice: either fall, as silent victims, or fight, as heroes, to the last drop of blood."[53] The Red Army was involved in the coordination of propagandizing Jewish workers; on April 16 a secret letter to this effect was sent from the People's Commissariat for War Affairs to the Jewish socialist parties in Ukraine.[54] Antisemitic tendencies in the Red Army were countered with internal propaganda. One lengthy proclamation addressed to soldiers of the Red Army in Ukraine attempted to dispel anti-Jewish attitudes by discussing Jewish oppression under the tsars.[55]

Certainly the motive of revenge for the pogroms was prominent among the new Jewish recruits. A memoir from the period records how a Red Army soldier began to decapitate wounded Directory soldiers:

> A Jewish soldier from Berdychiv ran amok. He would wipe his bayonet in the grass to remove the blood and with every head he cut off he screamed, "This is payment for my murdered sister, this is my retribution for my murdered mother!" The Jewish crowd...held its breath and kept silent.[56]

Of perhaps greater significance to the growing antagonism, Jews became particularly prominent in the dreaded Cheka, precursor to the NKVD and KGB.[57] The extent of Jewish membership is unclear; it is not impossible to imagine that revenge for the pogroms motivated some Jews to join the Cheka. This growing Jewish support for the Communists reinforced antisemitic attitudes among Ukrainians, "[f]or the most prominent and colourful figure after Lenin was Trotsky, in Petrograd the dominant and hated figure was Zinoviev, and...anyone who had the misfortune to fall into the hands of the Cheka stood a very good chance of finding himself confronted with and possibly shot by a Jewish investigator."[58] Statistics for Cheka membership, while fragmentary and limited, support this contention. Roughly 75 percent of the Kyiv Cheka in 1919 were Jews, a figure that most likely declined sharply in the twenties with the influx of new members.[59]

The collapse of the Austro-Hungarian Empire in late 1918 also provided the Ukrainians living in eastern Galicia with the opportunity for state-building. Demographically, the Ukrainian-Jewish situation in eastern Galicia was broadly similar to that in the territories immediately to the east with one exception: instead of a Russian presence, there was a significant Polish population. In 1910 Jews constituted approximately 11 percent of the total Galician population, Poles numbered 47 percent, and Ukrainians 42 percent.[60] The Polish population was concentrated in western Galicia (west of the San river), where they constituted 89 percent of the population. The Ukrainian and Jewish presence was most pronounced in eastern Galicia, where they represented, respectively, 63 percent and 12 percent; Poles were in the minority with only 25 percent of the population. The occupational distribution of Ukrainians, Jews, and Poles in eastern Galicia also bears a striking similarity to the situation in the territories to the east. Ukrainians in Galicia were involved overwhelmingly in agriculture and forestry, with less than 7 percent in other occupations. Jews were somewhat more involved in agriculture than their co-religionists elsewhere, some 14 percent making their living directly from the land, but the majority of the population was involved in trade and industry. The Polish occupational structure was more diversified than the Ukrainian, yet still predominately agricultural.[61]

Fundamental distinctions should be made between the Ukrainian experience in the Austro-Hungarian Empire and in the Tsarist Empire. Unlike the repressive and reactionary tsars, the Austro-Hungarian monarchies were comparatively benevolent and sometimes even progressive with regard to questions of religion and ethnicity. Joseph II (ruled 1780–1790), for example, had issued the famous Patent of Toleration, extending considerable rights to Jews as citizens and eliminating the ghettos.[62] Although the emperors were Catholic, tolerance was also extended to Protestants, as institutional church power was limited.[63] This was particularly significant for Galician Ukrainians, the majority of whom were members of the Uniate Church, the result of a late sixteenth-century agreement between the Catholic and Orthodox Churches. The Uniate Church became part of the Catholic hierarchy but retained certain distinctive features of the Orthodox, including a married priesthood. In 1774 the Uniates were officially given status equal to the much larger Roman Catholic Church; also, they were referred to as "Greek Catholics" to reflect both their Orthodox origins and their Catholicity.[64]

For Ukrainians, the conflict over statehood was not so much with the Austrian government as with their Polish neighbors. Polish nationalist sentiment regarded Galicia as an integral part of the Polish homeland. Despite the predominant Ukrainian presence in eastern Galicia, cities such as L'viv (Lwów in Polish, Lemberg in German) were considered essential parts of historic Poland. The Austrian government, as one of the parties in the eighteenth-century partitions that cynically removed Poland from the map, understood Polish animosity and often favored Ukrainian national aspirations to blunt the edge of Polish demands.[65]

Galician Jews had little affinity with Ukrainian causes until the beginning of the twentieth century. As in the eastern territories, Galician Jewish representatives in the Diet tended to be far more acculturated to Polish and/or Austrian society in contrast to the pious masses of traditional Orthodoxy, and most Galician Jews remained untouched by the political activities of the few Jews who sat in the parliament in Vienna.[66] In 1905, however, the Ukrainian Iuliian Romanchuk made an open call for an alliance with the Jews in a speech in the Diet, arguing that Jews had a right to be recognized as a nationality.[67] Romanchuk's speech provoked uproarious laughter in the Diet, but the Jews were listening, and an alliance was eventually formed that resulted in a signficant increase of Jewish members elected to the subsequent Diet.[68] Bringing the Jews over to a Ukrainian orientation was a significant coup, since this damaged the Polish position in the Diet.[69]

Soon after its surrender in October 1918, the Austro-Hungarian Empire collapsed. The Poles scrambled to take L'viv and declare it part of a resurrected Poland, but by November 1 eastern Galicia was in Ukrainian hands as part of a secret agreement between the former Austrian governor of Galicia and the Central Rada. The territory, including northwestern Bukovina and Sub-Carpathian Rus', was named the Western Ukrainian National Republic (WUNR).[70] War soon broke out between the Poles and the Ukrainians, and the WUNR was forced to abandon L'viv for Stanislaviv (modern Ivano-Frankivs'k). Early in 1919 the WUNR proclaimed union with the UNR to the east.

Jewish organizations coalesced to form local "Jewish National Councils" to express communal concerns, a development characteristic of postwar German and Austrian territories.[71] A general Jewish National Council (JNC) was cobbled together to act as an umbrella group for the Jewish population of eastern Galicia, although local JNCs continued to operate.[72] Elections held later in 1919 confirmed Zionist dominance.[73]

The general JNC was divided on how to deal with the Polish-Ukrainian conflict over eastern Galicia. The Zionist delegates were traditionally polonophiles, but the Ukrainian movement had made significant overtures to the JNC.[74] After a conference in which both pro-Polish and pro-Ukrainian views were aired, a decision was taken to adopt a position of neutrality in the conflict, while nevertheless demanding national-personal autonomy.[75] The WUNR was not enthusiastic about the declaration of neutrality, but it nevertheless recognized the JNC and invited it to send representatives to the newly formed government in Stanislaviv.[76] The JNC refused, fearing that open participation in the WUNR would impugn its declaration of neutrality.

Nevertheless, both the Poles and the Ukrainians considered Jewish neutrality as implicit support for the Ukrainian cause.[77] The Poles considered the Ukrainian claim to eastern Galicia to be much weaker than their own, and viewed Jewish reluctance to support the Polish position with hostility. Occasional tensions arose between Ukrainians and Jews as well, the former charging that the Jewish community allowed more polonized Jews to fight in Polish ranks, thereby breaking the principle of neutrality (as if the JNC had such power over individual Jews).[78] One popular rumor claimed that Jewish families had poured hot gruel (in another version, boiling water) down on Polish soldiers fighting in the streets below them.[79] The JNC-sponsored Jewish militia was often cited as violating neutrality, usually in favor of the Ukrainians. Although the JNC asserted its strict adherence to neutrality, the Jewish militia often found itself fighting off attacking Polish troops.[80]

Polish troops perpetrated widespread pogroms, particularly in November 1918.[81] The bloodiest pogrom occurred when the Ukrainians were driven out of L'viv on November 22. Although this pogrom was mild compared to the devastation that was to occur in the eastern regions in coming months, the death toll of over seventy had a tremendous impact on Galician Jewry.[82] Neutrality was maintained on an official level, but it was clear that the JNC was squarely within the Ukrainian camp. Isolated pogroms committed by Ukrainians did not change this attitude, despite the fact that the JNC was not entirely satisfied with WUNR anti-pogrom declarations.[83]

The Ukrainian orientation was championed by Dr. Israel Waldmann, editor of the influential *Lemberger Zeitung*.[84] Over a period of several months, the JNC moved closer and closer to abandoning neutrality and declaring open support for the WUNR. In lieu of the Ministry of Jewish Affairs that operated in the UNR, a Department of Jewish Affairs was set up in Stanislaviv. This allowed the JNC to maintain the fiction of neutrality while at the same time exercising a large role in the regulation of Jewish affairs in the WUNR. Waldman was appointed its Commissioner.[85] In a secret meeting in March, the JNC resolved that it was time to formally drop the declaration of neutrality and ally with the WUNR, once hostilities between the Poles and Ukrainians had ceased.[86] By the time hostilities finally did cease, however, circumstances were no longer favorable to such an alliance. The Poles were successful in their conquest of eastern Galicia and the destruction of the WUNR, and the possibility of Jewish autonomy in a Ukrainian government was removed.

Throughout this period, a Minister of Jewish Affairs continued to operate in the Ukrainian territories of the former Tsarist Empire ruled by the Directory. Pinkhos Krasny, a member of the Folkspartey, took the position immediately upon Revutsky's resignation.[87] His candidacy was not supported by any Jewish political body; he merely requested that Revutsky allow him to take over the post:

> "I hear [said Krasny] that you are resigning from the Ministry. Why are you doing this? Don't you think that with the prolonged development of national autonomy and the fight against pogroms, you should remain?..."
>
> "If, however, you think [replied Revutsky] that the pogrom question will be solved even in the current political situation in the Directory, and if the alliance with the Entente is possibly in the interest of the Jewish masses—then come and take my office. My party considers the current platform as shameful and will basically not work with the Directory. The place, however, is free for another."
>
> Krasny immediately answered:
>
> "Good, I agree. I consider it my duty to rescue the national autonomy. But how can 'the cat cross the water?'" [*vi kumt di kats ibern vasser*, i.e., how can I win this post without popular support?]
>
> "Very simple. I will appoint you as a member of my council, and immediately upon my resignation you will be given the provisional administration of the Ministry."[88]

This characterization of Krasny as an opportunist is corroborated by a former prime minister of the Ukrainian National Republic, Serhii Ostapenko. Apparently Krasny had approached Ostapenko asserting that without a Jewish minister, "Europe will not talk with you...if you like, friend, I will be the minister."[89] Krasny's actions were condemned by several Jewish political parties, including his own. At the initiative of Wolf Latsky, former Minister of Jewish Affairs, the Folkspartey issued a statement revealing that Krasny had earlier been thrown out of an organ of that party for disciplinary reasons.[90]

Krasny's Ministry has been characterized as a "Jewish Red Cross" mainly involved in pogrom relief.[91] Although most of Krasny's activities were in the traditional realm of *shtadlones*, or "intercession" with more powerful figures, Krasny attempted to keep the Jewish schools running as well, although with limited success.[92] His politics were highly partisan, and in one declaration he sent out a circular reminding all *kehiles* that the use of Hebrew in their protocols was strictly illegal; these documents were to be recorded in only Yiddish and Ukrainian.[93] Krasny also attempted to hold new elections in the *kehiles*, demanding detailed voters' lists from all communities.[94]

Krasny's tenure coincided with the Kam'ianets'-Podil's'kyi period of the Directory, roughly June to November 1919, when the Ukrainians held with some security a small triangle of territory in west-central Ukraine. The fragments of the socialist parties that had not adopted Communism continued to support Krasny's ministry with much hesitation, despite their earlier protests and the Directory's steady movement to the right.[95] While Krasny was decried by the Jewish political parties and many communities, some still sought his aid in pogrom defense.[96] Besides his activity as the "Jewish Red Cross," Krasny also produced some extremely optimistic legislation organizing the *kehiles*.[97]

In the summer of 1919, however, the Directory was increasingly implicated as a major perpetrator of the anti-Jewish violence. With the Great War over, the attention of the world turned to the ongoing civil war in Ukraine. A major demonstration held in New York City drew roughly half a million protestors, including 25,000 U.S. and British soldiers wearing black bands as a sign of mourning.[98] The U.S. Secretary of State received a delegation protesting the pogroms,[99] and a public letter of protest in France was signed by numerous dignitaries.[100] Campaigns to aid the pogrom victims were organized all over Europe and North America, with such slogans as "Our boys FREED them, won't you FEED them? Jewish War Sufferers."[101] One interesting American poster was specifically directed at Christians:

Because Christ Commands It

WE URGE EVERYONE TO HELP THE JEWISH SUFFERERS

Because they need it. Because we believe in paying our debts.

Humanity Owes Much to The Jews

Moses gave us the Moral Law; David voiced every cry of joy or sorrow of the human heart to God; Christ, after the flesh, born a Jew, taught in the Good Samaritan story—

THAT WHO NEEDS MY HELP IS MY NEIGHBOR

So for Christ's sweet sake, help the Jewish sufferers overseas with an open hand. In the U.W.W. [United War Work] campaign the Jews, knowing they would only get three million dollars out of the contributions, gave about twenty million dollars, and the Y.M.C.A. and the Red Cross were the beneficiaries of their liberality to about seventeen million dollars.

If not for sweet charity's sake, at least not to be put to shame, let us help those who, while giving to ours, never before have asked to give to theirs.

We Urge all Methodists to Give in the Name of Christ Born of the House of David

—First Methodist Church[102]

The Directory, no doubt influenced by world opinion and threatened with an increasingly successful Red Army, began to respond by stepping up the campaign against antisemitism. To improve its image abroad, the Ministry of Press and Information sought out materials on the Ministry of Jewish Affairs to publish in the West.[103] Minutes of meetings with Jewish delegations were published, and stronger antipogrom decrees were issued, many signed by Petliura himself.[104] Two in particular bear quoting at length. The following one was issued to the Directory forces:

Officers and Soldiers!

It is time for you to realize that the Jews, together with the majority of the Ukrainian population, have recognized the evil of the Bolshevist-Communist invasion, and know already where the truth lies. The most important Jewish parties, such as the Bund, Fareynikte, Poale-Tsion and Folkspartey, have decidedly placed themselves on the side of the Ukrainian independent state and are working together hand-in-hand for its good.[105]

It is time for you to understand that the peaceful Jewish population, their children and women the same as ourselves, have been oppressed and deprived of national freedom. They can not be alienated from us, they have of old been always with us and they have shared with us their joys and sorrows.

The gallant army which brings brotherhood, equality, and freedom to all peoples of Ukraine should not be lending an ear to various adventurers and provocateurs who long for human blood. Likewise, the Army should not be a party in bringing a hard lot on the Jews. Whoever is guilty of permitting such a heavy crime is a traitor and enemy of the country and must be thrust out of human society.

Officers and Soldiers! The whole world cannot but admire our heroic deeds in the struggle for freedom. Do not stain those deeds—not even accidentally—by disgraceful actions and do not bring down burning shame upon our state in the face of the whole world. Our many enemies, external as well as internal, are already profiting by the pogroms; they are pointing their fingers at us and inciting against us, saying that we are not worthy of an independent national existence and that we deserve to be again forcefully harnessed to the yoke of slavery.

I, your Commander-in-Chief, tell you that this very moment the question of to be or not to be for our independent existence is being decided before the International Tribunal. [106]

Officers and Soldiers! The judgment on this question rests in your hands, so decide it by showing an armed fist against our enemies, remembering always that a clean cause demands clean hands. Be sure that a severe and lawful punishment by a people's court will overtake all enemies of our country; but remember also that vengeance—often the result of want of careful consideration—is not the way of the Ukrainian Cossacks. I most positively order that all those who are instigating you to pogroms be thrust out of the army, and as traitors to the fatherland be handed over to the court. Let the court punish them according to their crimes by giving them the severest lawful penalty.

The Government of the Ukrainian National Republic, recognizing the harm done to the state by the pogroms, has issued an appeal to the whole population of Ukraine to withstand all attempts of the enemies who might arouse it to anti-Jewish pogroms.

I command the whole army to obey this appeal and to provide for its widest possible dissemination among comrades-in-arms and among the population.

This Army Order is to be read to all divisions, brigades, regiments, garrisons, and squadrons of the Dnipro and Dnistr armies as well as the partisan detachments.

The Commander in Chief
Petliura
The Chief of Staff of the Supreme Commander
Junakiv[107]

Another proclamation was issued to the population at large:

Soldiers of the Ukrainian Army!

The Ukrainian Republican People's Army of the Dnipro and Dnister territories, now united into one army, is advancing victoriously, is crushing the enemy, gaining each day new territories of the Ukraine to liberate them from the Bolshevist brigands, bringing them with freedom to the Ukrainian people as well as the certainty of happy days of living in a peaceful and orderly state.

The Bolshevist anarchy and maladministration, the horrible Red terror, the tyranny of the extraordinary inquiry commission [Cheka] and of other criminals for whom there is nothing sacred in life—have sapped our people's strength to the utmost and have flooded our steppes with human tears and with streams of blood of the innocent.

Amidst a peal of church bells, with bread and salt,[108] with flowers and tears of joy the weary, oppressed and pillaged Ukrainian people are greeting you, their valiant warriors, as liberators from the yoke and from Bolshevist atrocities, as flesh of their flesh and blood of their blood...

Our enemies, however, are not sleeping but only watching our every step in order to sow discord among us in one way or another, and thus to frustrate the immediate realization of our people's efforts.

The Bolshevists themselves consider Ukraine Moscow's inheritance—with the difference that formerly it was the heritage of a black Moscow, now of a Red one.

They see that the end of their rule in the Ukraine is already approaching because the Ukrainian people themselves have risen against them: but they do not give up yet their hope of subjugating the Ukrainian masses. By provocations for which they are spending enormous sums of money they want to divide us from within, hiring criminal elements who are inciting our soldiers to all sorts of outrages and pogroms against the innocent Jewish population; in this way they want to stamp our soldiers as pogrom-mongers, although these soldiers are bringing liberty to all peoples of Ukraine.

Our enemies intend thus to split the Ukrainian and Jewish laboring masses whose ways, in fact, have been bound together by three hundred years of Russian tsarist yoke.

Our national army must bring equality, brotherhood and freedom to the Ukrainian as well as the Jewish citizens who are also supporting actively the government of the Ukrainian National Republic. All their parties, i.e., the Bund, Fareynikte, Poale-Tsion and Folkspartey are standing on the principles of the independence of Ukraine, and are participating in the reconstruction of the republic.

I know myself how the representatives of the Jewish population have helped our army and supported our legal republican government...

I have the highest esteem for the sacrifices made during this war upon the altar of the fatherland by the Jewish population.

From the reports by the commanders of our brave divisions and corps as well as from reports by State Inspectors I have already learned that the Jewish population brought help to our wounded and sick soldiers, in the hospitals which had been built hastily 3–5 kilometers behind the battlefronts.[109]

I have been touched deeply by tears of thankfulness in the eyes of our soldiers for the loving care and human aid given them by the Jews, and I have noted with satisfaction how the soldiers of our army were standing guard at the shops and stores of Jews in order to protect them against plunderers.

The restoration of a bridge at Starokonstantyniv—which had been destroyed by the Bolshevists—by the Jewish population in an exceedingly short time, as well as their help with foodstuffs and underwear testify also to the loyal conduct of Jews in relation to our army...[110]

Officers and soldiers of the Ukrainian army! The Ukrainian-Jewish laboring masses see in you their liberation, and future generations will not forget your services rendered to them; history will with pride record on its pages your achievements in this struggle. Beware of provocations, and have no mercy on provocateurs or on those who execute pogroms, or incite the weakest among you to this action.

Let the death sentence overtake the perpetrators of pogroms and provocateurs. I demand the strictest discipline from you so that not even a hair of an innocent's head be touched.

Bear in mind that you are the elite sons of your great nation which wants to live its independent life and to be subjugated by no one, and therefore keep an unflinching watch on its interests as well as on the

> interests of all those who help you and are well-disposed to you and to the liberation of your people.
>
> Those who are guilty before the Ukrainian nation and before the republic, no matter what their nationality, shall suffer the severest punishment according to law prevailing in the territory of the Ukrainian republic; to the innocent, however, you must bring liberation from the hated Bolshevist yoke.
>
> The Republic's and my own cordial thanks to and high esteem for your martial bravery, devotion, and self-sacrifice which you offer upon the altar of the fatherland, while liberating our Ukraine and the nationalities living there—including the Jews—from the Bolshevists.
>
> May God help us in the great and sacred cause of liberating the nations from the heavy yoke of the Bolshevists!
>
> August 27, 1919
> Commander in Chief: Petliura[111]

The pogrom wave subsided after the issuance of these declarations, and it is reasonable to assume that they had a significant effect on troops loyal to Petliura. Other factors, such as the increasing consolidation of Ukrainian territory under the more organized Soviet control, the war-weariness of the population, and the formation of local Jewish self-defense groups certainly reduced the level of community violence in Ukraine. Petliura later forged an alliance with the Poles and staged a massive counterattack, but the Soviets drove the Ukrainians westward again.[112] The Ukrainian revolution had failed, and its leaders went into exile.

The Jewish Ministry simply fizzled out sometime at the end of 1920. Like a forgotten relative, its passing was not significantly remarked upon. In November 1920, the Ukrainians were finally driven west of the Zbruch river by the Red Army's advance.[113] The Ministry apparently continued to operate after November, sporadically producing an amateurish mimeographed newsletter entitled "Bulletin of the Jewish Press Bureau of Ukraine," which listed Krasny as a "representative" until 1922.[114] After the consolidation of Red Army control over the region, Krasny remained in Soviet Ukraine, and later wrote a treatise condemning Petliura and the Ukrainian movement.[115]

The year 1919 marked the end of the Ukrainian-Jewish experiment. The resurgent Ukrainian National Republic renewed the Ministry of Jewish Affairs almost immediately after the German retreat, but the pogrom wave had largely discredited the Directory in Jewish eyes. That year also saw a groundswell of Jewish support for the Red Army, whose troops were much more effective in maintaining order. This was accompanied by upheaval within the Jewish political parties as most of them split with their left wings joining the Communist movement. A Minister of Jewish Affairs continued to operate in the Directory for months after the Proskuriv-Felshtin massacres, organizing some attempts at pogrom relief and acting as a consultant to the Directory on Jewish issues. The military tide, however, had turned against the Ukrainian movement. The Red Army successfully pushed the Directory westward, ending the Ukrainian attempt at statehood. The Ministry of Jewish Affairs had its true end in the spring of 1919, when the Jewish parties fractured and the wave of pogroms made it impossible for them to fully support the Ministry. Although it limped on for nearly two more years, it was never regarded as anything but a shadow of the potential it once held. The Ukrainian-Jewish experiment had come to an ignoble end.

Conclusion

With the fall of the tsar, Ukrainians and Jews attempted to establish a noble experiment in human rights, but despite good will on both sides, the experiment was a disastrous failure. There are several reasons for this. First, the stratum of society that participated in the *rapprochement* was too thin; it was not well grounded in the population at large. The Jewish socialist parties, the primary architects of Jewish autonomy, were simply too divorced from ordinary Ukrainian Jewry to adequately represent its needs. Most Ukrainian Jews were devoid of political inclinations, and those who had such sensibilities were more traditionally inclined. The election results, although partial, indicate that when Jews expressed their political will it was mainly Zionist and/or religious. The average Jew was mistrustful of the grand schemes for social reform advanced by the socialists. The pogrom waves influenced a significant portion of Jewish youth to move further left, but the shift was abrupt and far more radical than the moderate Jewish socialist leaders could handle.

More serious was the chasm that separated the Ukrainian political leadership from the peasantry. The Ukrainian peasant could understand the struggle against Russian domination and the reassertion of local rights of self-rule. More sophisticated ideas, such as autonomy for minorities, were considerably less important than the satisfaction of more immediate demands such as land reform. As the Great War dragged into revolution, foreign occupation, and again revolution, the unrest and disorder provided an opportunity for hooligans and criminals to terrorize the population. These thugs—whether in military uniform or not—found minorities to be an attractive target. Political pretexts for attacks were concocted, and as it became apparent that there was no greater authority checking the violence, the pogroms multiplied. The Ukrainian revolutionary movement failed to communicate its position on minorities adequately to the population at large, and even to its own troops. With some exceptions, there is little evidence to suggest that the Directory leadership actively instigated the anti-Jewish violence, yet it must bear responsibility for not taking sufficient measures to stop the carnage. It is possible to argue that in a period of anarchy and confusion, such an attempt would have been pointless—a mere waste of energy. Analysis of the pogrom waves, however, suggests that this was not the case, since declarations against the pogroms had some impact. Furthermore, on a more idealistic level, it is relevant to recall the words of Symon Petliura in his August 1919 proclamation cited in Chapter 5: "a clean cause demands clean hands."

The Jewish political parties, however, must share some responsibility for the violence, since their quarreling prevented them from taking measures early enough to allow adequate self-defense. The Zionist boycott of the Jewish Nationality Council and the later socialist boycott of the Nationality Secretariat were great obstacles to effective representation of Jewish interests and to coordination of self-defense efforts in the Jewish community. Most serious perhaps was the socialist rejection of the December 1918 Zionist demand for self-defense units.

Nevertheless, even if these obstacles had been overcome, the prognosis for Jewish autonomy in Ukraine was poor. The political situation was simply too unstable for such complex schemes to be instituted, particularly in a young state confronted with belligerent neighbors. Even if the Jewish parties had not been hesitant to support the Ukrainian declaration of independence proclaimed in the Fourth Universal, it is unlikely that their allegiance would have had any impact on the eventual success of the Red Army's conquest of the region. Likewise, even if the events described here had turned out in favor of the Ukrainian movement, the experience of other Jewish autonomy plans does not support the idea that this one would have survived the increasingly intolerant atmosphere of the interwar period. Lithuania, Latvia, and Estonia all instituted Jewish autonomies of various types, but with limited success.

For example, the Jews comprised almost 8 percent of the population of the emerging Lithuanian state and had a long and active history in the region.[1] In particular, Jews made up one-third of the population of Vilnius, a city at the center of a fierce border dispute between

Lithuania and neighboring Poland.[2] Lithuanians hoped to win the Jews over to their side, certain that Jewish influence at the Paris Peace Conference would be decisive in granting Vilnius to the Lithuanians.[3] As in Ukraine, Jews were over-represented in the commercial sphere and other urban professions, while Lithuanians were primarily rural agriculturalists. Lithuanians hoped to forge a workable alliance for the economic health of their young state.[4] Finally, the fact that the Lithuanians wanted to preempt any developing Jewish sympathy for German, Polish, or Russian self-identification also was analogous to the Ukrainian situation.[5] A Polish pogrom against Jews in Vilnius accelerated the process, and Jews participated in the Lithuanian governments from the earliest days of the new state.

Lithuanian leaders at the Paris Peace Conference issued a formal statement in August 1919 expressing their strong support for the principles of Jewish autonomy and for a structure and competency broadly similar to the Ukrainian model.[6] Since the preceding December, a Ministry of Jewish Affairs had been functioning in the Lithuanian government, organizing a congress of *kehiles* that elected a Jewish National Council.[7] By January 1920, a law was passed making the decisions of this body binding on members of the Jewish community.[8] Jewish autonomy grew in leaps and bounds for a few years, then entered a period of steady decline. Lithuanian enthusiasm for the experiment waned as Jewish support failed to deliver Vilnius from the Poles. Furthermore, Lithuanians made great strides in the commercial sector, and the Jewish role in the economy grew less pronounced. In 1922 Lithuania issued a declaration to the League of Nations guaranteeing the equal rights of all its citizens but failed to make any mention of the institutions of Jewish autonomy, and in subsequent legislation the autonomy was also ignored.[9] The Ministry of Jewish Affairs was progressively eliminated, and by 1924 the Lithuanian government was passing discriminatory legislation and using police to break up clandestine meetings of the dissolved Jewish National Council.[10] The *kehiles* were similarly undermined with legislation that allowed Jews to set up rival *kehiles* in a single community and to remain outside of the membership and control of any *kehile*. In March 1926, after a struggle with the existing Jewish leadership, the *kehiles* themselves were declared illegal and ordered to disband.[11] Jewish autonomy in Lithuania was finished.

Latvia, with its smaller Jewish population, showed similar initial promise for Jewish autonomy. The early Latvian state guaranteed Jewish autonomy in late 1918, and Jewish delegates represented Jewish interests in the parliament.[12] By December 1919 legislation enshrined a Law of Autonomy for the Minorities that dealt almost exclusively with education.[13] More comprehensive authority for the Jewish autonomy was not considered, particularly within a constitutional framework, possibly out of the concern that potentially hostile neighbors such as Germany or the Soviet Union might cite Latvian failure to observe the legislation as a pretext for invasion. The so-called "minority treaties" imposed on several postwar states were viewed with much distrust and animosity; in general they were accepted only grudgingly, and compliance with their stipulations was increasingly lax through the interwar period.[14] A diverse network of Jewish schools teaching in Hebrew, Yiddish, Russian, and German flourished until 1934, when the liberal constitution that supported it was abolished.[15] A remnant of this system nevertheless continued to function without the Law of Autonomy until the Soviet period under the control of the Agudas Yisroel.[16]

Estonia's Jewish population was tiny, and a good portion of these Jews were veterans of the Tsarist army or their descendants who were allowed to live in this territory outside the Pale of Settlement. These veterans, commonly known as *kantonisten*, were often taken from their homes as children and forcibly inducted into the army for decades; typically they had little formal Jewish education but retained a strong attachment to the Jewish nationality.[17] Although Jewish religious parties were not especially strong in Estonia, which might suggest a lukewarm attitude toward Jewish ritual, fully 97 percent of Estonian Jews declared themselves "Jewish" by religious persuasion in 1934.[18] Unlike Lithuanians and Latvians, Estonians had little reason to actively court an alliance with their small Jewish population. Although their economic profile was similar to their southern neighbors, there were simply too few Jews (4,566, or 0.41 percent of the population in 1922)[19] to make a critical difference to the national economy.

Jewish autonomy disappeared from Lithuania in the late twenties and from Latvia and Estonia in the next decade. It seems that the idea was not in harmony with what were to be the major trends of the twentieth century. The notion of Jewish autonomy was simply too close to medieval corporatism to survive in a changing social climate.

The first-century Rabbi Hanina, the Deputy High Priest of the Temple in Jerusalem, said, "Pray for the welfare of the government, for were it not for the fear of it, people would swallow each other alive" (Avot 3:2). Fortunately, the dissolution of empires is not always intrinsically connected with communal violence, as the closing decade of this century has demonstrated. The so-called "Velvet Revolution" in Czechoslovakia and the fall of the Berlin Wall serve as examples. These are felicitous occasions in which humanity, for one reason or another, abstained from bloodletting, but they remain the exceptions that prove the rule. The more common pattern of human behavior remains amply evident throughout the world. One abomination is exchanged for another as Satan "wanders the earth, strolling about" (Job 1:7). The planet we share has not become a better place since the beginning of the century; indeed, it has arguably become worse. The Talmud records a sobering debate between the Schools of Hillel and Shammai (*Eruvin* 13b) on the question of whether or not the creation of humanity had a positive or a negative impact on the universe. After two and a half years of inconclusive argument, they uncharacteristically held a vote to decide the issue. The majority opinion ruled that humanity would have been better off not having been created at all, "but now that we have been created—one should scrutinize one's actions."

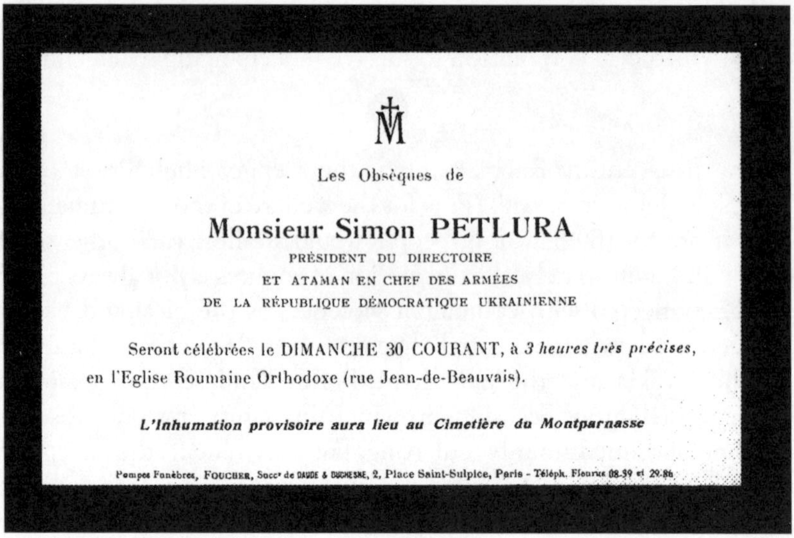

Les Obsèques de

Monsieur Simon PETLURA

PRÉSIDENT DU DIRECTOIRE
ET ATAMAN EN CHEF DES ARMÉES
DE LA RÉPUBLIQUE DÉMOCRATIQUE UKRAINIENNE

Seront célébrées le DIMANCHE 30 COURANT, à *3 heures très précises*, en l'Eglise Roumaine Orthodoxe (rue Jean-de-Beauvais).

L'Inhumation provisoire aura lieu au Cimetière du Montparnasse

Pompes Funèbres, FOUCHER, Succr de DAUDE & DUCHESNE, 2, Place Saint-Sulpice, Paris - Téléph. Fleurus 08.39 et 29.86

Top: Invitation to Petliura's Funeral. *Bottom:* Schwartzbard's Trial. (Schwartzbard is circled; the public prosecutor, Mr. Campinchi, is standing to the left; Henri Torrés is seated in front of the accused.)
Source: (Both) Tokarzewski-Karaszewicz Archives at the Research Library of the Harvard Ukrainian Research Institute. Bottom photo originally published in *Le Monde Illustré*, October 29, 1927.

Bibliographic Postscriptum[1]

> On the 25th of May, 1926, at 2:15 P.M., Rue Racine, several meters from Boulevard Saint-Michel, a man came out of a restaurant as another passed him going in the opposite direction, bare-headed and wearing a white shirt.
> The man in the white shirt looked at the first man, then, turning round, approached him and said:
> *"Pan Petliura?"*
> The first man ignored him and continued on his way, so the second asked a second time:
> *"You are Monsieur Petliura?"*
> At the same time, he withdrew a revolver from his pocket. Without answering, the first man raised his cane in an instinctive gesture of defense. The man in the white shirt fired five times, crying:
> *"Assassin! This is for the massacres! This is for the pogroms!"*[2]

Symon Petliura died several hours later in a Paris hospital. His assassin was Samuel Schwartzbard, a Jew from Bessarabia with a colorful past.[3] The case came to trial amid considerable publicity—the murder itself made the front page of the *New York Times*[4]—with the well-known attorney Henri Torrés defending Schwartzbard. Torrés adopted a clever line of argument at the trial. Rather than deal with the issue of Schwartzbard's guilt or innocence, Torrés focused on the murdered Petliura, contending that Schwartzbard was driven to an act of revenge for the pogroms that Petliura had orchestrated during the revolution, and that his act should therefore be seen as a crime of passion, an understandable expression of righteous indignation.

Historians with pro-Ukrainian sympathies have traditionally considered this a clever ruse and have followed the argument of the prosecution, which viewed Schwartzbard as a secret agent sent from Moscow to damage the Ukrainian anti-Communist movement. Current

Funeral Procession for Symon Petliura, May 30, 1926, departing from the Romanian Orthodox Church at rue Jean-de-Beauvais. Petliura was buried at Montparnasse Cemetery.
Source: Tokarzewski-Karaszewicz Archives at the Research Library of the Harvard Ukrainian Research Institute.

Top: Drawing by Marc Chagall for a Cover to a Planned Commemorative Volume on the Shalom Schwartzbard Trial, 1927. The text on the Torah scroll reads "Schwartzbard." *Bottom:* Title Page from Shalom Schwartzbard's Memoir *In'm loif fun yorn*.

Source: (Top) Archives of the YIVO Institute for Jewish Research. *Reproduced with permission. (Bottom)* Author's collection

research in French archives is confirming the extent of his Communist ties, but Schwartzbard seems to have had a sufficient motive to engineer the murder without any provocation.[5] Torrés' line of defense dominated the proceedings, which captivated Paris for over a year. The trial concentrated on the guilt or innocence of the victim Petliura rather than on the accused, and Torrés brought scores of witnesses forward to testify concerning the pogroms of 1917–1920.

In a judgment that caused considerable elation in Jewish circles and great consternation in the Ukrainian world, the French jury acquitted Schwartzbard after only twenty-four minutes of deliberation. As an added insult, Petliura's widow and brother-in-law were ordered to pay the court costs, while Schwartzbard was required to pay them each only one franc in damages.[6] It is possible that the Paris jury was unconsciously influenced by the trials of Alfred Dreyfus thirty years earlier, in which an innocent Jew was shamefully treated by French justice, and sought somehow to right this wrong by acquitting a Jew who was clearly guilty of the crime of which he was accused. Ukrainians and Jews had received, in the verdict, yet another reason to perpetuate their traditional animosities. Fourteen years later, the Nazis are reputed to have engineered a pogrom in L'viv called *Aktion Petliura* intended as "revenge" for the slaying of the Ukrainian leader.[7]

The Schwartzbard affair is of great relevance to the historiography of the revolutionary era, since both Ukrainian and Jewish historical scholarship were mobilized to provide evidence at the trial. Works published before Petliura's assassination tend to grapple with the issues in a forthright and reasonably balanced fashion, but many of those published after 1926 have followed, in the main, the arguments presented by either the prosecution or the defense instead of carefully examining the historical record. Recent historiography, however, has shown an encouraging trend toward an honest reevaluation of the polemics of earlier generations. The following is a brief review of the more important works on this topic.

In the immediate aftermath of the failed revolution, the major issue of concern to most scholars of Ukrainian Jewry was not the pogroms or the question of Petliura's personal responsibility for them. A political issue was of far greater import to these early researchers—the nature of the split between the Socialist and the Zionist blocs in Ukrainian Jewry in the debate over *doikeyt*, a Yiddish term meaning "here-ness."[8]

The Zionists argued that the ultimate expression of Jewish nationalism could only be realized in a Jewish state in Palestine. The socialists held that Jewish national aspirations must also be pursued in the Diaspora, with or without a Jewish state. This debate had several implications for the Jewish response to newly independent Ukraine. The socialists argued that Jews should take complete advantage of Ukrainian offers of national-personal autonomy, including the creation of the Ministry of Jewish Affairs, while the Zionists hesitated, feeling that the deeper the involvement in the fledgling Ukrainian state, the more energy would be diverted from the building of the Jewish homeland in Palestine.

Nevertheless, all shades of Jewish political opinion agreed that some form of participation with the Ukrainian government was desirable, and fixed organs of Jewish representation in the Ukrainian parliament were established soon after the fall of the tsar. Until the spring of 1919 these organs were led by members of the more moderate Jewish socialist parties, who have left a considerable memoir literature about their experience. The first significant work of this nature was published by Moshe Zilberfarb, who was active in Ukrainian-Jewish politics from the founding of the Central Rada until the resignation of the Vynnychenko government in January 1918.[9] Zilberfarb concerned himself for the most part with the struggle for leadership among the Socialist and Zionist blocs, and how political compromises were negotiated over the composition of the various governing bodies. The subject of antisemitism in the Ukrainian government in particular, and within the population in general, is treated only sporadically. The few pogroms during Zilberfarb's term of office were committed mainly by demobilizing Provisional Government troops on the Western front, making them a cause of concern, but not crisis, for Ukrainian-Jewish politics. Wolf Latsky-Bertholdi briefly became Minister for Jewish Affairs shortly after Zilberfarb's resignation; however, his memoir deals less with the experience of the Jews in the Ukrainian revolution *per se* than with the pogroms perpetrated by the White Army.[10]

The memoir of the third Minister of Jewish Affairs, Avraham Revutsky, is useful for understanding the relationship between Jews and the Ukrainian government.[11] Although Revutsky was active in the Ukrainian government mainly in late 1918 and early 1919, he provides an interesting account of the months since Zilberfarb held the position. The issue of pogroms perpetrated by Ukrainian forces became especially important in February 1919, and Revutsky devotes several chapters to the Proskuriv-Felshtin violence and its aftermath,[12] but his focus is primarily the internal Jewish political concerns of the day. Finally, the memoirs of Eliyohu Gumener, a local official of the Kam'ianets'-Podil's'kyi Jewish community, complete the treatment of the Jews in the Ukrainian government with an account of the final period of the Directory's activity in that region.[13]

The Zionist opposition was not silent during this period and in 1920 published a major work criticizing the socialist bloc's policy of heavy involvement with the Ukrainian government.[14] This work reproduced many decrees implicating Ukrainian government forces in pogrom activity, particularly in relation to the Proskuriv-Felshtin massacres perpetrated by Otaman Semesenko. It is crucial to note, however, that despite this evidence, the Zionist bloc did not condemn the Ukrainian government as a whole and still argued for Jewish participation in the Ukrainian revolutionary movement. The major point on which the Zionist bloc and the socialists differed was that, while the socialists accepted the position of a Minister of Jewish Affairs, the Zionists argued for a senior civil servant who would perform essentially the same functions. By not sitting in the cabinet, this "State Secretary" would not be so heavily involved in national, non-Jewish political issues. This debate is also reflected in the few writings on Jewish autonomy in Western Ukraine, which was also deeply concerned with the issue of neutrality in the Polish-Ukrainian conflict.[15]

With the rise of Ukrainian participation in the growing wave of pogroms during the spring of 1919, cooperation between Jewish and Ukrainian political parties came to an end. The Zionists moved further away from the government while the socialists contended with the growing success of communism. All the Jewish socialist parties split over the controversy, their left wings joining the Communist movement.[16] The Soviets welcomed Jewish socialists who had left the Ukrainian movement and were willing to repent in print; several prominent figures, such as Moshe Rafes of the Bund, published memoirs critical of the Ukrainian revolution under Soviet auspices.[17] Other socialists, who had not joined the pro-Communist factions of their parties, notably Solomon Goldelman and Arnold Margolin, continued to publish pro-Ukrainian works in the West. Although the works of Goldelman and Margolin are not as informative as other sources, such as Zilberfarb and Revutsky, they have enjoyed considerable popularity among Ukrainian researchers, not only because of their staunch pro-Ukrainian interpretations but also because they were published in other European languages besides Yiddish.[18]

The most significant center of scholarship on the topic was in Western Europe, where the noted scholar Elias (Eliyohu) Tcherikower had emigrated. Tcherikower, one of the editors of the pro-Zionist 1920 collection *Di idishe avtonomie un der natsionaler sekretariat in Ukrayne*, had amassed a considerable volume of documents while working in Kyiv, including a large collection of papers from the Ministry of Jewish Affairs and a wide assortment of newspaper clippings from the short-lived periodicals of the day. Tcherikower set up the "Eastern Jewish Historical Archive" and continued to collect eyewitness reports of pogroms, intending to embark on an ambitious multi-author study under the title *History of the Pogrom Movement in Ukraine, 1917–1921* which was to include these seven volumes:

1. Elias Tcherikower, *Antisemitism and Pogroms in Ukraine in the Years 1917–1918 (On the History of Ukrainian-Jewish Relations)*, published in 1923.[19]

2. Elias Tcherikower, *The Ukrainian Pogroms of 1919*, published posthumously in 1965.[20]

3. Joseph Schechtman, *The Pogroms of the Volunteer Army in Ukraine*, published in 1932.[21]

4. Nakhum Shtif, "The Pogroms of the Rebels (The Year 1920 in Ukraine—Civil War and Pogroms)," extant only in manuscript.[22]

5. Jacob Lestschinsky, "The Results of the Pogroms (Statistical-Economic Enquiry)," never completed.[23]

6. Nakhum Gergel, "The Pogroms in the Ukraine in 1918–1921," published as an article in 1928.[24]

7. "Materials on the History of Self-Defense," never completed.[25]

The series is generally critical of the Ukrainian revolutionary movement, in part because of the moderate Zionist approach of most of the authors, but it is more balanced than most publications that appeared after World War II. This is particularly evident in Tcherikower's first volume, which treats the activity of the Jewish political parties in the Ukrainian governments in great detail, and discusses pogroms perpetrated by all forces in Ukraine rather than focusing exclusively on those perpetrated by pro-Ukrainian forces.

The assassination of Petliura and Torrés' line of argument that Schwartzbard was acting out of revenge created a need for a new body of supporting scholarship, and a group of scholars, including Tcherikower and Schechtman, quickly assembled a publication that argued for Petliura's complicity in the pogroms. Issued in both English and French, the work published by the "Committee of the Jewish Delegations" proved to be both highly influential and highly effective.[26] Not only was Schwartzbard acquitted, but the work's argument has colored decades of Jewish scholarship and even the popular view of Jews and Ukrainians during the revolution.

The Committee publication relied heavily on both Tcherikower's *Antisemitizm un pogromen in Ukrayne* and the earlier *Di idishe avtonomie un der natsionaler sekretariat in Ukrayne*, reproducing many documents from those volumes in English and French translation. Several documents were edited, however, to support Torrés' argument that Petliura was the architect of the pogroms. Other documents that might have to some degree exculpated Petliura were not included.[27]

For the next sixty years, most published works that ostensibly dealt with the history of the Jews in Ukraine during the revolutionary years were in fact concerned more with condemning or upholding the 1927 Paris verdict. Soviet and Western Jewish scholars found common ground in their critique of Ukrainian nationalism, and most publications lacked the moderation present in the better works of the pre-Schwartzbard era. Even Pinkhos Krasny, the last Minister of Jewish Affairs in Petliura's government, published a stinging attack on Ukrainian nationalism that included an open letter to Schwartzbard's judges in Paris urging a decision in his favor.[28] This historiographic trend, which tended to ignore the positive activity of Jewish representatives in the Ukrainian government and to emphasize the pogroms committed by troops ostensibly loyal to that same government (often also ignoring pogroms committed by other forces such as the Whites and the Red Army), was given renewed vigor after the Holocaust, when Jewish historians examined Ukrainian complicity in war crimes. The Hebrew language journal *He'avar* marked the fiftieth anniversary of the 1919 pogroms by devoting two issues to this trend in the historiography.[29] Petliura had become, in the popular mind, only one in a long line of Ukrainian national leaders and rabid antisemites stretching back to Bohdan Khmel'nyts'kyi. The most vivid example of this popular view in the West is Saul Friedman's polemic *Pogromchik: The Assassination of Simon Petliura.*[30]

Ukrainian researchers were slow to defend their cause. Some important material had already been published on this issue by Batchinsky, Lewitzkyj, and Specht, and there were important general works by Khrystiuk and later by Doroshenko, but no new significant publication on Jews in Ukraine during the revolution appeared until well after World War II.[31] Two small collections relied heavily on previously published material.[32*]

In 1969 an important article by Taras Hunczak in *Jewish Social Studies*, a respected Jewish journal, signaled the beginning of a new phase in the debate.[33] Although Hunczak did not uncover any important new sources, nor did he advance any radically new arguments, he moved the level of debate to a higher plane as he eloquently presented the case for a "reappraisal of Symon Petliura and Ukrainian-Jewish relations." In the spirit of adversarial scholarly debate, the journal invited the rebuttal of Zosa Szajkowski, a long-standing proponent of the Jewish interpretation.[34] Szajkowski's impassioned article identified several major flaws in Hunczak's argument, but it preferred inflammatory language to the generally more academic tone of Hunczak. In the subsequent volume of *Jewish Social Studies* the debate regressed to increasingly bitter personal attacks.[35]

---

* As this work was going to press, Drs. Patricia Kennedy Grimsted and Yaroslav Hrytsak brought to my attention Volodymyr Serhiichuk's recent collection of documents from Ukrainian archives, *Pohromy v Ukraïni: 1914–1920, vid shtuchnykh stereotypiv do hirkoï pravdy, prykhovuvanoï v radians'kykh arkhivakh* [Pogroms in Ukraine: 1914–1920, from Artificial Stereotypes to the Bitter Truth, Hidden in Soviet Archives] (Kyiv, 1998). Despite the rather sensationalist subtitle, this work is quite useful, particularly in presenting documents from regional archives. Serhiichuk's analysis of the pogroms, however, is limited by the fact that he makes very little use of the significant research and primary sources available in non-Slavic languages.

In recent years, a new generation of scholars examined Hunczak's argument with renewed interest. Most Ukrainian researchers did not have the linguistic training to evaluate the documents adequately, and it took scholars with training in Yiddish and Hebrew to complete the task.[36] Recent scholarship has de-emphasized Petliura and examined the period from a broader perspective.[37] The pogroms perpetrated by Ukrainian forces are not ignored; rather, they are placed in the context of the brutal violence of the era as a whole. Furthermore, the activity of Jewish politicians in the Ukrainian parliaments is taken seriously as a bona fide attempt, however unsuccessful, at a *rapprochement* between these nationalities. The center of this revisionist approach to Ukrainian-Jewish relations was in Israel, where the scholars Matityahu Mintz (Minc) and Arie Zaidman produced significant works challenging the post-1926 traditional Jewish interpretation.[38] Similar research was presented at a 1983 conference on Ukrainian-Jewish history held at McMaster University in Hamilton, Ontario, which significantly advanced the state of scholarship on this topic.[39] My own research on this topic, first published in a 1991 article and culminating in the present monograph, represents my contribution to this trend of synthesizing Ukrainian and Jewish historiography of the revolutionary years.[40]

Abbreviations

Avtonomie	Grosman, M., Y. Grinfeld, Elias Tcherikower, Wolf Latsky, Joseph Schechtman, eds., *Di idishe avtonomie un der natsionaler sekretariat in Ukraine: materialn un dokumentn*, Kyiv: Idisher Folks-Farlag, 1920.
MKY	Mahleket kitvei-yad shel bet ha-sefarim ha-leumi ve-ha-universitai, Jerusalem.
Perepis'	Tsentral'nyi statisticheskii komitet, *Pervaia vseobshchaia perepis' naseleniia rossiiskoi imperii 1897 g.*, 89 vols. St. Petersburg, Izd. Tsentral'nogo, 1899–1905.
Statistik	Yidisher gezelshaftlikher komitet tsu helfen di gelitene fun pogromen (Yidgezkom), *Statistik fun pogromirte, heft 1: haymloze in Bohuslav (Kiev. gub.)*, Kyiv: Mlukhe-farlag, 1921.
TA	Tcherikower Archive, YIVO Institute for Jewish Research, New York City.
TsDAHOU	Tsentral'nyi derzhavnyi arkhiv hromads'kykh ob'iednan' orhanizatsii Ukraïny.

Notes

Foreword

1. Kurt Stillschweig, "Nationalism and Autonomy among Eastern European Jewry: Origin and Historical Development up to 1939," *Historia Judaica* 6 (New York, 1944): 59. This article is an adaptation of his more sophisticated "Zur neueren Geshichte des jüdischen Autonomie," *Monatsschrift für Geschichte und Wissenschaft des Judentums* 83 (Berlin, 1939): 509–32.
2. See the perceptive criticism of my early research in John-Paul Himka, "The National and the Social in the Ukrainian Revolution of 1917–1920: The Historiographical Agenda," *Archiv für Sozialgeschichte* 34 (1994): 104–105. I have attempted to address some of his concerns here.
3. See Henrik Birnbaum, "Some Problems with the Etymology and Semantics of the Slavic *Žid* 'Jew,'" *Slavica Hierosolymitana* 7 (Jerusalem, 1985): 1–11; John D. Klier, "*Zhid:* Biography of a Russian Epithet," *Slavonic and East European Review* 60:1 (1982): 1–15; and Roman Serbyn, "The Sion-Osnova Controversy of 1861–1862," in Peter Potichnyj and Howard Aster, eds., *Ukrainian-Jewish Relations in Historical Perspective* (Edmonton, 1988): 85–110.

Chapter 1

1. Early Jewish settlement is discussed in Philip Friedman, "The First Millennium of Jewish Settlement in the Ukraine and in the Adjacent Areas," *Annals of the Ukrainian Academy of Arts and Sciences in the U.S.* 7:1/2 (1959): 1483–1516; B. Nadel, *Yidn in Mizrekh-Eyropa fun di elteste tsaytn biz der mongolisher invazie (1240)* (Warsaw, 1960); Vsevolod Vikhnovich, "From the Jordan to the Dnieper," *Jewish Studies/Madaei ha-Yahadut* 31 (Jerusalem, 1991): 15–24. See also D. Goberman, *Evreiskie nadgrobiia na Ukraine i v Moldove* (Moscow, 1993).
2. See D. M. Dunlop, *The History of the Jewish Khazars* (Princeton, 1954); see also Norman Golb and Omeljan Pritsak, *Khazarian Hebrew Documents of the Tenth Century* (Ithaca, NY, 1982).
3. *The Russian Primary Chronicle: Laurentian Text*, trans. and ed. Samuel H. Cross and Olgerd Sherbowitz-Wetzor (Cambridge, MA, 1973),

p. 97, sub anno 6494 (986 CE). For a critical discussion of this account, see Petro Tolochko, "Volodimer Svjatoslavič's Choice of Religion: Fact or Fiction?" *Harvard Ukrainian Studies* 12/13 (1988–89): 816–19. It is interesting to note that the motif of a king entertaining the representatives of several faiths is also a central element of Jewish accounts of the Khazar conversion, most notably the twelfth-century Spanish classic of Jewish philosophy *Ha-Kuzari* by Yehuda Ha-Levi. An English version can be found in Isaak Heinemann et al., ed., *Three Jewish Philosophers* (New York, 1969).

4. See Omeljan Pritsak, "The Pre-Ashkenazic Jews of Eastern Europe in Relation to the Khazars, the Rus' and the Lithuanians," in Peter Potichnyj and Howard Aster, eds., *Ukrainian-Jewish Relations in Historical Perspective* (Edmonton, 1988), p. 8; Mykhailo Hrushevs'kyi, *Istoriia Ukraïny-Rusy*, 8 vols. (New York, 1959), map following vol. 2, p. 596. A useful overview of Jewish settlement in Kyiv may be found in Michael Hamm, *Kiev: A Portrait, 1800–1917* (Princeton, 1993), pp. 117–34.

5. For Moses of Kyiv, see A. Epstein, "Das talmudische Lexicon Yihuse tannai'im va-amoraim und Jehuda b. Kalonymos aus Speier," *Monatsschrift für Geschichte und Wissenschaft des Judentums* 39 (Breslau, 1895): 511; idem, "Moses aus Kiew," *Monatsschrift für Geschichte und Wissenschaft des Judentums* 40 (Breslau, 1896): 134. Isaac of Chernihiv is mentioned in Joseph Jacobs, *The Jews of Angevin England* (London, 1893), p. 73; he is also discussed in Avraham Harkavy, *Ha-yehudim u-sfat ha-slavim* (Vilnius, 1867), p. 62, and A. Drabkin, "Itse (Isaak) iz Chernigova," *Evreiskaia entsiklopediia* (St. Petersburg, n.d.), vol. 8, p. 523.

6. Petahia mi-Regensfurg [*sic*], in Elazar Grinhut, ed., *Sivuv* (Frankfurt am Main, 1905), pp. 2–3; J. Mann, *The Jews in Egypt and in Palestine under the Fatimid Caliphs*, 2 vols. (Oxford, 1922), vol. 2, p. 194 A.C. 12.2, see also vol. 1, pp. 165–66.

7. See Bernard Weinryb, "The Beginnings of East-European Jewry in Legend and Historiography," *Studies and Essays in Honour of Abraham A. Neuman* (Philadelphia, 1962), pp. 445–502. Weinryb argues that the Jewish settlement in Ukraine was not continuous from ancient times, having been disrupted by the Mongol invasion and other events.

8. A thumbnail sketch of the *arenda* is provided in *Encyclopaedia Judaica* (Jerusalem, 1972), vol. 3, pp. 402–404. More detailed information is provided in Moshe Rosman, *The Lords' Jews: Magnate-Jewish Relations in the Polish-Lithuanian Commonwealth during the Eighteenth Century* (Cambridge, MA, 1990), and Bernard Weinryb, *The Jews of Poland: A Social and Economic History of the Jewish Community in Poland from 1100 to 1800* (Philadelphia, 1973).

9. Rosman, *Lords' Jews*, pp. 95–105.

10. Rosman, *Lords' Jews*, pp. 48–51.

11. See Bernard Weinryb, "Hebrew Chronicles on Bohdan Khmel'nyts'kyi and the Cossack-Polish War," *Harvard Ukrainian Studies* 1 (1977): 153–77. Traditional Jewish prayer books for the holiday cycle include a special blessing for those who refrain from unnecessary speech during times of prayer, a transgression that is regarded as one of the reasons for the Khmel'nyts'kyi massacres. See, for example, *Bet tefilah mahzor ha-shalem he-hadash: Rosh ha-shanah (nusah ashkenaz)* (Jerusalem, 1989), p. 174.

12. The historiography on and writings of the Judaizers is discussed in Salo W. Baron, *The Russian Jew under Tsars and Soviets*, 2nd ed. (New York, 1987), pp. 7, 344–45, and Moshe Taube, "The 'Poem on the Soul' in the *Laodicean Epistle* and the Literature of the Judaizers," *Harvard Ukrainian Studies* 19 (1995): 671–85. See also Andrei Pliguzov, "Archbishop Gennadii and the Heresy of the Judaizers," *Harvard Ukrainian Studies* 16:3/4 (1992): 269–88.

13. See John Klier, *Russia Gathers Her Jews: The Origins of the "Jewish Question" in Russia, 1772–1825* (Dekalb, IL, 1986); Richard Pipes, "Catherine II and the Jews: The Origins of the Pale of Settlement," *Soviet Jewish Affairs* 5:2 (1975): 3–20.

14. See Chava Weissler, "Prayers in Yiddish and the Religious World of Ashkenazic Women," in Judith Baskin, ed., *Jewish Women in Historical Perspective* (Detroit, 1991), pp. 159–81.

15. The most notorious example of this is Johann Eisenmenger (1654–1704), who spent a considerable portion of his life—perhaps masquerading as a potential convert—studying Rabbinic literature, only to produce *Entdecktes Judenthum* ("Judaism Revealed"), a two thousand-page condemnation of Jewish attitudes toward non-Jews. See Jacob Katz, *From Prejudice to Destruction: Anti-Semitism, 1700–1933* (Cambridge, MA, 1980), pp. 13–16.

16. This is found in the opening blessings of the morning prayers (*Birkat ha-Shahar*). The word for non-Jew used here is *goy*, a term that has acquired an offensive connotation but is not instrinsically derogatory. The word is literally translated as "people" or "person," and takes on additional meaning only in context. Here it clearly refers to non-Jews, but in the *tahanun* section, for example, it is even used to refer to Jewish people (*goy kadosh*).

17. See, for example, *Mishnah Brurah* § 46:4, notes 15–16.

18. For basic reference works on traditional Jewish religious life, see Joseph Telushkin, *Jewish Literacy: The Most Important Things to Know About the Jewish Religion, Its People, and Its History* (New York, 1991) and Nachum Amsel, *The Jewish Encyclopedia of Moral and Ethical Issues* (Northvale,

NJ, 1994). These are popular works written for a contemporary audience, but have much value as general guides to Judaism as practiced in Eastern Europe.

19. This phrase is from Arcadius Kahan, "The Impact of Industrialization in Tsarist Russia on the Socioeconomic Conditions of the Jewish Population," in Roger Weiss, ed., *Essays in Jewish Social and Economic History* (Chicago, 1986), p. 10.

20. "*Niiakoï ukraïns'koï movy ne bulo, nemaie, i buty ne mozhe.*" Volodymyr Vynnychenko, *Vidrodzhennia natsiï* (Kyiv, 1990 [f.p. 1920]), vol. 1, p. 35. See also George Shevelov, *The Ukrainian Language in the First Half of the Twentieth Century* (Cambridge, MA, 1989), pp. 5–10, 42–57.

21. According to one account, 5,054,324 out of the 5,216,017 persons who declared Judaism as their religion spoke Yiddish as their mother tongue. See Henning Bauer, Andreas Kappeler, and Brigitte Roth, eds., *Die Nationalitäten des Russischen Reiches in der Volkszählung von 1897* (Stuttgart, 1991), vol. 1, p. 316.

22. See Max Weinreich, *History of the Yiddish Language*, trans. S. Noble (Chicago, 1980). Material specific to Ukrainian Yiddish is briefly discussed in Henry Abramson, "Yiddish," *Encyclopedia of Ukraine* (Toronto, 1993), vol. 5, pp. 773–74.

23. Bauer, Kappeler, and Roth, eds., *Nationalitäten*, vol. 1, p. 316.

24. Compare, for example, the recipes in Bessie Batist, *A Treasure for My Daughter* (Montreal, 1984, f.p. 1950), pp. 42, 83–84, 85; and Savella Stechishin, *Traditional Ukrainian Cookery* (Winnipeg, 1987, f.p. 1957), pp. 199, 222, 213, 276.

25. This notion is touched upon in Martha Bohachevsky-Chomiak, "Jewish and Ukrainian Women: A Double Minority," in Potichnyj and Aster, eds., *Ukrainian-Jewish Relations*, pp. 355–69.

26. See Mordechai Altshuler, *Soviet Jewry since the Second World War: Population and Social Structure* (New York, 1987), p. 239n1. Detailed figures of the Jewish population are provided in Arcadius Kahan, "The Impact of Industrialization," pp. 48–49. Although Bohdan Krawchenko argues for an overall increase of 33.2 percent in the population of permanent residents in Ukraine between 1897 and 1917, including a massive 101.9 percent growth in the urban population, this does not directly challenge Altshuler's calculations regarding emigration, since this increase was due mainly to Russian migration to the steppe regions. See Bohdan Krawchenko, "The Social Structure of the Ukraine in 1917," *Harvard Ukrainian Studies* 14:1/2 (1990): 97–112.

27. There is some reason to suspect that population figures for the Russian nationality are slightly exaggerated. See Robert Lewis, Richard Rowland, and Ralph Clem, *Nationality and Population Change in Russia*

and the USSR: An Evaluation of Census Data, 1897–1970 (New York, 1976), p. 161. Furthermore, the size of the Jewish population may be somewhat larger due to Jewish reluctance to enroll on the census. See Yakov Lestschinsky, "Di sotsial-ekonomishe antviklung fun Ukraynishn yidntum," *Yidn in Ukrayne*, 2 vols. (New York, 1961), vol. 1, pp. 183–85.

28. The world Jewish population at the end of the nineteenth century was roughly 10.3 million. For a graphic presentation, see Evyatar Friesel, *Atlas of Modern Jewish History* (New York, 1990), p. 15.

29. Lestschinsky, "Di sotsial-ekonomische antviklung," p. 186.

30. Jonathan Boyarin, *A Storyteller's Worlds: The Education of Shlomo Noble in Europe and America* (New York, 1994), p. 28. See also Elias Tcherikower, *Antisemitizm un pogromen in Ukrayne 1917–1918 (tsu der geshikhte fun Ukraynish-Yiddishe batsihungen)* (Berlin, 1923), pp. 23–24.

31. See Shevelov, *The Ukrainian Language*, pp. 5–6, 34–36, 54.

32. *Zakon pro vos'mohodynnyi rabochyi den'*, Kherson Kooperatyvnoho Tovarystva, 25 January 1918. Tsentral'nyi derzhavnyi arkhiv hromads'kykh ob'iednan' Ukraïny (TsDAHOU, formerly known as the Partiinyi arkhiv Instituta istorii partii pri TsK kompartii Ukrainy, Filiala Instituta marksizma-leninizma pri TsK KPSS), Kyiv, 41.1.9.26–41.

33. Patricia Herlihy, "Ukrainian Cities in the Nineteenth Century," in Ivan Rudnytsky and John-Paul Himka, eds., *Rethinking Ukrainian History* (Edmonton, 1981), p. 136. See also the article there by Steven L. Guthier, "Ukrainian Cities during the Revolution and the Interwar Era," pp. 159–61.

34. Out of a total population of 468,000, there were 77,000 Ukrainians (16.4 percent) and 87,000 Jews (18.6 percent). Forty-nine percent of the city was Russian (231,000), with other minorities making up the remaining 15.4 percent (73,000). Krawchenko, "The Social Structure of the Ukraine," p. 104.

35. Krawchenko, "The Social Structure of the Ukraine," pp. 106–107.

36. Lestschinsky, "Di sotsial-ekonomische antviklung," p. 209, table 23.

37. A useful introduction to the topic of pogroms, particularly in the tsarist period, is the collection edited by John Klier and Shlomo Lambroza, *Pogroms: Anti-Jewish Violence in Modern Russian History* (Cambridge, 1992). In connection with the 1881–1884 pogroms, I. Michael Aronson argued that although the pogroms took place on Ukrainian ethnolinguistic territory, the principal pogromists were Russians. See his *Troubled Waters: The Origins of the 1881 Anti-Jewish Pogroms in Russia* (Pittsburgh, 1990), pp. 101–107. For an extensive collection of pogrom-related documents, see Volodymyr Serhiichuk, *Pohromy v Ukraïni: 1914–1920, vid stuchnykh stereotypiv do hirkoï pravdy, prykhovuvanoï v radians'kykh arkhivakh* (Kyiv, 1998).

38. Walter Zenner, *Minorities in the Middle: A Cross-Cultural Analysis* (Albany, 1991), pp. 24–26.

39. Kahan, "The Impact of Industrialization," pp. 2–4.

40. Altshuler, *Soviet Jewry*, vol. 2, p. 240n5.

41. Kahan, "The Impact of Industrialization," pp. 6–7, 36–43.

42. Socialist thinking on the Jewish situation in the Russian Empire, particularly in the context of the pogroms of the late nineteenth century, is explored in Moshe Mishkinsky's "Black Repartition and the Pogroms of 1881–1882," in Klier and Lambroza, eds., *Pogroms*, pp. 62–98; also in that collection, see Erich Haberer, "Cosmopolitanism, Antisemitism, and Populism: A Reappraisal of the Russian and Jewish Socialist Response to the Pogroms of 1881–1882," pp. 98–134. Until recently, the established interpretation of the pogroms was that the tsarist regime had secretly organized them to deflect peasant anger away from the ruling powers. This position has largely been abandoned by current research; see in particular Aronson's *Troubled Waters*.

43. For an overview of this period, see Solomon Grayzel, *A History of the Jews* (New York, 1968), pp. 263–367.

44. See Arthur Hertzberg, *The French Enlightenment and the Jews* (New York, 1968), R. Necheles, "L'émancipation des Juifs 1787–1795: Aspects intellectuels et politiques," in Bernhard Blumenkranz and Albert Sobol, eds., *Les Juifs et la Revolution Française* (Paris, 1976), pp. 71–86. For peculiarities of the Russian situation, see John Klier, "The Concept of 'Jewish Emancipation' in a Russian Context," in Olga Crisp and Linda Edmondson, eds., *Civil Rights in Imperial Russia* (Oxford, 1989), pp. 121–44.

45. The essential primary texts relating to this period are contained in Paul Mendes-Flohr and Jehudah Reinharz, eds., *The Jew in the Modern World: A Documentary History* (New York and Oxford, 1980), pp. 103–125.

46. See Jacob Raisin, *The Haskalah Movement in Russia* (Philadelphia, 1913).

47. The most significant works are Karl Renner, *Das Selbstbestimmungsrecht der Nationen* (Leipzig and Vienna, 1918); Otto Bauer, *Die Nationalitätenfrage und die Sozialdemokratie* (Vienna, 1924). Renner's works (under the pseudonym "Rudolph Springer") date to 1899.

48. Oscar Janowsky, *The Jews and Minority Rights (1898–1919)* (New York, 1933), p. 32n15; Bauer, *Die Nationalitätenfrage*, pp. 366–81.

49. See Isaac Levitats, *The Jewish Community in Russia, 1844–1917* (Jerusalem, 1981), p. 182.

50. See Louis Greenberg, *The Jews in Russia: The Struggle for Emancipation*, 2 vols. (New York, 1976), vol. 1, p. 57. By way of contrast, see Moshe

Mishkinsky, "The Attitudes of the Ukrainian Socialists to Jewish Parties in the 1870s," in Potichnyj and Aster, eds., *Ukrainian-Jewish Relations*, pp. 57–68, and Ivan Rudnytsky in the same collection, "Ukrainian-Jewish Relations in Nineteenth-Century Ukrainian Political Thought," pp. 69–84.

51. Ivan Rudnytsky, "Mykhailo Drahomanov and the Problem of Ukrainian-Jewish Relations," in his *Essays in Modern Ukrainian History*, ed. Peter Rudnytsky (Edmonton, 1987), pp. 283–85.

52. *Sobranie politicheskikh sochinenii M. P. Dragomanova*, ed. B. A. Kistiakovskii [B. O. Kistiakivs'kyi], 2 vols. (Paris, 1905–1906), vol. 2, p. 328; Jonathan Frankel, *Prophecy and Politics: Socialism, Nationalism and the Russian Jews, 1862–1917* (Cambridge, 1981), pp. 101–104, 173–74.

53. Rudnytsky, "Mykhailo Drahomanov and the Problem," in Potichnyj and Aster, eds., *Ukrainian-Jewish Relations*, p. 291.

54. A useful summary of Chaim Zhitlowsky's conceptions of national autonomy may be found in Janowsky, *The Jews and Minority Rights*, pp. 51–57. See also *Sotsiializm i natsional'ne pytannie* (1915), The Andry Zhuk Collection, National Archives of Canada (Ottawa), vol. 148, file 33.

55. *History of the Jews in Russia and Poland: From the Earliest Times until the Present Day*, 3 vols. (Philadelphia: Jewish Publication Society, 1916–1920); *Weltgeschichte des jüdisches Volkes*, 10 vols. (Berlin, 1925).

56. The minute books of the Council of Lands are collected in Israel Halperin, ed., *Pinkas va'ad arba aratsot* (Jerusalem, n.d. [f.p. 1945]), and Dubnow's *Pinkas ha-Medinah* (Berlin, 1925). See also Shmuel Tsigelman, *Yehudei Polin ve-Litah ad shnat ta"h (1648)* (Jerusalem, 1991). For a useful thumbnail survey see H.H.B.S. [Haim Hillel ben Sasson], "Council of the Lands," *Encyclopaedia Judaica* (Jerusalem, 1972), pp. 995–1003.

57. The preeminent studies of the *kehile* are Isaac Levitats, *The Jewish Community in Russia, 1772–1844* (New York, 1943), and *The Jewish Community in Russia, 1844–1917* (Jerusalem, 1983).

58. These articles by Dubnow were later collected into book form and translated by Koppel Pinson under the title *Nationalism and History: Essays on Old and New Judaism* (New York, 1970).

59. See Pinson, Introduction to Dubnow, *Nationalism and History*, pp. 40–67.

60. Dubnow, *Nationalism and History*, p. 80. Other ethnic groups such as the Roma may also fit this description. I am grateful to Professor Paul Robert Magocsi for this observation.

61. For a useful summary of the Jewish political parties, see Benjamin Pinkus, *The Jews of the Soviet Union: The History of a National Minority* (Cambridge, 1988), pp. 39–47. Jewish liberalism, a short-lived but influential phenomenon, is examined in Christoph Gassenschmidt, *Jewish Liberal Politics in Tsarist Russia, 1900–1914: The Modernization of Russian Jewry* (New York, 1995).

62. See Moshe Mishkinsky, "Regional Factors in the Formation of the Jewish Labor Movement in Czarist Russia," in Ezra Mendelsohn, ed., *Essential Papers on Jews and the Left* (New York, 1997), pp. 79–80.

63. See Mishkinsky, "Regional Factors," pp. 89–96.

64. This shift in opinion is analyzed in Alexander Orbach, "Zionism and the Russian Revolution of 1905: The Commitment to Participate in Domestic Political Life," *Bar-Ilan Studies in the History and Culture of East European Jewry* 24–25 (1989): 7–23.

65. Cited in Janowsky, *The Jews and Minority Rights*, p. 111. The resolution is discussed on pp. 109–112.

66. In a platform published in connection with elections to the Jewish Provisional Parliament, the Tseire Tsion declared that national-personal autonomy was "our great national heritage from the recent revolution." TsDAHOU 41.1.236.4.

67. Jabotinsky's relationship with the Ukrainian national movement receives a brief and qualified mention in Shmuel Katz, *Lone Wolf: A Biography of Vladimir (Ze'ev) Jabotinsky*, 2 vols. (New York, 1996), vol. 1, pp. 751–58. See also Olga Andriewsky, "*Medved' iz berlogi:* Vladimir Jabotinsky and the Ukrainian Question, 1904–1914," *Harvard Ukrainian Studies* 14:3/4 (1990): 249–67.

68. At the 1901 Bialystok conference the principle of Jewish nationality was accepted, but the resolutions of that conference added: "it is yet too early to present the demand of national autonomy for Jews, the convention holds that for the present it is advisable to fight only against all exceptional laws against Jews, to...protest against every oppression of the Jewish nation, but at the same time to guard against the inflation of national consciousness that can only dim class consciousness and may lead to chauvinism." Cited in Janowsky, *The Jews and Minority Rights*, pp. 79–80.

69. Janowsky, *The Jews and Minority Rights*, p. 218.

70. "Di program fun Bund," Brochure No. 1, 1917, TsDAHOU 41.1.4.

71. See Pinkus, *The Jews of the Soviet Union*, p. 43; Janowsky, *The Jews and Minority Rights*, pp. 72–85. General histories of the Bund include Henry Tobias, *The Jewish Bund in Russia: From Its Origins to 1905* (Stanford, 1972), and Y. Sh. Hertz, *Di geshikhte fun Bund*, 5 vols. (New York, 1960).

72. See *Iuzhnaia oblastskaia konferentsiia Bunda 5–10 Avgusta 1917 g.*, TsDAHOU 41.1.5.

73. See Pinkus, *The Jews of the Soviet Union*, p. 41.

74. *Programa Evreiskoi Sotsial-Demokraticheskoi Rabochei Partii ("POALEI-TSION")*, Petrograd: Izdanie Petrogradskago Komiteta, n.d., TsDAHOU 41.1.126.25,31.; Janowsky, *The Jews and Minority Rights*, pp. 132–34.

75. See Pinkus, *The Jews of the Soviet Union*, p. 45; Mark Kiel, "The Ideology of the Folks-partey," *Soviet Jewish Affairs* 5:2 (1975): 75–89.

76. Pinkus, *The Jews of the Soviet Union*, pp. 43–44.

77. Janowsky, *The Jews and Minority Rights*, pp. 219n10, 232n24.

78. See Mordechai Altshuler, "Ha-politika shel ha-mahane ha-dati ve-ha-haredi be-Rusyah be-shnat 1917," *Shvut* 15 (1992): 195–234; Levitats, *The Jewish Community in Russia*, p. 180.

79. "Di yidishe ministerium kehiles in Ukrayne," in *Di yidishe ministerium avtonomie un der natsionaler sekretariat in Ukrayne: Materialn un dokumentn*, ed. M. Grosman, Y. Grinfeld, Elias Tcherikower, Wolf Latsky, J. Schechtman (Kyiv, 1920), p. 210n. Some of the programs of many of the parties mentioned here are reproduced in *Ha-ma'avak le-shovi-zkhuyot le-umiyot u-le-otonomiyah be-kerev yehudei Rusyah be-ma'avar min ha-meah ha-19 u-va-meah ha-20*, ed. Matityahu Mintz (Mints), (Tel-Aviv University, 1978). See also Pinkus, *The Jews of the Soviet Union*, pp. 45–47.

80. A thumbnail sketch of other Jewish parties is provided in Levitats, *The Jewish Community in Russia, 1844–1917*, pp. 179–89.

81. See examples cited in Richard Pipes, *Russia under the Bolshevik Regime* (New York, 1993), pp. 103–104.

82. Personal correspondence cited in Joseph Nevada, *Trotsky and the Jews* (Philadelphia, 1972), p. 28, see also p. 47. On the other hand, Trotsky was obsessed with the pogroms (pp. 48–69), and also taught himself Yiddish in order to read Bundist literature (p. 36).

83. Nevada, *Trotsky and the Jews*, pp. 133–59.

84. See Pinkus, *The Jews of the Soviet Union*, pp. 77–79.

85. Pinkus, *The Jews of the Soviet Union*, p. 43.

86. Altshuler, *Soviet Jewry*, pp. 208–209.

87. I have discussed some of the aspects of Ukrainian antisemitism, and the scholarship on it, in "The Scattering of Amalek: A Model for Understanding the Ukrainian-Jewish Conflict," *East European Jewish Affairs* 24:1 (1994): 39–47.

88. Zvi Gitelman, "Contemporary Soviet Jewish Perceptions of Ukrainians: Some Empirical Observations," in Potichnyj and Aster, eds., *Ukrainian-Jewish Relations*, pp. 454–55. Gitelman uses the word "myth" here in terms of a theoretical construct and not in the sense of a fable or untruth.

89. *Chy vorohy ievrei robitnykam ta selianam?* (Kyiv, 1919), p. 4.

90. George Fedotov, *The Russian Religious Mind*, 2 vols. (Belmont, MA, 1966), vol. 1, p. 91. See also Gerhard Podskalsky, *Christentum und Theologische Literatur in der Kiever Rus' (988–1237)* (Munich, 1982), pp. 78–80.

91. Muriel Heppel, trans., *The Paterik of the Kievan Caves Monastery* (Cambridge, MA, 1989), p. 73.

92. Henrik Birnbaum, "On Some Evidence of Jewish Life and Anti-Jewish Sentiments in Medieval Russia," *Viator* 4 (1973): 225, 235–37. See in this context the introduction of Simon Franklin in *Sermons and Rhetoric of Kievan Rus'* (Cambridge, MA, 1991), p. xxxviii.

93. Simon Dubnow, *History of the Jews in Russia and Poland from the Earliest Times until the Present Day*, trans. I. Friedlander, 3 vols. (Philadelphia, 1916–1920), vol. 1, p. 142.

94. Nathan Hannover, *Abyss of Despair (Yeven Metsulah)*, trans. Abraham Mesch (New York, 1950), pp. 27–28. Mesch adds in a note that "the lowliest" is a reference to Jews.

95. See Weinryb, "Hebrew Chronicles," p. 170; Jaroslaw Pelenski, "The Cossack Insurrection in Jewish-Ukrainian Relations," in Potichnyj and Aster, eds., *Ukrainian-Jewish Relations*, p. 37; Daniel Krochmalnik, "Juden und Kosaken," *Diskussions-beitrage aus dem jüdischen Lehrhaus in Frankfurt am Main* (Frankfurt am Main, 1986), pp. 88–89; Theodor Mackiw, "Die Situation der jüdischen Bewohner in den Konflikten um die Ukraine im 17. Jahrhundert," *Studien zu Nationalitätenfragen* 2 (1986): 56–57.

Chapter 2

1. The stone-throwing incident is recorded in Richard Stites, *The Women's Liberation Movement in Russia: Feminism, Nihilism, and Bolshevism, 1860–1930* (Princeton, 1978), p. 288. St. Petersburg, named after the saint in whose name Tsar Peter I had been baptized, was renamed Petrograd with the beginning of World War I. The change from the German-sounding "Peter's City" to the Russian was intended to reflect the anti-Central Powers position of the tsarist empire. During most of the Soviet period St. Petersburg was known as Leningrad.

2. Dmytro Doroshenko, *Istoriia Ukraïny 1917–1923 rr.*, 2 vols. (Uzhhorod, 1932, reprinted New York, 1954), vol. 1, p. 40.

3. A. A. Gol'denveizer, "Iz Kievskikh vospominanii (1917–1922 gg.)," *Arkhiv russkoi revoliutsii* 6 (Berlin, 1922): 164–65.

4. The declaration is translated in *A Source Book for Russian History from Early Times to 1917*, ed. George Vernadsky, 3 vols. (New Haven, 1972), vol. 3, pp. 881–82. See also W. E. Mosse, "A. F. Kerensky and the Emancipation of Russian Jewry," *Bulletin on Soviet and East European Jewish Affairs* 6 (1970): 33–38.

5. Cited in Mordechai Altshuler, "Ha-politika shel ha-mahane ha-dati ve-ha-haredi be-Rusyah be-shnat 1917" *Shvut* 15 (1992): 198.

6. For the text of this declaration, see Doroshenko, *Istoriia Ukraïny*, vol. 1, p. 43. See also Wolodymyr Stojko, "Ukrainian National Aspirations and the Russian Provisional Government," in Taras Hunczak, ed., *The Ukraine, 1917–1921: A Study in Revolution* (Cambridge, MA, 1977), pp. 4–6.

7. The Society of Ukrainian Progressives later changed its name to the Union of Ukrainian Autonomists-Federalists and shortly thereafter to the Ukrainian Party of Socialist-Federalists. John Reshetar, *The Ukrainian Revolution, 1917–1920: A Study in Nationalism* (New York, 1972), p. 48; Stojko, "Ukrainian National," p. 8.

8. See his "Chy Ukraïna til'ku dlia Ukraïntsiv?" in Mykhailo Hrushevs'kyi, *Vybrani pratsi: vydano z nahody 25-richchia z dnia ioho smerty (1934–1959)* (New York, 1960). See also Bohdan Klid, "The Struggle over Mykhailo Hrushevs'kyi: Recent Soviet Polemics," *Canadian Slavonic Papers* 33:1 (1991): 39; Serhii Plokhy, "The History of a 'Non-historical' Nation: Notes on the Nature and Current Problems of Ukrainian Historiography," *Slavic Review* 54:3 (1995): esp. 710–13.

9. George Grabowicz, "Ukrainian Studies: Framing the Contexts," *Slavic Review* 54:3 (1995): 679.

10. See Jurij Borys, "Political Parties in the Ukraine," in Hunczak, ed., *The Ukraine*, pp. 132–35. Although the article contains much useful information, the data on Jewish parties contain some minor inaccuracies. Vynnychenko's relationship with Jews was also personal, as his wife Rozalia was Jewish. See Iakiv Suslens'kyi, *Spravzhni heroi: pro uchast' hromadian Ukraïny u riatuvanni ievreïv vid fashists'koho henotsydu* (Kyiv, 1993), pp. 118–19.

11. George Liber, "Ukrainian Nationalism and the 1918 Law on National-Personal Autonomy," *Nationalities Papers* 15:1 (1987): 31. See also the resolution of the 1917 conference of the USDLP in Volodymyr Vynnychenko, *Vidrodzhennia natsiï*, 4 vols. (Kyiv, 1990; f.p. 1920), vol. 1, p. 45.

12. Liber, "Ukrainian Nationalism," p. 32.

13. Oscar Janowsky, *The Jews and Minority Rights (1898–1919)* (New York, 1933), p. 223.
14. See V. Yaniv, "Mikhnovsky, Mykola," *Encyclopedia of Ukraine* (Toronto, 1984–1993), vol. 3, p. 406.
15. Jurij Borys, "Political Parties in the Ukraine," in Hunczak, ed., *The Ukraine*, p. 143.
16. See Committee of Jewish Delegations, *The Pogroms in the Ukraine under the Ukrainian Governments (1917–1920): Historical Survey with Documents and Photographs* (London, 1927), p. 12.
17. See the observations of Avraham Revutsky, *In di shvere teg oif Ukrayne: zikhroines fun a yidishn minister* (Berlin, 1924), pp. 12–25.
18 Vynnychenko, *Vidrodzhennia natsiï*, vol. 1, pp. 255–56; translation from Liber, "Ukrainian Nationalism," p. 37. See also Revutsky, *In di shvere*, pp. 26–31.
19. See Elias Tcherikower, *Antisemitizm un pogromen in Ukrayne 1917–1918 (tsu der geshikhte fun ukraynish-yidishe batsihungen)* (Berlin, 1923), p. 24, for several examples of towns with populations that were over 90 percent Jewish.
20. I am grateful to Professor Orest Subtelny for this observation. See also Matityahu Mintz, "The Secretariat of Internationality Affairs *(Sekretariiat mizhnatsional'nykh sprav)* of the Ukrainian General Secretariat (1917–1918)," *Harvard Ukrainian Studies* 6:1 (1982): 29.
21. Some understood the move as implicitly indicating a future foreign ministry; see Mintz, "The Secretariat of Internationality Affairs," p. 27.
22. For a brief history of the Protocols of the Elders of Zion, see Norman Cohn, *Warrant for Genocide* (London, 1967).
23. Salo Baron, *The Russian Jew under Tsars and Soviets*, 2nd ed. (New York, 1987), p. 61. Ippolit Liutostanskii was able to generate additional sales of his antisemitic tracts by claiming that Jews had offered him 100,000 to refrain from publishing them. See Heinz-Dietrich Löwe, *The Tsars and the Jews: Reform, Reaction, and Antisemitism in Imperial Russia, 1772–1917* (New York, 1993), p. 59.
24. Shlomo Lambroza, "The Pogroms of 1903–06," in John Klier and Shlomo Lambroza, eds., *Pogroms: Anti-Jewish Violence in Modern Russian History* (Cambridge, 1992), pp. 222, 224.
25. The history of the blood libel myth is discussed in Joshua Trachtenberg, *The Devil and the Jews: The Medieval Conception of the Jew and Its Relation to Modern Antisemitism* (Philadelphia, 1983, f.p. 1943); see also R. Po-Chia Hsia, *The Myth of Ritual Murder: Jews and Magic in Reformation Germany* (New Haven, 1988). I have discussed some of the gender-related aspects of this myth in "A Ready Hatred: Depictions of the

Jewish Woman in Medieval Antisemitic Art and Caricature," *Proceedings of the American Academy for Jewish Research* 62 (1996): 1–18.

26. Löwe, *The Tsars and the Jews*, p. 287. The phrase "gruesome details left out here" is Löwe's.

27. Löwe, *The Tsars and the Jews*, p. 325.

28. I. Frumin was in the Executive Committee until late April (O.S.), when A. A. Gol'denveizer took the position. Gol'denveizer, "Iz Kievskikh," pp. 165, 169.

29. See Steven Guthier, "The Popular Base of Ukrainian Nationalism in 1917," *Slavic Review* 38:1 (1974): 30–47. This attitude, of course, was not universal. See Volodymyr Serhiichuk, *Pohromy v Ukraïni: 1914–1920, vid shtuchnykh stereotypiv do hirkoï pravdy, prykhovuvanoï v radianskykh arkhivakh* (Kyiv, 1998), p. 31.

30. Iakiv Zozulia, *Velyka ukraïns'ka revoliutsiia: materiialy do istoriï vidnovlennia ukraïns'koï derzhavnosty* (New York, 1967), p. 10.

31. See Solomon Goldelman's report back to his party, the Poale-Tsion: Minutes of the Kievskii Gubernskii Komitet Evreiskoi Sotsial-Demokraticheskoi Partii /ESDRP/ Poale-Tsion (entry March 16 old style), Tsentral'ny Derzhavnyi Arkhiv Hromads'kykh Ob'iednan' Ukraïny (TsDAHOU) 41.1.165. See also Gol'denveizer, "Iz Kievskikh," p. 166.

32. The Polish community also greeted the Congress. See Gol'denveizer, "Iz Kievskikh," pp. 168, 172. See also Committee of Jewish Delegations, *The Pogroms in the Ukraine*, p. 4.

33. W. E. Mosse, "A. F. Kerensky and the Emancipation of Russian Jewry," *Bulletin on Soviet and East European Jewish Affairs* 6 (1970): 38n24.

34. Ihor Kamenetsky, "Hrushevskyi and the Central Rada: Internal Politics and Foreign Interventions," in Hunczak, ed., *The Ukraine*, p. 34. For examples of Hrushevs'kyi's statements on the nationality question, see his *Vybrani pratsi*, pp. 117–18, 123, and 126–31.

35. See Wolodymyr Stojko, "Ukrainian National Aspirations and the Russian Provisional Government," in Hunczak, ed., *The Ukraine*, pp. 4–32.

36. Much of the following material is taken from a paper entitled "Notes on the Non-existence of Ukrainian Jewry," which I delivered at the conference on "Peoples, Nations, Identities: The Russian-Ukrainian Encounter," Columbia University, 1994.

37. *Mahzor min rosh-ha-shana ve-yom ha-kipurim* (Zhytomyr, 1858), p. 14.

38. *Shulhan arukh* [Code of Jewish Law], Orah Haiim § 224:8.

39. Löwe, *The Tsars and the Jews*, p. 28.

40. Some concise, useful biographies may be found in Avraham Finkel, *The Great Torah Commentators* (Northvale, NJ, 1990).

41. "Appendix: The Four Universals," in Hunczak, ed., *The Ukraine*, pp. 382–84. Emphasis in the original, translation slightly adapted.

42. Ibid., pp. 384–85. Emphasis in the original.

43. Moshe Rafes, *Dva goda revoliutsii na Ukraine (èvoliutsiia raskola "Bunda")* (Moscow, 1920), cited in Liber, "Ukrainian Nationalism," p. 38.

44. Liber, "Ukrainian Nationalism," p. 26. Liber remarks on the strange omission of the Poles from this commission.

45. See Mintz, "The Secretariat of Internationality Affairs," p. 29; Reshetar, *The Ukrainian Revolution*, p. 62.

46. Pavlo Khrystiuk, ed., *Zamitky i materiialy do istoriï ukraïns'koï revoliutsiï 1917–1920 rr.*, 4 vols. (Vienna, 1921), vol. 1, p. 92n.

47. Zozulia, *Velyka ukraïns'ka revoliutsiia*, p. 69.

48. Matityahu Minc (Mintz), "Kiev Zionists and the Ukrainian National Movement," in Peter Potichnyj and Howard Aster, eds., *Ukrainian-Jewish Relations in Historical Perspective* (Edmonton, 1988), p. 253.

49. Kievskii Gubernskii Komitet, TsDAHOU 41.1.165, under the entries March 27 and April 11, 1917 (O.S.).

50. Gol'denveizer, "Iz Kievskikh," pp. 183–84.

51. See, for example, the July 17, 1917 (O.S.) protest to the Central Rada by the Zionists of Polonnom', Volhynia, TsDAHOU 41.1.238–39.

52. Gol'denveizer, "Iz Kievskikh," p. 169.

53. Kievskii Gubernskii Komitet, TsDAHOU 41.1.165, see 25 April 1917 (O.S.).

54. These calculations are based on Doroshenko's figures (*Istoriia Ukraïny*, vol. 1, p. 123) with membership in the Central Rada totaling 822. The exact size of the Central Rada is a matter of debate; see Reshetar, *The Ukrainian Revolution*, p. 63n3.

55. On Jews participating in blocs, see Christoph Gassenschmidt, *Jewish Liberal Politics in Tsarist Russia, 1900–1914: The Modernization of Russian Jewry* (New York, 1995), p. 32.

56. Vynnychenko, *Vidrodzhennia natsiï*, vol. 1, p. 253.

57. Mintz, "The Secretariat of Internationality Affairs," p. 28; see the declaration of the General Secretariat to the Ukrainian Central Rada, 27 June 1917 (O.S.) in Vynnychenko, *Vidrodzhennia natsiï*, vol. 1, p. 266.

58. Doroshenko, *Istoriia Ukraïny*, vol. 1, pp. 124–25; Vynnychenko, *Vidrodzhennia natsiï*, vol. 1, p. 299.

59. See Khrystiuk, *Zamitky*, vol. 1, pp.114–15; Vynnychenko, *Vidrodzhennia natsiï*, vol. 1, pp. 315–18. See also Stojko, "National Aspriations," p. 24.

60. Mintz, "The Secretariat of Internationality Affairs," p. 31.

61. Khrystiuk, ed., *Zamitky*, vol. 1, pp. 144–45. I am grateful to Alan Rutkowski for sharing some of his translations with me.

62. See the text in Vynnychenko, *Vidrodzhennia natsiï*, vol. 1, pp. 338–42.

63. Vynnychenko, *Vidrodzhennia natsiï*, vol. 1, p. 303.

64. On the significance of these terms, see Mintz, "The Secretariat of Internationality Affairs," pp. 32ff.

65. Mintz, "The Secretariat of Internationality Affairs," p. 39.

66. Moshe Zilberfarb, *Dos idishe ministerium un di idishe avtonomie in Ukrayne (a bletl geshikhte)* (Kyiv, 1919), p. 1. Mintz remarks that there is no ready explanation for the delay of the Russian Vice-Secretariat, "The Secretariat of Internationality Affairs," p. 32n27.

67. Yosef Kruk, "Moshe Zilberfarb (meah shanah le-huladeto)," *He'avar* (Tel-Aviv, 1971): 276–79; Janowsky, *The Jews and Minority Rights*, 69; TsDAHOU 41.1.59.30.

68. Volodymyr Stojko, "Z'ïzd narodiv u Kyievi 1917 roku," *Ukraïns'kyi istorik* 3–4 (55–56) 1977: 15, 19.

69. Zilberfarb, *Dos idishe ministerium*, Appendix, pp. 1–8.

70. On the *kehile* and its demise, see Isaac Levitats, *The Jewish Community in Russia 1772–1844* (New York, 1933) and *The Jewish Community in Russia, 1844–1917* (Jerusalem, 1981).

71. Zilberfarb, *Dos idishe ministerium*, pp. 32, 67.

72. "Appendix: The Four Universals," p. 388. Text is also in Vynnychenko, *Vidrodzhennia natsiï*, vol. 2, pp. 74–80.

73. Ibid., p. 390. This paragraph was formulated by the Fareynikte; see Zilberfarb, *Dos idishe ministerium*, p. 47.

74. Henryk Jabłoński, *Polska autonomia narodowa na Ukrainie 1917–1918* (Warsaw, 1948), pp. 66–73.

75. Joseph Schechtman, "Jewish Community Life in the Ukraine (1917–1919)," in Gregor Aronson et al., eds., *Russian Jewry 1917–1967* (New York, 1969), p. 46.

76. The Ukrainian original of the law is reproduced in Doroshenko, *Istoriia Ukraïny*, pp. 274–76 and the Yiddish, with minor differences, in Zilberfarb, *Dos idishe ministerium*, Appendix, pp. 75–78. A partial Russian text is preserved in TsDAHOU 41.1.87.20–22. An English translation is reproduced in Walter Dushnyk, ed., *Ukrainians and Jews: A Symposium* (New York, 1966), pp. 154–56; a German translation in

Solomon Goldelman, *Juden und Ukrainer: Briefe Eines Jüdischen Sozialdemokraten* (Vienna, 1921), pp. 138–40. Textual variations are discussed in Matityahu Mintz (Mints), ed., *Ha-ma'avak le-shovi-zkhuyot le-umiyot u-le-otonomiyah be-kerev yehudei Rusyah be-ma'avar min ha-meah ha-19 u-va-meah ha-20* (Tel Aviv, 1978), pp. 126–32.

77. Zilberfarb discusses the possibility of groups breaking from one union and creating new ones but avoids the problem on the individual level. A draft document for establishing the unions is preserved in TsDAHOU 41.1.87.18–19. Not surprisingly, it is marred by numerous strikeouts.

78. This met with some opposition from USDLP, see Zilberfarb, *Dos idishe ministerium*, pp. 55–56.

79. See Joseph Schechtman, "Tsum gezets vegn natsional-personaler avtonomie," in M. Grosman et al., eds., *Di idishe avtonomie un der natsionaler sekretariat in Ukrayne: materiyaln un dokumentn* (Kyiv, 1920), pp. 57–58. Several other concerns are raised in this article, and a proposed revision is also supplied.

80. Schechtman, "Tsum gezets," pp. 63–64; Zilberfarb, *Dos idishe ministerium*, p. 60n67.

81. Zilberfarb, *Dos idishe ministerium*, p. 58.

82. Schechtman, "Jewish Community Life," p. 45. Schechtman later quotes an article from a Petrograd newspaper (*Rassvet*, January 31, 1918 [old style]): "To be sure, after a couple of days [the Rada] collected itself, buttoned up all of its buttons, and approved the bill, but the attitude of the Ukrainian representatives was disclosed precisely at this opening session, when the people gave voice to just what was on their minds."

83. John Hewko, "The Ukrainian-Jewish Political Relationship during the Period of the Central Rada—March 1917 to January 1918," M.Litt thesis, St. Anthony's College, Oxford, 1981, p. 172.

84. "Appendix: The Four Universals," p. 392. Text is also in Vynnychenko, *Vidrodzhennia natsiï*, vol. 2, pp. 244–52.

85. Tcherikower Archive, YIVO Institute for Jewish Research (TA) 50712; also Schechtman, "Jewish Community Life," p. 46.

86. Janowsky, *The Jews and Minority Rights*, p. 239.

87. Hewko, "The Ukrainian-Jewish Political Relationship," pp. 172–77.

88. Solomon Goldelman, *Jewish National Autonomy in Ukraine, 1917–1920* (Chicago, 1968), p. 50.

89. Zilberfarb, *Dos idishe ministerium*, p. 62.

90. Mintz, "The Secretariat of Internationality Affairs," p. 36; Zilberfarb, *Dos idishe ministerium*, p. 11n.

Chapter 3

1. The Law of National-Personal Autonomy is often referred to in the literature as "the Law of 9 January," after the official Julian date of its acceptance by the Rada. It should be noted, however, that in fact this law was not passed until two days later. See the "Appendix: The Four Universals," in Taras Hunczak, ed., *The Ukraine, 1917–1921: A Study in Revolution* (Cambridge, MA, 1977), p. 394n4.
2. Moses Silberfarb [Moshe Zilberfarb], *The Jewish Ministry and Jewish National Autonomy in Ukraine*, translated by David H. Lincoln (New York, 1993), pp. 106–112. This translation covers all of the text of the original with the exception of 12 appendices. The Yiddish original is Moshe Zilberfarb, *Dos idishe ministerium un di idishe avtonomie in Ukrayne (a bletl geshikhte)*, (Kyiv, 1919).
3. Zilberfarb, *Dos idishe ministerium*, p. 22.
4. One *karbovanets'* was calculated to have the value of 0.767 grams of pure gold, making the total budget equal to some 463 kilograms. Ye. Glovinsky, V. Shuhaievsky, "Currency and Coins," *Encyclopedia of Ukraine*, eds. Volodymyr Kubijovyc and Danylo Husar Struk (Toronto, 1984–1993), vol. 1, p. 631. State expenditures totaled 5.3 million *karbovantsi*; B. Wynar, "Budget," *Encyclopedia of Ukraine*, vol. 1, p. 309.
5. Proekt Shtativ Ministerstva Ievreis'kykh Sprav, Tcherikower Archive, YIVO Institute for Jewish Research, New York City (hereafter TA), 734–737. It should be noted, however, that these figures are drawn from the only extant budget for the Ministry, which is unfortunately only a proposed budget. Its date, which does not appear on the document, may be deduced from context: the term *Ministerstvo* [Ministry] was used no earlier than 24 January 1918, and the funds are expressed in terms of *karbovantsi*, which were replaced by *hryvni* as the basic monetary unit on March 1, 1918.
6. Zilberfarb, *Dos idishe ministerium*, p. 36.
7. Silberfarb, *Jewish*, p. 38; Zilberfarb, *Dos idishe ministerium*, p. 26.
8. TA 7.619-620, Ukrainian translation 11.798.
9. "...mit a motiv az a id hot nit keyn rekht erfolgen azelkher arbet."
10. "Take povodzhennia nachal'nyku ie tsil'kom nazakonne, bo na Ukraïni niiakykh natsional'nykh pravovykh obmezhen' ne mozhe buty." TA 11.797.
11. TA 5.475.
12. TA 6.493.
13. TA 5.477.

14. TA 5.481; 6.498.
15. TA 7.633; 7.638.
16. TA 7.533; 7.546–547; 7.556; 7.570–571. Mahleket kitvei-yad shel bet ha-sefarim ha-leumi ve-ha-universitai (Manuscripts Division of the National and University Library, Jerusalem; hereafter MKY) V772.583.
17. MKY V772.26, 108.1, 108.6.
18. TA 7.560.
19. Zilberfarb, *Dos idishe ministerium*, pp. 29, 77.
20. TA 11.746.
21. TA 11.742.
22. Christoph Gassenschmidt discusses the transformation of Jewish political expression from *shtadlones* (modern Hebrew: *shtadlanut*, Russian: *shtadlanstvo*) to other modes in his *Jewish Liberal Politics in Tsarist Russia, 1900–1914: The Modernization of Russian Jewry* (New York, 1995).
23. "Tefilah ahar amirat Tehilim." The English translation is from *The ArtScroll Tehillim*, translated and annoted by Rabbi Hillel Danziger with Rabbi Nosson Scherman (Brooklyn, 1988), p. 323.
24. The Ukrainian government was, at times, equally unprepared to deal with the Ministry of Jewish Affairs. As late as 1919 other offices were enquiring if the secular administration operated on the Jewish Sabbath (MKY V772.269).
25. See above, Chapter 2, pp. 46–53.
26. The Russians convened a similar council, although internal party friction prevented the Poles from doing so (Zilberfarb, *Dos idishe ministerium*, p. 22n).
27. Protokol No. 1, October 1, 1917 [old style] (TA 1.10). Zilberfarb mentions only that the Nationality Council "did not find it possible" to admit the Akhdes (*Dos idishe ministerium*, p. 23n2).

    This shunning of the Akhdes Yisroel was typical of the anti-clerical position of the socialist parties. In April the Akhdes would again complain to the Election Commission that no one had informed them of the possibility of sending a representative (Tsentral'nyi Derzhavnyi Arkhiv Hromads'kykh Ob'iednan' Ukraïny [formerly Partiinyi Arkhiv Instituta Istorii Partii pri TsK Kompartii Ukrainy, Filia Instituta Marksisma-Leninisma pri TsK KPSS], Kyiv [hereafter TsDAHOU] 41.1.239.6–9).
28. Nakhum Gergel, "Dos idishe ministerium un der natsional-rat," unpublished ms., TA 4.445.
29. Protokol No. 1, TA 1.6.
30. "...in itstign ibergangs-moment konen nit apgehit vern di taryag

mitsves fun demokratizm" (Protokol No. 1, TA 1.7). The allusion refers to the number of religious commandments applicable to Jews.

31. Gergel, "Dos idishe ministerium," TA 4.4.

32. The law regulating the *kehiles* is reproduced in Zilberfarb, *Dos idishe ministerium*, Appendix 5, pp. 48–56. For some of the institutional details, see also Joseph Schechtman, "Jewish Community Life in Ukraine (1917–1919)," in Gregor Aronson et al., eds., *Russian Jewry 1917–1967* (New York, 1966), pp. 39–57.

33. These concerns are discussed at length in M. Postan, "Zu der Shtats-Sekretar frage," in M. Grosman et al., eds., *Di idishe avtonomie un der natsionaler sekretariat in Ukrayne: materialn un dokumentn* (Kyiv, 1920), pp. 20–34.

34. See the interesting comments on this point in Arie Zaidman, "Ha-avtonomia ha-leumit ha-yehudit be-Ukrainah ha-atsmait ba-shanim 1917–1919," Ph.D. diss., Tel-Aviv University, 1980, pp. 45–46.

35. Gergel, "Dos idishe ministerium," TA 4.463.

36. See Oscar Janowsky, *The Jews and Minority Rights (1898–1919)* (New York, 1933), pp. 72–85.

37. "(Proiekt) Gezets vegn dem statut fun di idishe kehile," TsDAHOU 41.1.9.

38. TA 8.674.

39. Janowsky, *The Jews and Minority Rights*, pp. 109–111. See also Alexander Orbach, "Zionism and the Russian Revolution of 1905: The Commitment to Participate in Domestic Political Life," *Bar-Ilan Studies in the History and Culture of East European Jewry* 24–25 (1989): 7–23.

40. "Tsu ale idishe kehila-ratn: Tsu der idisher bafelkerung fun Ukrayne," TA 18.980.

41. Zilberfarb, *Dos idishe ministerium*, pp. 33–35.

42. See the useful chart in Zaidman, "Ha-avtonomie," p. 237n16, for a comprehensive overview of their positions and sources.

43. See the Protocols of the sixth sitting of the Smaller Nationality Assembly, January 21, 1919, TsDAHOU 41.1.119.3-5.

44. Salo Baron, *The Russian Jew Under Tsars and Soviets*, 2nd ed. (New York, 1987), p. 192.

45. Zaidman, "Ha-avtonomie," p. 52.

46. For an example, see the letter from the Ministry to the Jewish National Council in Vienna, January 20, 1919, TsDAHOU 41.1.119.8-9. Letterheads seemed to vary as regularly as the governments, however, and other formalities of correspondence also existed. Typewriters were also

in short supply. Ukrainian correspondence was often typed on Russian machines (using the number *1* to render the Ukrainian letter *i*, which is nonexistent in the Russian alphabet, etc.) and Yiddish and Hebrew was generally written by hand, even alongside a typed Cyrillic text. See, for example, the letter dated "27 travnia 1919" in MKY V772 69.1.

47. TsDAHOU 41.1.236.

48. See *Avtonomie*, p. viii.

49. TA 4.456: "...nit arbeten, nit shafn...v-lo saase." TA 4.460: "tsvey felker mit tsvey shprakhn."

50. See TsDAHOU 41.1.96 for some of the faculty and curriculum proposals. Plans for a Jewish university were common among Jewish activists in this era. See, for example, Gassenschmidt, *Jewish Liberal Politics*, pp. 74, 134–35.

51. See the remarks of Avraham Revutsky on the Zionist plans for teaching physics in Hebrew, *In di shvere teg oif Ukrayne: zikhroines fun a yidishn minister* (Berlin, 1924), pp. 91–98.

52. For information concerning the historical developments leading to the establishment of political rule of the Directory, see the Foreword, pp. xvii–xviii. For more on the importance of Petliura to historiography, see the Foreword and the Bibliographic Postscriptum herein.

53. Nakhum Gergel, "Di pogromen in Ukrayne in di yorn 1918–1921," *Shriftn far ekonomik un statistik* (Berlin, 1928), vol. 1, pp. 106–113. An English language version of this article was later published under the title "The Pogroms in the Ukraine in 1918–1921," *YIVO Annual of Jewish Social Science* 6 (1951): 237–52.

54. It is difficult to ascertain exactly how many of these were specifically anti-Jewish—as opposed to anti-Polish—pogroms, particularly because Volhynia had large pockets of various minority populations. The fact that the Ministry of Jewish Affairs recorded them, however, implies that at least the majority of the attacks were on predominately Jewish populations. Elias Tcherikower (Eliyohu Tsherikover), *Antisemitizm un pogromen in Ukrayne 1917–1918 (tsu der geshikhte fun ukraynish-yidishe batsihungen)* (Berlin, 1923), pp. 197–98; Committee of Jewish Delegations, *The Pogroms in the Ukraine under the Ukrainian Governments (1917–1920): Historical Survey with Documents and Photographs* (London, 1927), pp. 5–11; J. Hewko, "The Ukrainian-Jewish Political Relationship during the Period of the Central Rada—March 1917 to January 1918," unpublished M.Litt thesis, St. Anthony's College, Oxford, 1981, pp. 124–25. See also Volodymyr Serhiichuk, *Pohromy v Ukraïni: 1914–1920, vid shtuchnykh stereotypiv do hirkoï pravdy, prykhovuvanoï v radianskykh arkhivakh* (Kyiv, 1998), pp. 153–64.

55. Tcherkiower, *Antisemitzm*, p. 29.

56. Reproduced in Tcherikower, *Antisemitizm un pogromen*, p. 208. The Ukrainian text may be found in TA 1332.

57. Reproduced in Tcherikower, *Antisemitizm un pogromen*, p. 207.

58. Adapted from the English translation in Committee of Jewish Delegations, *The Pogroms in the Ukraine*, pp. 123–24. Yiddish text is in Tcherikower, *Antisemitizm un pogromen*, pp. 203–204. A Russian translation under the title "K evreiskomu naseleniiu ot Evreiskago General'-nago Sekretariata" is available, TA 1330–1331.

59. "General'nyi sekretar po viis'kovykh spravakh S. Petliura, 15 Lystopada 1917," *Symon Petliura: Statti Lysty Dokumenty*, 2 vols. (New York, 1956-1979), vol. 1, pp. 219–20. A Yiddish translation is available in Tcherikower, *Antisemitizm un pogromen*, p. 209.

60. The interpellation is reproduced in Tcherikower, *Antisemitizm un pogromen*, pp. 202–203.

61. Adapted from the English translation in Committee of Jewish Delegations, *The Pogroms in the Ukraine*, pp. 123–24. The Yiddish text is in Tcherikower, *Antisemitizm un pogromen*, pp. 203–204.

62. See, for example, TsDAHOU 41.1.94.39.

63. Tcherikower, *Antisemitizm un pogromen*, p. 204; see also Revutsky, *In di shvere*, pp. 283-284; Schechtman, "Jewish Community Life," p. 47.

64. TA 22.1732-1744. Trumpeldor, an officer in the Tsarist army, was also an energetic Zionist and activist for Jewish military formations. His death in a battle with Arabs at Tel Hai has become part of Israeli folklore. See Y.S., "Trumpeldor, Joseph," in *Encyclopedia Judaica* (Jerusalem, 1972), vol. 15, pp. 1410–1413; Yael Zerubavel, "The Politics of Interpretation: Tel Hai in Israel's Collective Memory," *AJS Review* 16:2 (1991): 133–60.

65. TA 21.1532

66. "Protokol delegatskago s"ezda Evreev Voinov Osoboi Armii," p. 5. TA 21.1536.

67. TsDAHOU 41.1.96.3; 41.1.96.4.

68. TsDAHOU 41.1.56.25.

69. Tcherikower, *Antisemitizm un pogromen*, p. 83.

70. Mattityahu Mintz, "The Recruitment of Jews for Ukrainian National Units in 1917, as Reflected in the Minutes of the Provisional Jewish Council," *Jews and Jewish Topics in the Soviet Union and Eastern Europe* 2:12 (1990): 8–14. Documents follow.

71. Mintz, "Recruitment," pp. 17–19; Tcherikower, *Antisemitizm un*

pogromen, pp. 222–23; see also Schechtman, "Jewish Community Life," p. 48.

72. Tcherikower, *Antisemitizm un pogromen*, pp. 90–91; Schechtman, "Jewish Communal Life," pp. 48–49.

73. See Committee of Jewish Delegations, *The Pogroms in the Ukraine*, pp. 96–97. This issue will be discussed in greater detail in Chapter 4. The shouting anecdote is from Lilian Gorenstein, "A Memoir of the Great War, 1914–1924," *YIVO Annual* 20 (Evanston, 1991), p. 131.

74. Orest Subtelny, *Ukraine: A History* (Toronto, 1988), pp. 348–49.

75. John Reshetar, *The Ukrainian Revolution, 1917–1920: A Study in Nationalism* (New York, 1972), p. 93.

76. N. I. Suprunenko et al., eds., *Istoriia Ukrainskoi SSR: Velikaia Oktiabr'skaia sotsialisticheskaia revoliutsiia i grazhdanskaia voina na Ukraine (1917–1920)* (Kyiv, 1984), p. 229.

77. "Arsenal," in I. F. Kuras et al., eds., *Velykyi zhovten' i hromadians'ka viina na Ukraïni: Entsyklopedychnyi dovidnyk* (Kyiv, 1987), p. 43.

78. See James E. Mace, *Communism and the Dilemmas of National Liberation: National Communism in Soviet Ukraine, 1918–1933* (Cambridge, MA, 1983).

79. Dominique Arel, "Ukraine: A Country Report," unpublished paper prepared for the Minority Rights Group (USA), draft dated December 12, 1995, p. 13. I am grateful to Professor Arel for sharing this work in progress with me.

80. See Zvi Gitelman, *Jewish Nationality and Soviet Politics: The Jewish Sections of the CPSU, 1917–1930* (Princeton, 1972).

81. A Pole was found for the post of Commissar for Polish Affairs. Jabłoński, *Polska autonomia*, p. 103.

82. Zilberfarb, *Dos idishe ministerium*, p. 65.

83. See, for example, Lenin's July 1918 decree condemning antisemitism in Simon Dimanshtein, ed., *Yidn in FSSR: Zamlbukh* (Moscow, 1935), p. 173.

84. Original poster TA 37.3488; emphasis in the original. The Russian text later uses the non-perjorative term *evrei* when referring to Jews, so the term *zhid* is unmistakeably derogatory.The most prominent individual in Soviet Ukrainian politics, Khrystyian Rakovs'kyi, was not ethnically Ukrainian. The poster dealt with his background by portraying him as working for a universal cause: "And, finally, Comrade Rakovskii—a Rumanian, who goes to struggle for the rights not only of Ukrainian workers, but for the rights of the workers of the entire world…"

85. Tcherikower, *Antisemitizm un pogromen*, p. 107.

86. January 30, 1918. Cited in Tcherikower, *Antisemitizm un pogromen*, p. 108.

87. *Naye tsayt*, January 31, 1918. Cited in Tcherikower, *Antisemitizm un pogromen*, pp. 108–109.

88. See Tcherikower, *Antisemitizm un pogromen*, pp. 109–110; Zaidman, "Ha-avtonomie," pp. 72–73; Schechtman, "Jewish Community Life," pp. 50–51.

89. Solomon Goldelman, *Jewish National Autonomy in Ukraine 1917–1920*, trans. Michael Luchkovich (Chicago, 1968), p. 22n3.

90. The complete text of the Brest-Litovsk treaty, in German with English translation, is provided in *Texts of the Ukraine "Peace,"* ed. Paul R. Magocsi (Cleveland, 1981).

91. Oleh S. Fedyshyn, *Germany's Drive to the East and the Ukrainian Revolution, 1917–1918* (New Brunswick, N.J., 1971), pp. 89–91.

92. Tcherikower, *Antisemitizm un pogromen*, pp. 134–35.

93. Moses Silberfarb, *The Jewish Ministry and the Jewish National Autonomy in Ukraine*, trans. David Lincoln (New York, 1993), p. 85; Zilberfarb, *Dos idishe ministerium*, p. 68.

94. Zilberfarb, *Dos idishe ministerium*, p. 67.

95. Zilberfarb, *Dos idishe ministerium*, p. 61.

96. Tcherikower, *Antisemitizm un pogromen*, pp. 116–17.

97. TA 18.990.

98. Tcherikower, *Antisemitizm un pogromen*, p. 142.

99. Tcherikower, *Antisemitizm un pogromen*, p. 118; Schechtman, "Jewish Community Life," p. 51.

100. Cited in Tcherikower, *Antisemitizm un pogromen*, p. 119.

101. Schechtman, "Jewish Community," p. 51.

102. Tcherikower, *Antisemitizm un pogromen*, pp. 119–30.

103. Goldelman, *Jewish National Autonomy*, pp. 59–62. Zilberfarb's resignation was submitted along with the entire government, as per conventional parliamentary etiquette.

104. Reproduced in Zilberfarb, *Dos idishe ministerium*, Appendix 5, pp. 48–56.

105. M. Grosman et al., eds., *Di idishe avtonomie un der natsionaler sekretariat in Ukrayne: materyaln un dokumentn* (Kyiv, 1920), p. 208, table 3.

106. M. Sadikov, *In yene teg: zikhroines vegen der rusisher revolutsie un di ukrayner pogromen* (New York, 1926), pp. 18–19.

107. Silberfarb, *Jewish*, pp. 91–92; Zilberfarb, *Dos idishe ministerium*, pp. 74–75. Second and third ellipses in the original.

108. See Fedyshyn, *Germany's Drive to the East*, pp. 133–57; Arthur Adams, *Bolsheviks in the Ukraine: The Second Campaign, 1918–1919* (New Haven, 1963), p. 8.

109. See Vynnychenko, *Vidrodzhennia natsiï*, vol. 3, pp. 61–66; see also Paul Robert Magocsi, *A History of Ukraine* (Seattle, 1996), pp. 487–93.

110. Tcherikower, *Antisemitizm un pogromen*, pp. 153–54.

111. TsDAHOU 41.1.86.4.

112. The text of Skoropads'kyi's April 29 (old style) declaration is reproduced in Vynnychenko, *Vidrodzhennia natsiï*, vol. 3, pp. 19, 23.

113. The vote of Gutnik, the finance minister, was decisive in this matter. See Eliyohu Gumener, *A kapitl Ukrayne* (Vilnius, 1921), p. 61. See also Vynnychenko, *Vidrodzhennia natsiï*, vol. 3, p. 39; Arnold Margolin, *The Jews of Eastern Europe* (New York, 1926), p. 18.

114. Zaidman, "Ha-avtonomie," p. 78. The date of repeal is normally given as July 9, 1918, including archival documents (see TA 4.470). Khurgin's chapter in Zilberfarb's memoir, however, gives July 8 as the date (Zilberfarb, *Dos idishe ministerium*, p. 81); Zilberfarb himself (p. 1) gives July 18.

115. Results from over 150 *kehiles* elections were available by April. "Di tsaytvaylike natsionaler farzamlung un der idisher natsionaler sekretariat in Ukrayne," *Avtonomie*, p. 5.

116. Nakhum Gergel, "Dos idishe ministerium un der natsional-rat," Unpublished ms., TA 4.446.

117. Joseph Schechtman, "Jewish Community Life in the Ukraine (1917–1919)," in G. Aronson et al., ed., *Russian Jewry 1917–1967* (New York, 1969), pp. 39–57.

118. TsDAHOU 41.1.86.

119. Zilberfarb, *Dos idishe ministerium*, p. 72.

120. Gergel, "Dos idishe ministerium," TA 4.465.

121. Zilberfarb, *Dos idishe ministerium*, pp. 68–69.

122. Gergel, "Dos idishe ministerium," TA 4.447; 449.

123. Zilberfarb, *Dos idishe ministerium*, p. 69. Latsky was born in 1881 in Kyiv and educated in Riga. He was a co-founder (with Nahum Syrkin) of the Herut movement. In 1920 he fled to Berlin, but in 1925 returned to Riga where he edited Jewish newspapers. In 1935 he settled in Palestine.

124. Gergel, "Dos idishe ministerium," TA 4.469.

125. See Zaidman, "Ha-avtonomie," pp. 77–78. The appendices of Zilberfarb, *Dos idishe ministerium*, reproduce some of Latsky's proposals.

126. *Avtonomie*, pp. 10–11.

127. Election flyer from Tula, July 28, Fareynikte. TsDAHOU 41.1.59. Emphasis in the original. I am grateful for the suggestions of Mr. Zachary Baker and Professor Zvi Gitelman in translating this document.

128. *Avtonomie*, p. 15.

129. *Avtonomie*, pp. 16, 204–206. This represented roughly 22 percent of the eligible *male* electorate above the age of 20. Suffrage was technically to have been extended to women as well, but it is possible that this was inconsistently followed.

130. *Avtonomie*, p. 213. The reference here does not clarify if it refers to male voters only.

131. *Avtonomie*, p. 211.

132. See TsDaHOU 41.1.18.

133. *Avtonomie*, p. 19.

134. Adams, *Bolsheviks in the Ukraine*, pp. 11–13.

135. Elias Tcherikower, *Di ukrayner pogromen in yor 1919* (New York, 1965), pp. 66–69.

136. TA 37.3467.

137. Reproduced in Tcherikower, *Antisemitizm un pogromen*, after p. 301. Emphasis in the original. Original in German and Russian.

138. Original proclamation, issued in German, Ukrainian, and Russian, is photoreproduced in Tcherikower, *Antisemitizm un pogromen*, before p. 302; emphasis in the original.

139. TsDAHOU 41.1.86.19.

Chapter 4

1. John Klier, "The Pogrom Paradigm in Russian History," *Pogroms: Anti-Jewish Violence in Modern Russian History*, eds. John Klier and Shlomo Lambroza (Cambridge, 1992), p. 34n1.

2. Klier, "The Pogrom Paradigm," p. 35n2.

3. Compare Map 2 (p. 108) with maps of pogroms in 1881–1884, 1903–1906 in Klier and Lambroza, eds., *Pogroms*, pp. 43, 194.

4. See, for example, D. Neufeld, *A Russian Dance of Death: Revolution and Civil War in the Ukraine* (Winnipeg, 1977).

5. Nakhum Gergel, "Di pogromen in Ukrayne in di yorn 1918–1921,"

Shriftn far ekonomik 1 (Berlin, 1928): 106–113; an English-language version appeared under the title "The Pogroms in the Ukraine in 1918–1920," *YIVO Annual of Jewish Social Science* 6 (1951): 237–51. For an example of early methods of data collection on the pogroms, see "Tsu ale kehiles in Ukrayne/le-kol kehilot Ukrainah," 23 March 1919, TA 17850. See also Zosa Szajkowski, "Di geshikhte fun dem itstikn bukh," in Elias Tcherikower, *Di ukrayner pogromen in yor 1919* (New York, 1965), pp. 333–49.

6. Gergel, "The Pogroms in the Ukraine," p. 249. Recently published documents from regional Soviet archives support Gergel's low estimate. See Volodymyr Serhiichuk, *Pohromy v Ukraïni: 1914–1920, vid shtuchnykh stereotypiv do hirkoï pravdy, prykhovuvanoï v radianskykh arkhivakh* (Kyiv, 1998), pp. 445–56. For some higher estimates, see, for example, *The Ukraine Terror and the Jewish Peril* (London, 1921), p. 5; Salomon Resnick, *Cinco Ensayos Sobre Temas Judios* (Buenos Aires, 1943), p. 24, Ilya Heifets, *Pogrom geshikhte (1919–1920), Band 1: Di Ukrainishe shkhite in 1919* (New York, 1921), p. 276; Jacob Letschinsky, *La Situation economique des Juifs depuis la Guerre Mondiale* (Paris, 1934), p. 148.

7. Paul Avrich, *Russian Rebels, 1600–1800* (New York, 1972), pp. 268–69.

8. Volodymyr Vynnychenko, "Ievreis'ke pytannia na Ukraïni," *Suchasnist'* 8 (Kyiv, 1992). Vynnychenko asserts that many of them were Russians, not Ukrainians.

9. This is not the case with earlier pogromists. See Michael Aronson, *Troubled Waters: The Origins of the 1881 Anti-Jewish Pogroms in Russia* (Pittsburgh, 1990). The chaos and political upheaval of the revolutionary era precluded the kind of systematic research and publication that would have yielded a similar portrait of the pogromists of 1919. See *Ievreiskie pogromy, 1918–1921* (Moscow, 1926); Committee of Jewish Delegations, *The Pogroms in the Ukraine under the Ukrainian Governments (1917–1920): Historical Survey with Documents and Photographs* (London, 1927), pp. 47–51, 106–120; and "Di insurgentn-bavegung (povstantshevsve) un di poierim-oifshtandn gegn der Ratn-Makht in Ukrayne (loit tsaytungs-mittaylungen un loitn arkhiv)," TA 7138-7229.

10. See Vynnychenko, "Ievreis'ke," p. 119.

11. On the history of antisemitic theory, see Rosemary Ruether, *Faith and Fratricide: The Theological Roots of Anti-Semitism* (Minneapolis, 1974); Jacob Katz, *From Prejudice to Destruction: Anti-Semitism, 1700–1933* (Cambridge, 1980); Gavin Langmuir, *Toward a Definition of Antisemitism* (Los Angeles, 1990) and *History, Religion and Antisemitism* (Berkeley, 1990).

12. I have discussed the specific nature of Ukrainian antisemitism in "The

Scattering of Amalek: A Model for Understanding the Ukrainian-Jewish Conflict," *East European Jewish Affairs* 24:1 (1994): 39–47.

13. "Chy vorohy ievrei robitnykam ta selianam?" (Kyiv, 1919), p. 4. The term used is *proty evreis'ka*.
14. See Vynnychenko's remarks on "socio-political" antisemitism in "Ievreis'ke," p. 117.
15. See, for example, Volodymyr Vynnychenko, *Vidrodzhennia natsiï*, 4 vols. (Kyiv, 1990, f.p. 1920), vol. 3, p. 366; Arnold Margolin, *The Jews in Eastern Europe* (New York, 1926), p. 126; M. Sadikow, *In yene teg: zikhroines vegen der rusisher revolutsie un di ukrayner pogromen* (New York, 1926), p. 83.
16. See "Do vol'nykh kazakovy budennago," Tcherikower Archive, YIVO Institute for Jewish Research, New York City (hereafter TA) 3594; "Do naselennia Liatychevs'koho povitu," TA 3141; "Vsim holovam volos'kykh ta sil's'kykh uprav, volos'kym komysaram, peredama [illegible]," TA 3155; "Vidozva," TA 5822. See also, in this context, "Vidozva do ievreis'koho naselennia," TA 3114; "Vsim holovam volos'kykh ta sil's'kykh uprav, volos'kym komysaram, peredaty po selakh," TA 3155; Solomon Goldelman, *Juden und Ukrainer: Briefe eines Jüdischen Sozialdemokraten* (Vienna, 1921), p. 55.
17. Both in TA 3595, "Novy zakony." See also Joseph Schechtman, "Jewish Community Life in Ukraine (1917–1919)," in G. Aronson et al., eds., *Russian Jewry 1917–1967* (New York, 1969), p. 51.
18. TA 5879.
19. "Seliane!" TA 5816; "Oholoshennia," TA 5913; "Nakaz" ch. 2, TA 5914; "Kozaky!" TA 3153.
20. "Do zbori Ukraïns'kyi Narode! Vstavai!," TA 1781. See also Richard Pipes, *Russia under the Bolshevik Regime* (New York, 1993), p. 107.
21. Benjamin Pinkus, *The Jews of the Soviet Union: History of a National Minority* (Cambridge, 1983), pp. 77–78.
22. Zvi Gitelman, *A Century of Ambivalence: The Jews of Russia and the Soviet Union, 1881 to the Present* (New York, 1988), p. 96. VTsIK stood for Vserossiiskii TSentral'nyi Ispolnitel'nyi Komitet.
23. See, for example, Robert Weinberg, *The Revolution of 1905 in Odessa: Blood on the Steps* (Bloomington, 1993), pp. 179–80; Michael Hamm, *Kiev: A Portrait, 1800–1917* (Princeton, 1993), p. 189; Peter Kenez, "Pogroms and White Ideology in the Russian Civil War," in Klier and Lambroza, eds., *Pogroms*, pp. 303–305.
24. Pipes, *Russia under the Bolshevik Regime*, pp. 100–101.
25. Arthur Adams, "The Great Ukrainian Jacquerie," in Taras Hunczak,

ed., *The Ukraine 1917–1921: A Study in Revolution* (Cambridge, MA, 1977), p. 262.

26. Gergel, "The Pogroms in the Ukraine, 1918–1921," *YIVO Annual of Jewish Social Science* 6 (1951): 241.

27. Avraham Revutsky, *In di shvere teg oif Ukrayne: zikhroines fun a yidishn minister*, (Berlin, 1924), pp. 133–34, 184.

28. Gergel, "The Pogroms in the Ukraine," pp. 238–39.

29. Gergel, "The Pogroms in the Ukraine," p. 243.

30. See Yehuda Slutski (Slutsky), "Ba'ayat ha-aharayut le-peraot Ukrainah," *He-avar* 17 (Tel Aviv, 1970), pp. 27–43.

31. Adams, "Jacquerie," pp. 255–56. Revutsky recalls some 250,000 soldiers gathered in the space of three weeks, probably an exaggeration (*In di shvere teg*, p. 39). See also Rudolf A. Mark, "Symon Petljura und die UNR. Vom Sturz des Hetmans Skoropadskyj bis zum Exil in Polen," *Forschungen zur osteuropaeischen Geschichte* 40 (1988): 41–42.

32. Revutsky, *In di shvere teg*, p. 134.

33. See the "receipts" in *Avtonomie*, pp. 134–37.

34. See Revutsky, *In di shvere*, pp. 134–35.

35. Cited in Elias Tcherikower, *Di ukrayner pogromen in yor 1919* (New York, 1965), pp. 77–79.

36. I am grateful to Professor Jonathan Frankel for this observation.

37. Ironically, the town was renamed Khmel'nyts'kyi during the Soviet period.

38. Tcherikower, *Di ukrayner pogromen*, p. 157.

39. Report of A. I. Hillerson [Gilerson], Barrister-at-Law, delegate of the Kyiv Pogrom Relief Committee, cited in Committee of Jewish Delegations, *The Pogroms in the Ukraine*, p. 176. Some sources spell his name "Semosenko," from Russian usage. See Serhiichuk, *Pohromy*, pp. 208–237.

40. Tcherikower, *Di ukrayner pogromen*, p. 135; see also pp. 154–55. Some of the survivors of the pogrom later wrote that "his entire body was covered in syphillis, and his soul was also covered with this disease, which he wished to cure by dousing in the blood of our brothers." *Khurbn Proskurov: Tsum andenken fun di heilige neshomes vos zaynen umgekumen in der shreklikher shkhitah, vos iz ongefirt gevorn durkh di Haidamakes* (New York, 1924), p. 20n.

41. Translation based on Committee of Jewish Delegates, *The Pogroms in Ukraine*, p. 187. Ukrainian original is in TA 675.5800, also reproduced in Pavlo Khrystiuk, *Zamitky i materiialy do istorii ukraïns'koi revoliutsii 1917-1920 rr.*, 4 vols. (Vienna, 1921), vol. 4, p. 105. The Khrystiuk

text has emphasis added (also the copy reproduced in M. Grosman et al., eds., *Di idishe avtonomie un der natsionaler sekretariat in Ukrayne: materialn un dokumentn* [Kyiv, 1920], p. 137). The originals held in TA 675.5800 and the Mahleket kitvei-yad shel bet ha-sefarim ha-leumi ve-ha-universitah (hereafter MKY) V772.526a do not have emphasis added. The TA text is incorrectly dated Feburary 16 rather than February 6, see Tcherikower *Di ukrayner pogromen*, p. 134.

42. I. Alekseev (Nebutev), *Iz vospominanii levogo zhera (Podpolnaia rabotana Ukraina)* (Moscow, 1922), pp. 33–35.
43. Tcherikower, *Di ukrayner pogromen*, pp. 119–20, 130–32.
44. *Khurbn Proskurov*, p. 18.
45. Tcherikower, *Di ukrayner pogromen*, p. 120.
46. *Khurbn Proskurov*, p. 19.
47. Tcherikower, *Di ukrayner pogromen*, p. 121.
48. Some details vary; *Khrurbn Proskurov* refers to 600 men, Tcherikower, *Di ukrayner pogromen* has the figure of 300 to 400.
49. Hillerson in Committee of Jewish Delegations, *The Pogroms in the Ukraine*, pp. 178–80.
50. Tcherikower, *Di ukrayner pogromen*, p. 124.
51. Tcherikower, *Di ukrayner pogromen*, p. 136. Ironically, Rakhman's original name meant "merciful one" in Hebrew.
52. TA 362.32995. See also Serhiichuk, *Pohromy*, pp. 237–44. Pogroms such as these had a devastating effect on Jewish children. For a heart-rending medical study of these child survivors, see Fischel Schneerson, *Die Katastrophale Zeit und die Heranwachsende Generation (Die Wirkung von Katastrophen auf die Seele des normalen und abnormalen Kindes)* (Berlin, 1924).
53. Tcherikower, *Di ukrayner pogromen*, p. 137.
54. The homes of massacred Jews were easily identified by the electric lights that burned all through the night of the 15/16. As was common there, electricity was not supplied at all hours but only at night, and since the majority of Proskuriv's Jews were strictly Orthodox, lights in the dining and living areas were simply left on Friday night to avoid desecration of the Sabbath. When the electric mains came on again Saturday evening, lights stayed on all night in the homes of the dead, a beacon for those who would do them greater disgrace. Hillerson in Committee of Jewish Delegations, *The Pogroms in the Ukraine*, p. 181.
55. Tcherikower, *Di ukrayner pogromen*, pp. 136–37; *Khurbn Proskurov*, p. 15.
56. Report of the Delegate of the Danish Red Cross, May 1919, reproduced in Committee of Jewish Delegations, *The Pogroms in the Ukraine*, p. 190.

57. "Nakaz," TA 5805.

58. TA 71.5803. The Ukrainian original and Yiddish translation are provided in *Avtonomie*, pp. 138–40. An English translation, which this is based upon, is found in Committee of Jewish Delegations, *The Pogroms in the Ukraine*, p. 188. Emphasis in these texts is not present in the TA text.

59. *Khurbn Proskurov* records a list of 878 names; the number of dead is most likely higher since it would be difficult for the émigrés who collected the list to recall all the victims. Most estimates are under 2,000 dead, however there are occasional estimates that are considerably higher, e.g., 6,000 in *Avtonomie*, p. 174. According to the 1897 census, 11,411 Jews lived in Proskuriv—constituting half of the town's population of 22,855. Ia. Shabag, "Podol'skaia gub.," *Evreiskaia entsiklopediia*, ed. A. Harkavy, L. Katsenel'son (St. Petersburg, n.d.), vol. 12, p. 647 Table 1.

60. "Nakaz" ch. 12, February 24, 1919, TA 5811. In Committee of Jewish Delegations, *The Pogroms in the Ukraine*: 300,000 rubles (p. 185).

61. Some receipts of this nature are reproduced in *Avtonomie*, pp. 136–37 in both the original Ukrainian and Yiddish translation.

62. "Nakaz" ch. 16, February 27, 1919, TA 5791.

63. Reported by Semesenko's physician in Proskuriv, Dr. Saliternik. Tcherikower, *Di ukrayner pogromen*, pp. 135–36.

64. Tcherikower, *Di ukrayner pogromen*, p. 136.

65. Revutsky, *In di shvere teg*, p. 153.

66. See, for example, Eliyohu Gumener, *A Kapitl Ukrayne: 2 Yor in Podolye* (Vilnius, 1921), esp. pp. 54–55, 94, 119, 125.

67. Taras Hunczak, "Preface," in Hunczak, ed., *The Ukraine, 1917–1921*, p. v.

68. Joseph Schechtman, *Ver iz farantvortlikh far di pogromen in Ukrayne: loit naye nit farefntlikhte materiyaln un dokumentn* (Paris, 1927), pp. 16–18. See also Tcherikower, *Di ukrayner pogromen*, p. 72. For clippings from *Ukraïns'ka stavka*, see TA 523.43355, 523.43352, 502.42387, 510.42166, 42167. The anti-Jewish articles mentioned here tend to have appeared in early January 1919.

69. January 19, 1919. TA 523.43355.

70. "Khto ahitue proty Directorii?" *Ukraïns'ka stavka* January 12, 1919, TA 43352; Tcherikower, *Di ukrayner pogromen*, p. 73.

71. See, for example, Tsentral'nyi Derzhavnyi arkhiv hromads'kykh ob'iednan' [orhanizatsii] Ukraïny, Kyiv (hereafter TsDAHOU) 41.1.19.24.

72. Matthew Stachiw and Nicholas Chirovskyy, *Ukraine and the European*

Turmoil, 1917–1919, 2 vols. (New York, 1973), vol. 2, p. 25; "Ievreis'ka demokratiina Vkraïny suchasnyi moment," TA 519.42731, and, for example, "Pohroma khvylia," *Ukraïns'ka stavka*, June 22, 1919, TA 524.43360; see also Committee of Jewish Delegations, *The Pogroms in the Ukraine*, pp. 26–28 and the comments of Arnold Margolin in Julian Batchinsky et al. *The Jewish Pogroms in Ukraine: Authoritative Statements on the Question of Responsibility for Recent Outbreaks Against the Jews of the Ukraine* (Washington, DC, 1919), p. 19.

73. For information on pogrom relief funds, see "Tsu di kehiles," TA 17849; Walter Dushnyk, ed., *Ukrainians and Jews: Articles, Testimonies, Letters and Official Documents Dealing with Interrelations of Ukrainians and Jews in the Past and Present: A Symposium* (New York, 1966), p. 151; Revutsky, *In di shvere*, pp. 182–88; Wladimir Lewitzkyj and Gustav Specht, eds., *Die Lage von der Juden in der Ukraine: Eine Dokumentensammlung*, (Berlin, 1920), p. 38. For information on commissions of inquiry, see "Ob'iava/Meldung/Obiavlenie," TA 17815; Dushnyk, *Ukrainians and Jews*, p. 150; Batchinsky *The Jewish Pogroms*, pp. 11–14, 24; Revutsky, *In di shvere*, pp. 197–99; Committee of Jewish Delegations, *The Pogroms in the Ukraine*, pp. 91–92; Lewitzkyj and Sprecht, eds., *Die Lage*, pp. 32–34.

74. Revutsky erroneously identifies him as Victor Andriievs'kyi. *In di shvere*, pp. 155, 219.

75. John Reshetar, *The Ukrainian Revolution, 1917–1920: A Study in Nationalism* (New York, 1972), p. 242; Revutsky, *In di shvere*: "er is geven a groyser khosid fun a guter mashke," p. 155.

76. Vynnychenko, *Vidrodzhennia natsiï*, vol. 3, pp. 237–39.

77. See the comments of Solomon Goldelman, *Juden und Ukrainer*, pp. 13–14.

78. See Committee of Jewish Delegations, *The Pogroms in the Ukraine*, pp. 31–40.

79. Tcherikower, *Di ukrayner pogromen*, p. 93–97.

80. Revustky, *In di shvere*, p. 285; see also Schechtman, *Ver iz farantvortlich*, pp. 35–39, and *Avtonomie*, pp. 132–34.

81. Taras Hunczak, "A Reappraisal of Symon Petliura and Ukrainian-Jewish Relations, 1917–1921," *Jewish Social Studies* 31:3 (New York, 1969): 176n67; see also Zosa Szjakowski, "'A Reappraisal of Symon Petliura and Ukrainian-Jewish Relations, 1917–1921 ': A Rebuttal," *Jewish Social Studies* 31:3 (1969): 194; Vynnychenko, *Vidrodzhennia natsiï*, vol. 3, p. 373; TA 35279, 39037; Committee of Jewish Delegations, *The Pogroms in the Ukraine*, pp. 46–49.

82. See Mark, "Symon Petljura," p. 49.

83. Hunczak, "Reappraisal," p. 172; see also Mark, "Symon Petljura," pp. 41–42, 49.

84. Martin Malia, *The Soviet Tragedy: A History of Socialism in Russia, 1917–1991* (New York, 1994), p. 120.

85. Vynnychenko, *Vidrodzhennia natsiï*, vol. 3, p. 187; see also pp. 369–70; also his "Ievreis'ke," p. 19; Revutsky, *In di shvere*, p. 291. See also TA 20704.

86. Cited in Szajkowski, "A Rebuttal," p. 193. Although it might seem odd that the Jews trusted Petliura enough to ask for his protection, anecdotal evidence suggests that this was the case. Szajkowski also indicates that a delegation of Jews was sent to salute Petliura under coercion. For another example of a Jewish delegation meeting Petliura, see "Verkhovnyi ataman v Kiev," *Kievskii den'*, May 25, 1920, TA 42801.

87. Saul Friedman, *Pogromchik: The Assassination of Simon Petlura* (New York, 1974), p. 153.

88. For a more nuanced impression, see Vynnychenko, *Vidrodzhennia natsiï*, vol. 3, p. 367.

89. Symon Petliura, "Peredmova: Uvahy pro zavdannia ukraïns'koho teatru," Ie. Chirikov, *Ievrei: p'esia na 4 dii*, translated from Russian to Ukrainian by Leonyd Pakharevs'kyi (Kyiv, 1907), pp. xvi-xvii.

90. "Ukraïns'ke selo i emihratsiia v Ameriku," (1907), in *Symon Petliura: Statti, Lysty, Dokumenty*, 2 vols. (New York, 1956-1979), vol. 1, p. 69; also there, "Revoliutsiia v Rosiï i Ievropeis'ka Presa," (1905), vol. 2, p. 18.

91. "Do naselennia Ukraïny i povstantsiv," *Symon Petliura: Statti Lysty Dokumenty*, vol. 1, p. 287.

92. Saul Friedman, however, has argued that post-revolutionary writings betray Petliura's deep antisemitism (*Pogromchik*, p. 277). Friedman's reading of these documents is tendentious, and is based mainly on Petliura's opposition to a Soviet plan to confiscate Ukrainian arable land to colonize Jewish farmers. The articles, some of which were written under a pseudonym, are available in part in *Statti, Lysty, Dokumenty*, vol. 2, pp. 424–32 and 449–51.

93. The text of the alleged wire was as follows: "*Secret and Important:* Everything indicates a Bolshevik uprising on the part of the Jewish population. Suppress absolutely with a strong armed might, that no Jewish hand might rise in Podolia against the aspiring Ukraine. Holovnyi Otaman." Tcherikower, who believed that the story was correct and that the document had in fact existed at one time, provided full disclosure of its history (*Di ukrayner pogromen*, p. 146n1). Szajkowski, his disciple at YIVO, cited the document in a polemical article published after Tcherikower's death, yet did not provide full details on its

authenticity, a breach of scholarly procedure ("Rebuttal," p. 194). Saul Friedman went even further. Not only did he not provide the background to the document, but he actually went on to claim that the telegram was held in File 360 of the Tcherikower Archive at YIVO (*Pogromchik*, p. 166n37). No such document exists in File 360. Furthermore, Szajkowski himself numbered each document in the Tcherikower Archive, and no document in that file is missing.

94. Avraham Revutsky, "Aynlaytung," in Sadikow, *In yene teg*, p. 15.

95. Julian Batchinsky, Ukrainian diplomatic representative to the United States of America, wrote in an open letter, "I must admit that information now in my possession fully establishes the fact that in one case—a very severe one (Proskurov)—soldiers from the Ukrainian People's Army were the perpetrators" (Batchinsky, *Jewish Pogroms*, p. 7).

96. Szajkowski, "A Rebuttal," pp. 206–208; Vynnychenko, *Vidrodzhennia natsiï*, vol. 1, pp. 187–88; vol. 3, p. 372. In correspondence related to the Schwartzbard trial, Vynnychenko wrote that this inaction was the primary measure of Petliura's culpability (TA 37245-66).

97. Petliura seemed to be ashamed to visit Proskuriv immediately after the pogrom, despite the fact that he was in the vicinity (Revutsky, *In di shvere*, pp. 287–88).

98. Petliura also issued a brief telegram regarding "excesses" on January 28, 1919 (TA 3203); Serhiichuk, *Pohromy*, p. 198. Also included in Serhiichuk's work is a Directory declaration condemning pogroms that is dated simply "February 1919" (pp. 250–51). It is difficult to estimate the impact this decree might have made, since it is mentioned in no other study of the period and was found only in one of the regional archives.

99. See Vynnychenko, *Vidrodzhennia natsiï*, vol. 3, p. 372.

100. Reshetar, *The Ukrainian Revolution*, p. 267.

101. Margolin, *The Jews of Eastern Europe*, p. 139.

102. On the other hand, it should be mentioned that a host of factors contributed to the decline in pogrom activity besides these declarations. The return of some form of *Rechtsstaat* under Soviet control, war-weariness, and greater attempts at self-defense among the Jewish population must be considered. See, Schechtman, *Pogromy*, p. 188, and discussion in Pipes, *Russia under the Bolshevik Regime*, p. 111.

103. "Sein politischer Dilletantismus, verbunden mit einer gewissen Popularität als Volksführer, setzten ihn deshalb in die Lage, Kompromisse zu akzeptieren und Entscheidungen zu fällen, wo sich seine sozialdemokratischen Partiegenossen allein aus ideologischen Gründen versagen mußten" (Mark, "Symon Petljura," p. 53).

104. Avraham Revutsky, "Aynlaytung," in Sadikow, *In yene teg*, p. 14.

Chapter 5

1. See the prominence given to National-Personal Autonomy in the December 26, 1918 declaration of the Directory in Volodymyr Vynnychenko, *Vidrodzhennia natsiï*, 4 vols. (Kyiv, 1990 [f.p. 1920]), vol. 4, pp. 168–76; A. Slavs'kyi, "Na vkolo ievreis'koho ministerstva," *Trybuna* 31 December 1919, Tcherikower Archive, YIVO Institute for Jewish Research, New York City (hereafter TA) 42735.

2. Avraham Revutsky, *In di shvere teg oif Ukrayne: Zikhroines fun a yidishn ministr* (Berlin, 1924), p. 33. While the actual document is no longer extant, Goldelman recalls the phrase "The Jews are our friends, they will string along with us," *Jewish National Autonomy in Ukraine, 1917–1920* (Chicago, 1968), p. 90. A similar decree was issued in Kremenchuk; see M. Grosman et al., eds., *Di idishe avtonomie un der natsionaler sekretariat in Ukrayne: Materyaln un dokumentn* (Kyiv, 1920), pp. 125–26. See also "Der gezets-proekt vegn oisrekhenen fun di mlukhe hoitsois oif di baderfenishn fun idisher bildung," *Naye tsayt* January 31, 1919, TA 42767. See also Matthew Stachiw and Nicholas Chirovskyy, *Ukraine and the European Turmoil, 1917–1919*, 2 vols. (New York, 1973), vol. 2, p. 19. See also "K narodam Ukrainy," TA 3110.

3. Texts of both decrees are provided in Goldelman, *Jewish National Autonomy*, pp. 88–89n45; German translation in his *Juden und Ukrainer: Briefe eines Jüdischen Sozialdemokraten* (Vienna, 1921), pp. 31–32.

4. Revutsky, *In di shvere*, pp. 47–48.

5. Goldelman, *Jewish National Autonomy*, p. 100.

6. Elias Tcherikower, *Di ukrayner pogromen in yor 1919* (New York, 1965), p. 92.

7. Revutsky, *In di shvere*, pp. 57–58; Tsentral'nyi derzhavnyi arkhiv hromads'kykh ob'iednan' [orhanizatsii] Ukraïny (hereafter TsDAHOU) 41.1.19.5.

8. *Avtonomie*, p. 38; see also Joseph Schechtman, "Jewish Community Life in Ukraine (1917–1919)," in Gregor Aronson et al., eds., *Russian Jewry 1917–1967* (New York, 1969), p. 55.

9. "Der Natsionaler Sekretariat un di Direktorie (der farhandlungen vegn der frage fun idishe avtonomie)," *Avtonomie*, pp. 36, 38–39.

10. Tcherikower, *Di ukrayner pogromen*, p. 45.

11. See Revutsky, *In di shvere*, pp. 68–69.

12. Two biographies of Solomon Goldelman have been written, both by Lev Bykovs'kyi [Bykovsky]: *Solomon Izraïlevych Gol'del'man, 1885–1974: bio-bibliohrafychni materiialy* (Denver, 1976) and a shorter English

version, *Solomon I. Goldelman: A Portrait of a Politician and Educator (1885–1974)* (New York, 1980). Born in Soroka, northern Bessarabia, Goldelman joined the Poale-Tsion after the 1905 pogrom in Chişinău (Kishinev). He was educated in Kyiv, specializing in economics and agriculture. After the revolution he emigrated to Vienna and then later to Prague, where he was very active in the Ukrainian Husbandry Academy and the YIVO Institute for Jewish Research, then based in Vilnius. In 1939 Goldelman and his family fled to Palestine, where he lived until his death in 1974.

13. Revutsky, *In di shvere*, pp. 35–41.

14. Revutsky, *In di shvere*, pp. 87–90; *Trybuna* December 31, 1918, TA 42735.

15. Avraham Revutsky was born in Smela, Kyiv province. His early childhood was spent in Palestine, but his family returned back to the Russian Empire for health reasons. After the revolution he moved to Palestine, but was expelled by the British for his publications criticizing British policy. He moved to the United States and Americanized his name to Revusky. He passed away in Yonkers, New York, in 1946. L. Tarnopoler, "Avraham Revutski—itonai, hoker, ve-lokhem," *He'avar* 17 (Tel-Aviv, 1970): 217–28. See also TA 42762.

16. *Avtonomie*, pp. 50–55.

17. See TA 20649; Revutsky, *In di shvere*, p. 138; *Avtonomie*, pp. 99–107.

18. See *Naye tsayt* January 9, 1919, TA 511.42267; January 14, 1919, TA 511.42267; January 15, 1919 TA 511.42273.

19. Stachiw and Chirovskyy, *Ukraine and the European Turmoil*, vol. 2, pp. 24–25.

20. Reproduced in "Di pogromen in Ukrayne un der Natsionaler Sekretariat," *Avtonomie*, p. 105.

21. Based on the translation in Committee of Jewish Delegations, *The Pogroms in the Ukraine under the Ukrainian Governments (1917–1920)* (London, 1927), pp. 169–70. The original Ukrainian text, dated January 11, is reproduced in *Symon Petliura: Statti, Lysty, Dokumenty*, 2 vols. (New York, 1956–1979), vol. 2, p. 353. Yiddish text in *Avtonomie*, pp. 105–106.

22. Revutsky, *In di shvere*, pp. 137–47.

23. Yiddish translation in *Avtonomie*, pp. 106–107 and Revutsky, *In di shvere*, pp. 146–47. Dated January 13, 1919.

24. Committee of Jewish Delegations, *The Pogroms in the Ukraine*, pp. 170–71.

25. Tcherikower, *Di ukrayner pogromen*, p. 70.

26. Eliyohu Gumener, *A kapitl Ukrayne: 2 yor in Podolye* (Vilnius, 1921), p. 65.
27. John Reshetar, *The Ukraine, 1917–1921: A Study in Revolution* (New York, 1952), p. 259.
28. TA 33.3205. This translation based on F. Pigido (Pihido), ed., *Material Concerning Ukrainian-Jewish Relations during the Years of the Revolution (1917–1921): Collection of Documents and Testimonies by Prominent Jewish Political Workers* (Munich, 1956), p. 52. German text in W. Lewitzkyj and G. Specht, eds., *Die Lage von der Juden in der Ukraine: Eine Dokumentensammlung* (Berlin, 1920), p. 41.
29. Reproduced in Arnold Margolin, *The Jews of Eastern Europe* (New York, 1926), p. 145; original in Volodymyr Serhiichuk, *Pohromy v Ukraïni: 1914–1920, vid shtuchnykh stereotypiv do hirkoï pravdy, prykhovuvanoï v radianskykh arkhivakh* (Kyiv, 1998), pp. 265–66.
30. TA 33.3132. The Ministry also disseminated anti-pogrom declarations by various Ukrainian leaders. See, for example, the April 1919 comments of Otaman Oskilko in "Der Rovner idishn kehile rat/Do Rivens'koï ievreis'koï hromads'koï rady," TA 3148.
31. See Taras Hunczak, ed., *Ukraïns'ka revoliutsiia 1919–1921: Dokumenty* (New York, 1984), pp. 107–110; Taras Hunczak, "A Reappraisal of Symon Petliura and Ukrainian-Jewish Relations, 1917–1921," *Jewish Social Studies* 31:3 (1969): 177–78, Alexandre Choulgine, *L'Ukraine et le Cauchemar Rouge: Les Massacres en Ukraine* (Paris, 1927), pp. 148, 151–55. See also Mahleket kitvei-yad shel bet ha-sefarim ha-leumi ve-ha-universitai, Jerusalem (hereafter MKY) V772.514 for a typical report of a local commission.
32. Joseph Schechtman, *Ver iz farantvortlikh far di pogromen in Ukrayne: Loyt naye nit farefntlikhte materiyaln un dokumentn* (Paris, 1927), pp. 90–91.
33. Gumener, *A kapitl Ukrayne*, p. 80. See also MKY V772.514, TA 20910.
34. See, for example, "Der gezets-proekt vegn oysrekhenen fun di mlukhe hoytsos oyf di baderfenishn fun idisher bildung," *Naye tsayt* January 31, 1919, TA 42767; "Programma ministerstva po evreiskim delam," *Posledniia novosti* January 25, 1919, TA 42762.
35. Revutsky, *In di shvere*, pp. 93–95.
36. See Revutsky, *In di shvere*, pp. 247–53; Schechtman, *Ver iz Farantvortlikh*, p. 57.
37. Reproduced in Goldelman, *Juden und Ukrainer*, pp. 30–31.
38. See, for example, "Presa," *Trybuna* January 24, 1919, TA 42760.
39. Arthur Adams, *Bolsheviks in the Ukraine: The Second Campaign, 1918–1919* (New Haven, 1963), pp. 79–81.

40. See Zvi Gitelman, *Jewish Nationality and Soviet Politics: The Jewish Section of the CPSU, 1917–1930,* (Princeton, 1972), pp. 169–83. See also Baruch Gurevitz, "The Bolshevik Revolution and the Foundation of the Jewish Communist Movement in Russia," *Slavic and Soviet Studies* 4 (1976): 12. See also "Shtimung un politik," *Folktsaytung* May 5, 1919, TA 45918; "Der idisher komisariat," April 3, 1919, TA 45913; "Di oyfgabn fun idishn komisariat," 11 March 1919, TA 45877.

41. "Der krizis in Bund," *Folkstsaytung*, February 19, 1919, cited in Baruch Gurevitz, *National Communism in the Soviet Union 1918–1928* (Pittsburgh, 1980).

42. Gurevitz, *National Communism*, p. 32.

43. TsDAHOU 41.1.22; 41.1.30.27. The Fareynikte had also considered uniting with the Poale-Tsion (Gitelman, *Jewish Nationality*, pp. 199–200).

44. TsDAHOU 41.1.29.17.

45. Gitelman, *Jewish Nationality*, p. 216.

46. Gurevitz, *National Communism*, p. 48.

47. See, for example, Khrystyian Rakovs'kyi's decree, "Bor'ba s antisemitizmom," Tsentral'nyi derzhavnyi arkhiv zhovtnevoï revoliutsiï (TsDAZhR) 2.1.46.

48. See, for example, the pamphlets "Dlia choho i iak kulaky ts'kuiut' proty ievreïv" (Kyiv, 1919) and "Slava Petliuri (na koho robyt' Petliura)" (n.p., n.d.); K. Kautskii, "Evreiskie pogromy i evreiskii vopros v Rossii" (St. Petersburg, 1919); I. Shelit, "Doloi pogromy," (Kyiv, 1919)—all held in the YIVO Institute for Jewish Research Library. Lenin's own decrees were less forceful; see Richard Pipes, *Russia under the Bolshevik Regime* (New York, 1993), p. 111. For Trotsky's work against pogroms, see Joseph Nevada, *Trotsky and the Jews* (Philadelphia, 1972), pp. 64–66, 165–66. See also "Resoliutsii zahal'noho zibrannia haryzona m. Cherkas," TA 3478.

49. TsDAHOU 41.1.47.

50. Gurevitz, *National Communism*, p. 49; Gitelman, *Jewish Nationality*, p. 165. The demand for specifically Jewish units was a heavily debated issue among Jewish Communists, see Nevada, *Trotsky and the Jews*, pp. 111–15. Units were approved, but not formed, as the Jewish Section disobeyed the order.

51. Peter Kenez, "Pogroms and White Ideology in the Russian Civil War," in John Klier and Shlomo Lambroza, eds., *Pogroms: Anti-Jewish Violence in Modern Russian History* (Cambridge, 1992), p. 301.

52. See, for example, *Komunistishe fon*, June 19, 1919, TA 42301, 47455; "Di prese," *Naye tsayt* May 25, 1919, TA 45935; "Mobilizatsie fun Bundistn

fun 18 biz 25 yor," April 29, 1919 TA 47441; "Nit in der roiter armey!," *Folkstsaytung* April 27, 1919 TA 47437; "Vegn der roiter armey," *Naye Tsayt* April 26, 1919 TA 47431; "Evreiskie rabochie idut v krasnuiu armiiu," *Krasnaia Armiia* May 7, 1919 TA 47416; "Prikaz," *Bor'ba* April 24, 1919 TA 47426; "Idisher arbeter, tsum gever!" *Naye tsayt* May 20, 1919 TA 47402; "Idisher arbeter in der roiter armey," TA 47456.

53. TA 544.47431.

54. TsDAHOU 41.132.26.

55. "Chto govoriat nashy vragi," TA 3472. The document has been dated by hand as the second of August, most likely of 1919. This declaration addresses the false notion that Jews were not joining the Red Army.

56. L. Shapiro, *Bakalakhat ha-Rusit: Pirkai zikhronot (1914–1924)*, (Jerusalem, 1952), p. 62; cited in Gitelman, *Jewish Nationality*, p. 165.

57. For anecdotal evidence, see Trotsky's complaints in Pipes, *Russia under the Bolshevik Regime*, p. 104; Nevada, *Trotsky*, pp. 157–58; Margolin, *Jews of Eastern Europe*, pp. 23–24.

58. Leonard Schapiro, "The Role of the Jews in the Russian Revolutionary Movement," in his *Russian Studies* (New York, 1987), p. 286.

59. See George Leggett, *The Cheka: Lenin's Political Police* (Oxford, 1981), p. 263.

60. Ivan Rudnytsky, "The Ukrainians in Galicia under Austrian Rule," in Andrei Markovits and Frank Sysyn, eds., *Nationbuilding and the Politics of Nationalism: Essays on Austrian Galicia* (Cambridge, MA, 1982), p. 38.

61. John-Paul Himka, "Ukrainian-Jewish Antagonism in the Galician Countryside During the Late Nineteenth Century," in Peter Potichnyj and Howard Aster, eds., *Ukrainian-Jewish Relations in Historical Perspective* (Edmonton, 1988), p. 115.

62. See Paul Mendes-Flohr and Jehuda Reinharz, eds., *The Jew in the Modern World: A Documentary History* (New York, 1980), pp. 34–35.

63. Andrei Markovits, "Introduction: Empire and Province," in Markovits and Sysyn, eds., *Nationbuilding*, pp. 4–5. See also Joseph A. Karniel, *Die Toleranzpolitik Kaiser Josephs II* (Stuttgart, 1986) and Klaus Lohrmann, *Das österreichische Judentum zur Zeit Maria Theresias und Josephs II* (Eisenstadt, 1980).

64. Rudnytsky, "Ukrainians in Galicia," in Markovits and Sysyn, eds., *Nationbuilding*, p. 25.

65. Reuven Fahn, *Geshikhte fun der yudisher natsional-oitonomie: in'm period fun der ma'arev-ukrainisher republik* (L'viv, 1933), p. 5.

66. Kurt Stillschweig, "Nationalism and Autonomy Among Eastern Euro-

pean Jewry: Origins and Historical Development up to 1939," *Historica Judaica* 6 (1944): 37–39.

67. Leila Everett, "The Rise of Jewish National Politics in Galicia, 1905–1907," in Markovits and Sysyn, eds., *Nationbuilding*, p. 162.

68. Stillschweig, "Nationalism and Autonomy," p. 39.

69. Frank Golczewski, *Polnisch-Jüdische Beziehungen 1881–1972: Eine studie zur geschichte des antisemitismus in Osteuropa* (Wiesbaden, 1981), p. 216, esp. note 184.

70. Nahum Gelber, "The National Autonomy of Eastern-Galician Jewry in the West-Ukrainian Republic, 1918–1919," in I. Lewin, ed., *A History of Polish Jewry During the Revival of Poland* (New York, 1980), pp. 230–34.

71. Moshe Landau, "Ha-yehudim ke-miut leumi be-shnoteha ha-rishonot shel Polin ha-atsmait (1918–1926)," unpublished Ph.D. diss., Hebrew University, Jerusalem, p. 1.

72. Ezra Mendelsohn, *Zionism in Poland: The Formative Years, 1925–1926* (New Haven, 1981), p. 97.

73. Zionists took 70 percent of the vote, and other pro-Zionist groups another 13 percent. The Jewish Socialist Party claimed only 9 percent, followed by the Poale-Tsion with 8 percent. Gelber, "National Autonomy," p. 282.

74. Mendelsohn, *Zionism in Poland*, p. 97.

75. Landau, "Ha-yehudim," p. 3; Gelber, "National Autonomy," p. 230.

76. Gelber, "National Autonomy," pp. 234–35.

77. See Golczewski, *Polnisch-Jüdische Beziehungen*, p. 186, esp. note 23.

78. Gelber, "National Autonomy," p. 235.

79. Israel Cohen, "My Mission to Poland (1918–1919)," *Jewish Social Studies* 13 (1951): 163.

80. Gelber, "National Autonomy," p. 238.

81. A detailed list is provided in *Evidence of Pogroms in Poland and Ukraina: Documents, Accounts of Eye-witnesses, Proceedings of the Polish Parliament, Local Press Reports, etc.* (New York, n.d.), pp. 48–54.

82. On the L'viv pogrom, see L. Chasanowitch, ed., *Les Pogromes Anti-Juives en Galicie et en Pologne en Novembre et Decembre 1918: Faits et Documents* (Stockholm, 1919); Joseph Tenenbaum, *Galitsie: Mayn alte haym* (Buenos Aires, 1952), pp. 229–53; Joseph Bendow (pseudonym of Joseph Tenenbaum), *Der Lemberger Judenpogrom (November 1918–Janner 1919)* (Vienna-Brünn, 1919).

83. Gelber, "National Autonomy," pp. 257–63, 284.

84. Landau, "Ha-yehudim," p. 3.

85. Gelber, "National Autonomy," pp. 289–91.

86. Gelber, "National Autonomy," p. 282.

87. Krasny was born in Kyiv in 1881. He became a Communist after the revolution. He was shot in 1939.

88. Revutsky, *In di shvere*, pp. 248–52.

89. Stenographic protocols of the meeting of the Ukrainian SRs, Dilo 259, cited in Tcherikower, *Di ukrayner pogromen*, p. 185.

90. Tcherikower, *Di ukrayner pogromen*, p. 163.

91. Gumener, *A kapitl Ukrayne*, p. 93; Pigido (Pihido), ed., *Material*, pp. 57–60, 65–67. See Krasny's comments on pogroms in "Ukraina i Antanta," *Odesskiia novosti* March 10, 1919, TA 3759.

92. See his letter to the war ministry TA 20804; Gumener, *A kapitl Ukrayne*, p. 96.

93. Reproduced as appendix 4 of Gumener, *A kapitl Ukrayne*, pp. 166–67.

94. Several were complied. For some lists and related materials, see MKY V772.52.4/1, 52.4/2a, 53.16, 53.35-37, 86.1, 86.15.12, 207.

95. Gumener, *A kapitl Ukrayne*, pp. 98–99, 121–22.

96. See Mordechai Altshuler, "Ukrainian-Jewish Relations in the Soviet Millieu in the Interwar Period," in Peter Potichnyj and Howard Aster, eds., *Ukrainian-Jewish Relations in Historical Perspective* (Edmonton, 1988), p. 284. For examples of aid requests sent to Krasny, see MKY V772.2, 26, 108.1, 108.6, 583.

97. Pigido (Pihido), ed., *Material*, pp. 78–102.

98. TA 46.3776-3779.

99. TA 47.3785-3791.

100. Reproduced in *The Ukraine Terror and the Jewish Peril* (London, 1921), pp. 15–16.

101. M. E. Ravage, *The Jew Pays: A Narrative of the Consequences of the War to the Jews of Eastern Europe* (New York, 1919), pp. 98–99.

102. Reproduced in ibid., pp. 130–31. Emphasis in the original.

103. MKY V772.251. See also Julian Batchinsky, "Jewish Pogroms in Ukraine and the Ukrainian People's Republic," typescript, TA 3304-3311.

104. "Ievreï ta Ukraïns'ka Respublika," TA 3091. For examples of the anti-pogrom decrees, see Dushnyk, *Ukrainians and Jews*, pp. 149–51, "S. Petliura do naselennia Ukraïny," *Ridnyi krai* March 28, 1921, TA 3233; "Do ievreis'koho hromadianstva i robitnytsva na Ukraïni/Tsu der

idisher birgershaft un arbaytershaft oyf Ukrayna" TA 30801; "Verordnungen des Rates der Volksminister," Goldelman, *Juden und Ukrainer*, p. 62, "Die Ukrainische Regierung an die Jüdische Bevölkerung," ibid., pp. 72–80; "Do zhydivs'koho naselennia," TA 5918; "Ofitsiial'no," TA 3240-3241; "Ofitsiial'no," TA 3156; Lewitzkyj and Specht, eds., *Die Lage*, pp. 44–52; Serhiichuk, *Pohromy*, pp. 268–71.

105. At this point (August 1919) all the parties had effectively abandoned the Ukrainian movement, and only isolated individuals such as Krasny remained.

106. A reference to the ongoing negotiations in Paris regarding the future of post-war eastern Europe.

107. Army Order of the Supreme Command of the Ukrainian National Republic, August 26, 1919, No. 131. This translation is based on Pigido (Pihido), ed., *Materials*, pp. 68–69. Ukrainian original text is in *Symon Petliura: Statti, Lysty, Dokumenty*, vol. 2, pp. 228–30. See also texts in Dushnyk, *Ukrainians and Jews*, pp. 151–52; Batchinsky et al., *The Jewish Pogroms*, pp. 15–16.

108. Traditional Ukrainian gifts of welcome.

109. The Jewish community of Proskuriv registered a complaint with the Ministry of Jewish Affairs that soldiers had taken over the Jewish hospitals (MKY V772/2, 4, 7).

110. It is possible that these "gifts" refer to the so-called "contributions," bribes that Jewish communities paid to avert pogroms.

111. TA 225.20705, *Ukraïna*, September 2, 1919. This translation based on Pigido (Pihido), *Material*, pp. 70–72. Ukrainian original text is also in *Symon Petliura: Statti, Lysty, Dokumenty*, vol. 2, pp. 360–63. See also Dushnyk, *Ukrainians and Jews*, pp. 152–54.

112. See Michael Palij, *The Ukrainian-Polish Defensive Alliance, 1919–1921: An Aspect of the Ukrainian Revolution* (Edmonton, 1995).

113. Goldelman, *Jewish National Autonomy*, p. 113.

114. Biuleten' Ievreis'koho Presovoho Biuro na Ukraïni, TA 47.3819-3821. See also TA 47.3822-3826; 47.3832-3836; 39041.

115. *Tragediia ukrainskogo evreistva (k protsessu Shvartsbarda)* (Kharkiv, 1928).

Conclusion

1. Statistics on Jewish population in the Baltic states are available in *The Baltic States*, Royal Institute of International Affairs (Westport, 1970 [f.p. 1938]), pp. 30, 33, 36.

2. See Raphael Mahler, *Yehudei Polin bein shtei milhamot ha-olam* (Tel-Aviv, 1968), p. 35.

3. See A. Strazhas, "Das nationale Erwachen des litauischen Volkes und die Judenheit," in A. Loit, ed., *National Movements in the Baltic Countries during the 19th Century* (Stolkholm, 1985), esp. 177–80; M. Sodarsky, "Lita in ir kamf far Vilne," in M. Sudarsky, A. Katzenelenbogen, and J. Kisin, eds., *Lite,* 3 vols. (New York, 1951), vol. 1, pp. 295–306; M. Kahan, "Vilna bein Lita ve-Polin," in Y. Olaiski et al., eds., *Yahadut Litah,* 4 vols. (Tel-Aviv, 1972), vol. 2, pp. 84–90.

4. See Jacob Lestschinsky's "Di ekonomishe lage fun di yidn in Lite (1919–1939)," *Lite*, vol. 1, p. 850; Hebrew and English adaptations are available under the titles "Ha-kalkalah ve-ha-demografiah shel yahadut Litah (1919–1939)," in Olaiski et al., eds., *Yahadut Litah,* vol. 2, pp. 91–100 and "The Economic Struggle of the Jews in Independent Lithuania," *Jewish Social Studies* 8:4 (1946): 267–96.

5. See S. Gringauz, "Jewish National Autonomy in Lithuania (1918–1925)," *Jewish Social Studies*14:3 (1952): 233–34.

6. L. Garfunkel, "Ma'avakam shel yehudei Litah al zekhuyot le-umiot," in Olaiski et al., eds., *Yahadut Litah,* vol. 2, p. 41.

7. The history of the Ministry is described in Shaul (Paul) Radensky, "Der ministerium far yidishe inyonim un di yidishe oitonomie in Lite, 1919–1923," *YIVO Bleter* (New Series) 2 (1994): 127–46.

8. Gringauz, "Jewish National Autonomy," pp. 233–36. See also M. Friedman, "The *Kehillah* in Lithuania 1919–1926: A Study Based on Panevezys and Ukmerge (Vilkomir)," *Soviet Jewish Affairs* 6:2 (1976): 83–103.

9. See Olaiski et al., eds., *Yahadut Litah,* vol. 2, pp. 58–61 for the text of the declaration in English. See also Gringauz, "Jewish National Autonomy," pp. 237–38. Paragraphs 73 and 74 of the constitution allowed minorities to establish their own institutions of culture, and even to tax their membership. The relationship of these organs to the state, and the manner in which the state would enforce and support this, however, was not stipulated.

10. Gringauz, "Jewish National Autonomy," pp. 239–41.

11. Friedman, "The *Kehillah* in Lithuania," pp. 101–102; Gringauz, "Jewish National Autonomy," pp. 239–41. See also the useful survey by Ezra Mendelsohn, *The Jews of East Central Europe between the World Wars* (Bloomington, 1983), pp. 213–41.

12. See M. Laserson, "The Jews and the Latvian Parliament, 1918–1924," in M. Bobe, S. Levenberg, I. Maor, Z. Michaeli, eds., *The Jews in Latvia* (Tel-Aviv, 1971), p. 95; M. Garleff, "Ethnic Minorities in the Estonian and Latvian Parliaments: The Politics of Coalition," in V. Vardys and

R. Misiunas, eds., *The Baltic States in Peace and War 1917–1925* (University Park, PA, 1978), pp. 81–94.

13. See Z. Michaeli (Michelson), "Jewish Cultural Autonomy and the Jewish School Systems" in Bobe, ed., *Jews in Latvia*, pp. 186–87.

14. See J. Robinson et al., eds., *Were the Minorities Treaties a Failure?* (New York, 1939), in this context especially p. 166; also Kurt Stillschweig, *Die Juden Osteuropas in den Minderheiten-vertragen* (Berlin, 1936) and "Nationalism and Autonomy Among Eastern European Jewry: Origin and Historical Development up to 1939," *Historia Judaica* 6 (1944): 27–68.

15. See S. Gringauz, "The Jewish National Autonomy in Lithuania, Latvia and Estonia," in G. Aronson, J. Frumkin, A. Goldenweiser, J. Lewitan, eds., *Russian Jewry 1917–1967* (New York, 1969), p. 69.

16. See M. Beth, "Men and Deeds," in Bobe, ed., *Jews in Latvia*, pp. 301–302, also in that collection, see I. Maor (Meirson), "The Communal Image of Latvian Jewry," p. 84.

17. See K. Jokton (Yokton), *Geshikhte fun di yidn in Estland* (Tartu, 1927), pp. 12–14. On the *kantonisten*, see Michael Stanislawski, *Tsar Nicholas I and the Jews: The Transformation of Jewish Society in Russia 1825–1855* (Philadelphia, 1983).

18. H. Reiman, "Kirikuelu 1930–34," *Eesti Statistika Kuukiri* 160 (March 1935): 126, cited in T. Parming, "The Jewish Community and Inter-Ethnic Relations in Estonia, 1918–1940," *Journal of Baltic Studies* 10:3 (Fall 1979): 243.

19. *The Baltic States in Peace and War*, p. 36.

Bibliographic Postscriptum

1. An earlier version of this chapter was published under the title "Historiography on the Jews and the Ukrainian Revolution," *Journal of Ukrainian Studies* 15:2 (1990): 33–45. I am grateful to Mr. Roman Senkus and the *Journal* for allowing me to publish a revised version here.

2. Henri Torrés, *Les Procès des Pogromes* (Paris, 1928), pp. i–ii.

3. Much of the historiography on Schwartzbard is simply incorrect, and written with a view either to lionize or to defame him. Even basic data such as his place of birth are subject to debate in some circles. His name is also erroneously transliterated as Schwartsbart, and in one case a dubious pseudonym ("Walsberger") is supplied without any supporting information. The most detailed studies, although not necessarily the most reliable, are Meir Kotik, *Mishpat Shvartsbard: retsah-nakam 'al reka' ha-pogromim be-Ukrainah* ([Hadera], 1972) and Saul Friedman, *Pogromchik: The Assassination of Simon Petlura* (New York, 1974).

4. "General Petlura is Fatally Shot in Paris by Russian Student Seeking Revenge," *New York Times* May 26, 1926: 1.

5. See Marko Antonovych and Roman Serbyn, "Dokumenty pro uchast' Shvartsbarda v komunistychnii iacheitsi v Paryzhi," in *Naukovyi Zbirnyk (1945–1950–1995)*, vol. IV (1999), ed. Marko Antonovych (New York, 1999), pp. 334–46. See also Sebastien de Gasquet's notes in the *Bulletin de l'Association Française d'Études Ukrainiennes* 1(11) 1999. As this work was going to press, I was informed of recent research by Mikhail Liubimov that adds further weight to this contention. Unfortunately, I have not been able to secure copies of his publications to examine the work personally. See his *Shpiony, kotorykh ia liubliu i nenavizhu* (Moscow, 1998), p. 297. See also Stepan Lenkavsky, "Soviet Russian Political Murders Abroad and Attempts to Camouflage Them," *Murdered by Moscow: Petlura-Konovalets-Bandera, Three Leaders of the Ukrainian National Liberation Movement Assassinated at the Orders of Stalin and Khrushchov* (London, 1962), pp. 9–10. More useful is the brief mention of this argument in Taras Hunczak, "A Reappraisal of Symon Petliura and Ukrainian-Jewish Relations, 1917–1921," *Jewish Social Studies* 31:3 (New York, 1969): 164n4.

6. "Schwartzbard le meurtier de l'hetman Petlura est acquitté par le jury de la Seine," *Le Journal* October 27, 1927: 1. "Paris Jury Acquits Slayer of Petlura," *New York Times* October 27, 1927: 1. The *Times* asserts that the jury deliberated for thirty-five minutes.

7. Philip Friedman, "Ukrainian-Jewish Relations During the Nazi Occupation," *YIVO Annual of Jewish Social Science* 12 (1958/1959): 279. Taras Hunczak, however, maintains that there was no *Aktion* named after Petliura.

8. Ezra Mendelsohn, *The Jews of East Central Europe between the World Wars* (Bloomington, 1983), pp. 43–49.

9. Moshe Zilberfarb, *Dos idishe ministerium un di idishe avtonomie in Ukrayne (a bletl geshikhte)* (Kyiv, 1919). This work recently appeared in a slightly abridged English translation: Moses Silberfarb, *The Jewish Ministry and Jewish National Autonomy in Ukraine*, trans. David Lincoln (New York, 1993).

10. Wolf Latsky-Bertholdi, *Gzeyrat Denikin* (Berlin, 1922).

11. Avraham Revutsky, *In di shvere teg oif Ukrayne: zikhroines fun a yidishn ministr* (Berlin, 1924).

12. Two commemorative books published in memory of the pogrom victims of Proskuriv and Felshtin mark the beginning of a new genre in twentieth-century Jewish historiography: the semi-scholarly Yizkerbukh, which became very popular after the destruction of thousands of Jewish communities in the Holocaust. *Khurbn Proskurov: Tsum andenken fun di heilige neshomes vos zaynen umgekumen in der shreklikher*

shkhitakh, vos iz ongefirt gevorn durkh di Haidamakes (New York, 1924); Boim, Y. and A. Katz, *Felshtin*, (New York, 1937). Zachary Baker, "Memorial Books as Sources for Eastern European Jewish Local History," paper presented to the Centre for Russian and East European Studies, University of Toronto, 17 January 1992.

13. Eliyohu Gumener, *A kapitl Ukrayne: 2 yor in Podolye* (Vilnius, 1921).

14. M. Grosman, Y. Grinfeld, E. Tcherikower, W. Latsky, J. Schechtman, eds., *Di idishe avtonomie un der natsionaler sekretariat in Ukrayne: materialn un dokumentn* (Kyiv, 1920).

15. The relationship between Ukrainian and Jewish political activists in Western Ukraine was quite involved, yet a comprehensive treatment is made difficult by a paucity of published primary sources. The principal memoirs are Nahum Michael Gelber, "The National Autonomy of Eastern-Galician Jewry in the West-Ukrainian Republic, 1918–1919," in I. Lewin, ed., *A History of Polish Jewry During the Revival of Poland* (New York, 1990), pp. 223–326; and Reuven Fahn, *Geshikkhte fun der yudisher natsional-oitonomie in'm period fun der maarev-ukrainisher republik* (L'viv, 1933). See also Frank Golczewski, *Polnisch-Jüdische Bezieungen 1881–1882: Eine Studie zur Geschichte des Antisemitismus in Osteuropa* (Wiesbaden, 1981); and Moshe Landau, "Ha-yehudim ke-miut leumi be-shnoteha ha-rishonot shel Polin ha-atsmait (1918–1926)," unpublished Ph.D. dissertation, The Hebrew University of Jerusalem, 1972. The pogroms of the period are treated in L. Chasanowitch, ed., *Les Pogromes Anti-Juifs en Galicie et en Pologne en Novembre et Decembre 1918: Faits et Documents* (Stockholm, 1919); Joseph Tenenbaum, *Galitsie: Mayn alte haym* (Buenos Aires, 1952); Josef Bendow [Tenenbaum], *Der Lemberger Judenpogrom (November 1918–Janner 1919)* (Vienna–Brunn, 1919).

16. This process is treated in the works of Baruch Gurevitz, "The Bolshevik Revolution and the Foundation of the Jewish Communist Movement in Russia," *Slavic and Soviet Studies* 4 (1976): 3–20; and his *National Communism in the Soviet Union 1918–1928* (Pittsburgh, 1980). See also Zvi Gitelman, *Jewish Nationality and Soviet Politics: The Jewish Sections of the CPSU* (Princeton, 1972).

17. Moshe Rafes, *Dva goda revoliutsii na Ukraine (èvoliutsiia raskola "Bunda")* (Moscow, 1920).

18. Goldelman's works include *Jewish National Autonomy in Ukraine 1917–1920* (Chicago, 1968), originally published in Ukrainian; and *Lysty zhydivs'koho sotsial-demokrata pro Ukraïnu: Materiialy do istoriï ukraïns'ko-zhydivs'kykh vidnosyn za chas revoliutsiï* (Vienna, 1921). Margolin wrote *Ukraina i politika Antanty* (Berlin, 1921); *The Jews of Eastern Europe* (New York, 1926); and *From a Political Diary: Russia, the Ukraine, and America 1905–1945* (New York, 1946).

19. *Antisemitizm un pogromen in Ukraine 1917–1918 (tsu der geshikhte fun ukraynish-yidishe batsihungen)* (Berlin, 1923); a Russian-language version also appeared. See also Zosa Szajkowski, "Di geshikhte fun dem itstikn bukh," in Elias Tcherikower, *Di Ukrayner pogromen in yor 1919*, (New York, 1965), pp. 341–43.
20. *Di Ukrayner pogromen in yor 1919* (New York, 1965).
21. I. V. Shekhtman [Joseph Schechtman], *Pogromy dobrovol'cheskoi armii na Ukraine* (Berlin, 1932).
22. "Di pogromen fun di povstantses: Dos yor 1920 in Ukraine, birgerkrig un pogromen."
23. Lestschinsky dealt with this topic in the Yiddish press as well as devoting the odd chapter in several of his demographic studies. For references, see Szajkowski, "Geshikhte," p. 342n25.
24. "Di pogromen in Ukrayne in di yorn 1918–1920," *Shriftn far ekonomik un statistik* 1 (Berlin, 1928): 106–113. An English-language version appeared in the *YIVO Annual of Jewish Social Science* 6 (New York, 1951): 237–52.
25. Szajkowski argues that Tcherikower intended to write this work himself; see "Di geshikhte," p. 343.
26. Committee of Jewish Delegations, *The Pogroms in the Ukraine under the Ukrainian Governments (1917–1920): Historical Survey with Documents and Photographs* (London, 1927); Comité des Delegations Juives, *Les Pogromes en Ukraine sous les Gouvernements Ukrainiens (1917–1920): Aperçu historique et documents* (Paris, 1927).
27. See, for example, the omission of Petliura's support for Jewish self-defense and related anti-pogrom statements which appear in Tcherikower, *Antisemitizm un pogromen*, pp. 203–204, 209.
28. Pinkhos Krasny, *Tragediia ukrainskogo everistva (k protsessu Shvartsbarda)* (Kharkiv, 1928). His letter is reproduced on pp. 65–72.
29. *He'avar* 16, 17 (Tel-Aviv, 1969, 1970).
30. New York, 1976.
31. J. Batchinsky, A. Margolin, M. Vishnitzer, I. Zangwill, *The Jewish Pogroms in Ukraine: Authoritative Statements on the Question of Responsibility for Recent Outbreaks against the Jews in Ukraine, Documents, Official Orders, and Other Data Bearing on the Facts as They Exist Today* (Washington, DC, 1919); W. Lewitzkyj and G. Specht, eds., *Die Lage der Juden in der Ukraine: Eine Dokumentsammlung* (Berlin, 1920); Dmytro Doroshenko, *Istoriia Ukraïny 1917–1923 rr.*, 2 vols (Uzhhorod, 1932); Pavlo Khrystiuk, ed., *Zamitky i materiialy do istoriï ukraïns'koï revoliutsiï 1917–1920 rr.*, 4 vols. (Vienna, 1921).
32. Fedir Pigido (Pihido), ed., *Material Concerning Ukrainian-Jewish Rela-*

tions during the Years of the Revolution (1917–1921): Collection of Documents and Testimonies by Prominent Jewish Political Workers (Munich, 1956); W. Dushnyk, ed., *Ukrainians and Jews: Articles, Testimonies, Letters and Official Documents Dealing with Interrelations of Ukrainians and Jews in the Past and Present: A Symposium* (New York, 1966).

33. Taras Hunczak, "A Reappraisal of Symon Petliura and Ukrainian-Jewish Relations, 1917–1921," *Jewish Social Studies* 31:3 (1969): 163–83.

34. Zosa Szajkowski, "'A Reappraisal of Symon Petliura and Ukrainian-Jewish Relations, 1917–1921': A Rebuttal," *Jewish Social Studies* 31:3 (1969): 184–213.

35. "Communications," *Jewish Social Studies* 32:3 (1970): 246–63. See also the comment by Joseph Schechtman in "Communications," *Midstream* 15:9 (1969): 59–61.

36. A very signficant exception to this rule is the excellent work by John Hewko, "The Ukrainian-Jewish Political Relationship During the Period of the Central Rada—March 1917 to January 1918," unpublished M.Litt thesis, Oxford, 1981. Although Hewko could use neither Yiddish nor Hebrew sources, he spent considerable time in the archives of the YIVO Institute for Jewish Research (New York City) leafing through for the odd Ukrainian and Russian newspaper clipping, with very positive results.

37. A brief but useful bibliographic overview of the subject in general is provided in Avraham Greenbaum's "Bibliographic Essay," in John Klier and Sholmo Lambroza, eds., *Pogroms: Anti-Jewish Violence in Modern Russian History*, (Cambridge, 1992), especially pp. 380–82.

38. Matityahu Mintz' publications include *Ha-maavak le-shovi-zkhuyot leumiot u-le-otonomie be-kerev yehudei Rusyah be-maavar min ha-meah ha-19 u-ba-meah ha-20* (Tel-Aviv, 1978); "The Secretariat of Internationality Affairs (*Sekretariat mizhnatsionalnykh sprav*) of the Ukrainian General Secretariat (1917–1918)," *Harvard Ukrainian Studies* 6:1 (1982): 25–42; "The Recruitment of Jews for Ukrainian National Units in 1917, as reflected in the minutes of the Provisional Jewish Council," *Jews and Jewish Topics in the Soviet Union and Eastern Europe* 2:12 (1990): 8–14. See also Arie Zaidman's Ph.D. dissertation, "Ha-avtonomie ha-leumit ha-yehudit be-Ukraina ha-atsmait ba-shanim 1917–1919," Tel-Aviv, 1980.

39. Matityahu Minc (Mintz), "Kiev Zionists and the Ukrainian National Movement," in Peter Potichnyj and Howard Aster, eds., *Ukrainian-Jewish Relations in Historical Perspective* (Edmonton, 1988), pp. 247–62; also in that collection, Jonathan Frankel, "The Dilemmas of Jewish Autonomism: The Case of Ukraine 1917–1920," pp. 263–80.

40. "Jewish Representation in the Independent Ukrainian Governments of 1917–1920," *Slavic Review* 50:3 (1991): 542–50; "Jews and Ukrainians in Revolutionary Times: Autonomy, Statehood, and Civil War, 1917–1920," Ph.D. dissertation (University of Toronto, 1995).

Selected Bibliography

Primary Sources

1. Archives

Mahleket kitvei-yad shel bet ha-sefarim ha-leumi ve-ha-universitai, Jerusalem.

Tcherikower Archive, YIVO Institute for Jewish Research, New York City.

Tsentral'nyi derzhavnyi arkhiv hromads'kykh ob'iednan' [orhanizatsii] Ukraïny, formerly known as the Partiinyi arkhiv institutu istoriï partiï pry TsK kompartiï Ukraïny, Filiala institutu marksyzmu-leninizmu pry TsK KPRS, Kyiv [=Tsentral'nyi gosudarstvennyi arkhiv grazhdanskikh obedinenii (organizatsii) Ukrainy].

Tsentral'nyi derzhavnyi arkhiv zhovtnevoï revoliutsiï, currently known as the Tsentral'nyi derzhavnyi arkhiv vyshchykh orhaniv derzhavnoï vlady i orhaniv derzhavnoho upravlinnia Ukraïny, Kyiv.

Tsentral'nyi derzhavnyi istorichnykh arkhiv, Kyiv.

Zhuk Collection, National Archives of Canada, Ottawa.

2. Newspapers

Arbeter shtime, Petrograd.

Bor'ba, Kyiv.

Der telegraf, Kyiv.

Der Yidisher arbeter, Kyiv.

Der Yidisher proletarier, Kyiv.

Dos naye lebn, Odesa-Kyiv.

Evreiskaia mysl', Odesa.

Folkshtime, Vilnius.

Folkstsaytung, Kyiv.

Haynt, Warsaw.

Kievs'kyi den', Kyiv.

Kievskaia mysl', Kyiv.

Krasnaia armiia, Kyiv.

Nay Lebn, Kyiv.

Naye tsayt, Kyiv.

The New York Times, New York.

Nova rada, Kyiv.

Novyi put', Moscow.

Odesskiia novosti, Odesa.

Ridnyi krai, L'viv.

Robitnycha hazeta, Kyiv.

Rus', Kyiv.

Trybuna, Kyiv.

Ukraïns'ka stavka, Kyiv.

Visti z Ukraïns'koï Tsentral'noï Rady, Kyiv.

Yidishe folksblat, Kyiv.

3. Published Documents

"Appendix: The Four Universals," in *The Ukraine 1917–1921: A Study in Revolution*, ed. Taras Hunczak, Cambridge, MA: Harvard Ukrainian Research Institute–Harvard University Press, 1977, 382–95.

Antonovych, Marko and Roman Serbyn, "Dokumenty pro uchast' Shvartsbarda v komunistychnii iacheitsi v Paryzhi," in *Naukovyi Zbirnyk (1945–1950–1995)*, vol. IV, ed. Marko Antonovych, New York: Ukraïns'ka Vil'na Akademiia Nauk u SShA, 1999, pp. 334–46.

Batchinsky, J., A. Margolin, M. Vishnitzer, I. Zangwill, *The Jewish Pogroms in Ukraine: Authoritative Statements on the Question of Responsibility for Recent Outbreaks Against the Jews in Ukraine: Documents, Official Orders, and Other Data Bearing on the Facts as They Exist Today*, Washington, DC: The Friends of Ukraine, 1919.

Bauer, Henning, Andreas Kappeler, Brigitte Roth, eds., *Die Nationalitäten des Russischen Reiches in der Volkszählung von 1897*, 2 vols. Stuttgart: Franz Steiner Verlag, 1991.

Chasanowitch, L., ed., *Les Pogromes Anti-Juifs en Galicie et en Pologne en Novembre et Decembre 1918: Faits et Documents*, Stockholm: Bokforlaget Judaea, 1919.

"Chy vorohy ievreï robitnykam ta selianam?" Kyiv: Vseukraïns'ke vydnavnytstvo pry VTsVK rad robitnychykh, selians'kykh ta chervono-armiis'kykh deputativ, 1919.

Committee of Jewish Delegations, *The Pogroms in the Ukraine under the Ukrainian Governments (1917–1920): Historical Survey with Documents and Photographs*, London: Bale, 1927 [French translation: *Les Pogromes en Ukraine sous les Gouvernements Ukrainiens (1917–1920): Aperçu Historique et Documents*, Paris: Beresniak, 1927].

Cross, Samuel H. and Olgerd Sherbowitz-Wetzor, eds. *The Russian Primary Chronicle: Laurentian Text*, Cambridge, MA: Harvard University Press/ Mediaeval Academy of America, 1973.

Dimanshtein, Simon, ed., *Revoliutsiia i natsional'nyi vopros*, vol 3: *1917 fevral'-oktiabr'*, Moscow: Izdatel'stvo Kommunisticheskoi Akademii, 1930.

"Dlia choho i iak kulaky ts'kuiut' proty ievreiv," Kyiv: Vydavnytstvo politychnoho upravlinnia narodn'oho viis'kovykh sprav komisariiaty Ukraïny, 1919.

Dragomanov [Drahomanov], Mikhailo, *Sobranie politicheskikh sochinenii*, 2 vols. Paris: Société Nouvelle de Librarie et D'edition, 1906.

Dubnow, Simon, *Nationalism and History: Essays on Old and New Judaism*, ed. K. Pinson, New York: Atheneum, 1970.

Dushnyk, W., ed., *Ukrainians and Jews: Articles, Testimonies, Letters and Official Documents Dealing with Interrelations of Ukrainians and Jews in the Past and Present: A Symposium*, New York: Ukrainian Congress Committee of America, 1966.

Evidence of Pogroms in Poland and Ukraina: Documents, Accounts of Eye-witnesses, Proceedings of the Polish Parliament, Local Press Reports, etc., New York: Information Bureau of the Committee for the Defense of Jews in Poland and Other East European Countries, American Jewish Congress, n.d.

Franklin, Simon, trans. and intro., *Sermons and Rhetoric of Kievan Rus'*, Cambridge, MA: Harvard Ukrainian Research Institute–Harvard University Press, 1991 [=Harvard Library of Early Ukrainian Literature, English trans., vol. 5].

Goldberg, Israel, ed., *The Massacres and Other Atrocities Committed Against the Jews in Southern Russia: A Record Including Official Reports, Sworn Statements, and Other Documentary Proof*, New York: American Jewish Congress, Committee on Protest Against the Massacres of Jews in Ukrainia and Other Lands, 1920.

Grosman, M., Y. Grinfeld, Elias Tcherikower, Wolf Latsky, Joseph Schechtman, eds., *Di idishe avtonomie un der natsionaler sekretariat in Ukraine: materialn un dokumentn*, Kyiv: Idisher Folks-Farlag, 1920.

Hannover, Nathan, *Abyss of Despair (Yeven Metsulah)*, trans. Abraham Mesch, New York: Bloch, 1950.

Heifetz, A. [E.], *Pogrom geshikhte (1919–1920)*: Band 1, *di Ukrayner shkhite in 1919*, New York: Arbeter Ring, 1921 [English translation: *The Slaughter of the Jews in the Ukraine in 1919*, New York: Seltzer, 1921].

Heppell, Muriel (trans. and intro.), *The Paterik of the Kievan Caves Monastery*, Cambridge, MA: Harvard Ukrainian Research Institute–Harvard University Press, 1989 [=Harvard Library of Early Ukrainian Literature, English trans., vol. 1].

Hornykiewicz, T., ed., *Ereignisse in der Ukraine 1914–1922: deren Bedeutung und historische Hintergrunde*, 4 vols. Horn, Austria and Philadelphia: Berger, 1966.

Hrushevs'kyi, Mykhailo, *Vybrani pratsi*, New York: Holovna uprava OURDP v SShA, 1960.

Hunczak, Taras, ed., *Ukraïns'ka revoliutsiia 1919–1921: dokumenty*, New York: Ukrainian Academy of Arts and Sciences in the United States, 1984 [= Sources of Modern History of Ukraine, eds. Yaroslav Bilinsky et al.].

Ievreiskie pogromy 1918–1921, Moscow: Shkola i kniga, 1926.

Khrystiuk, Pavlo, ed., *Zamitky i materiialy do istoriï ukraïns'koï revoliutsiï 1917–1920 rr.* 4 vols. Vienna: Vernay, 1921.

Kirzhnits, A. and Moshe Rafes, eds., *Der idisher arbeter: khrestomatye tsu der geshikhte fun der idisher arbeter, revolutsionerer un sotsialistisher bavegung in Rusland*, 4 vols. Moscow: Tsentraler farlag far di felker fun FSSR, 1925.

Lewitzkyj, W. and G. Specht, eds., *Die Lage von den Juden in der Ukraine: Eine Dokumentensammlung*, Berlin: Ukrainischer Pressedienst, 1920.

Lodyzhenskii, Iurii, *Mezhdunarodnaia pomoshch' zhertvam grazhdanskoi bor'by*, Kyiv: Kantselariia Mezhdunarodnogo Krasno-Krestnogo Komiteta Pomoshchi Zhertvam Grazhdanskoi Bor'by Pomyshchaetsia, 1919.

Magocsi, Paul Robert, ed., *Texts of the Ukraine "Peace" with Maps*, Cleveland: J.T. Zubal, 1981.

Manilov, V., ed., *1917 god na Kievshchine: khronika sobytii*, Kyiv: Gos. izd-vo Ukrainy, 1928.

Materialy ob antievreiskikh pogromakh, Moscow: EvobShchESTKOM, 1922.

Mints [Minc, Mintz], Matityahu, ed., *Ha-ma'avak le-shovi-zkhuyot leumiyot u-le-otonomiyah be-kerev yehudei Rusyah ba-ma'avar min ha-meah ha-19 u-va-meah ha-20*, Tel-Aviv: Tel-Aviv Univeristy, 1978.

Nathansen, Henri, *Protest Against the Jewish Pogroms: Speech Held at the Protest Meeting in Copenhagen on November the 27th 1918 On Occasion of the Pogroms in Poland*, Copenhagen: Zionist Organization, 1919.

Petliura, Symon, "Peredmova," *Ievreï: p'iesa na 4 diï*, Ie. Chirikov, Kyiv: S.A. Borisov, 1907, iii–xviii.

———, *Symon Petliura: Statti, lysty, dokumenty*, 2 vols. New York: Ukraïns'ka vil'na akademiia nauk u SShA–Biblioteka im. Symona Petliury v Parizhi, 1956–1979.

Pigido [Pihido], F., ed., *Material Concerning Ukrainian-Jewish Relations during the Years of the Revolution (1917–1921): Collection of Documents and Testimonies by Prominent Jewish Political Workers*, Munich: Ukrainian Information Bureau, 1956.

Serhiichuk,Volodymyr, *Pohromy v Ukraïni: 1914–1920, vid stuchnykh stereotypiv do hirkoï pravdy, prykhovuvanoï v radians'kykh arkhivakh*, Kyiv: Vydavnytstvo imeni Oleny Telihy, 1998.

Shelit, I., *Doloi pogromy*, Kyiv: Izdatel'stvo Narodnogo Komissariata po Voennym Delam Ukrainy, 1919.

"Slava Petliuri (na koho robyt' Petliura)" [Kyiv?]: Bil'shovyk, [1919?].

Tcherikower, Elias, *Antisemitizm un pogromen in Ukrayne 1917–1918 (tsu der geshikhte fun ukraynish-yidishe batsihungen)*, Berlin: Mizrakh-yidish Historisher Arkhiv, 1923.

———, ed., *In der tkufe fun revoliutsie (memoarn, materialn, dokumentn): zamlbukh*, Berlin: Yidisher literarisher farlag, 1924.

Tetigkeyt barikht 1921, London: Federation of Ukrainian Jews in Aid of the Pogrom Sufferers in Ukraine, [1921?].

The Ukraine Terror and the Jewish Peril, London: The Federation of Ukrainian Jews in Aid of the Pogrom Sufferers in the Ukraine, 1921.

Tsentral'nyi statisticheskii komitet, *Pervaia vseobshchaia perepis' naseleniia rossiiskoi imperii 1897 g.*, 89 vols. St. Petersburg, Izd. Tsentral'nogo, 1899–1905.

Tsvey yohr hilfs-arbayt: tetikgayt-barikht fun dem farband fun ukrayner iden in London, April 1923–Marts 1925, London: Federation of Ukrainian Jews, 1925.

Unterman, Yitskhak, *Fun di shkitah-shtet 1919–1922: Ayndrike, bilder, fakten un materiyaln*, Hudson City, NJ: Hudson Jewish News, 1925.

Vernadsky, George, ed., *A Source Book for Russian History from Early Times to 1917*, 3 vols. New Haven, CT: Yale University Press, 1972.

Yidisher Gezelshaftlikher komitet tsu helfen di gelitene fun pogromen (Yidgezkom), *Statistik fun pogromirte, heft 1: haymloze in Bohuslav (Kiev. gub)*, Kyiv: Mlukhe-farlag, 1921.

"Zakon pro vos'mohodynnyi rabochyi den'," Kherson: Kherson kooperatyvnoho tovarystva, Ukraïns'ka knyharnia, 1918.

Zhitlovsky, Kh., *Gezamelte shriftn*, 10 vols. New York: Yubilos, 1912–1919.

Zilberfarb, Moshe, *Evreiskii vopros na stranitsakh sotsialisticheskoi pechati*, St. Petersburg: Bor'ba, 1906.

4. Memoirs

Agurski, S., *Der idisher arbeter in der komunistisher bavegung 1917–1921*, Minsk: Mlukhe-farlag fun Vaysrusland, 1925.

Berman, Joseph, *Un juif en Ukraine au temps de l'Armée rouge: des pogroms à la guerre civile*, Paris: L'Harmattan, 1993 [=*Memoires du XXème siècle*, ed. Alain Forest].

Boim, Y., and A. Katz, eds., *Felshtin: zamlbukh tsum ondenk fun di Felshtiner kedoshim*, New York: Felshtiner Farband, 1937.

Boyarin, Jonathan, *A Storyteller's Worlds: The Education of Shlomo Noble in Europe and America*, New York: Holmes and Meier, 1994.

Charnofsky, M., *Jewish Life in the Ukraine: A Family Saga*, New York: Exposition Press, 1965.

de Lubersac, Jean, *The Ukraine Inferno: Recital of an Eye-Witness*, London: Fund for the Relief of the Jewish Victims of the War, 1922.

Gol'denveizer, A. A., "Iz Kievskykh vospominanii (1917–1921 gg.)," *Arkhiv russkoi revoliutsii* 6 (Berlin, 1922): 161–303.

Goldelman, Solomon, *Jewish National Autonomy in Ukraine 1917–1920*, trans. Michael Luchkovich, Chicago: Ukrainian Research and Information Institute, 1968 [Yiddish version: *Di yidishe natsionale oitonomie in Ukrayne (1917–1920)*, in *Yidn in Ukrayne*, 2 vols. New York: Ankenk fun Ukrayner Yidn, 1961, 1:119–62].

———, *Juden und Ukrainer: Briefe eines Jüdischen Sozialdemokraten*, Vienna: Hamojn, 1921 [Ukrainian translation: *Lysty zhydivs'koho sotsial-demokrata pro Ukrainu: materialy do istorii ukraïns'koho zhydivs'kykh vidnosyn za chas revoliutsii*].

Gorenstein, Lillian, "A Memoir of the Great War, 1914–1924," *YIVO Annual* 20 (Evanston, IL, 1991): 125–83.

Gumener, Eliyohu, *A kapitl Ukrayne: 2 Yor in Podolye*, Vilnius: Sh. Shreberk, 1921.

Krasnii [Krasny], Pinkhos, *Tragediia ukrainskogo evreistva (k protsessu Shvartsbarda)*, Kharkiv: Gos. izd-vo Ukrainy, 1928.

Lestschinsky, Jacob, *Tsvishn lebn un toit: tsen yor yidish lebn in Sovet-Rusland*, Vilnius: Kletskin, 1930.

Makhno, Nestor, *Vospominaniia*, Moscow: Respublika, 1992.

Margolin, Arnold, *From a Political Diary: Russia, the Ukraine, and America, 1905–1945*, New York: Columbia University Press, 1946.

———, *The Jews of Eastern Europe*, New York: Thomas Seltzer, 1926.

———, *Ukraina i politika Antanty*, Berlin: Efron, [1921].

Mozun, M., "V krovavom chadu (k istorii Dobrovol'cheskoi pogromshchiny)," Kyiv: Kievskii Gorodskoi Komitet ESDRP (Poalei-Tsion), n.d.

Neufeld, D., *A Russian Dance of Death: Revolution and Civil War in the Ukraine*, Winnipeg: Hyperion Press, 1977.

Rafes, Moshe, *Dva goda revoliutsii na Ukraine (èvoliutsiia raskola "Bunda")*, Moscow: Gos. izd-vo, 1920.

Revutsky, Avraham, *In di shvere teg oif Ukraine: zikhroines fun a yidishn ministr*, Berlin: Yidisher literarisher farlag, 1924.

Sadikow, M., *In yene teg: zikhroines vegen der rusisher revolutsie un di ukrayner pogromen*, New York: n.p., 1926.

Schechtman, Joseph, "Jewish Community Life in Ukraine (1917–1919)," in *Russian Jewry 1917–1967*, ed. G. Aronson, J. Frumkin, A. Goldenweiser, and J. Lewitan, New York: Yoseloff, 1969, pp. 39–57.

Schoenfeld, J. *Shtetl Memoirs: Jewish Life in Galicia under the Austro-Hungarian Empire and in the Reborn Poland, 1898–1939*, Hoboken, NJ: KTAV, 1985.

Tenenbaum, Joseph, *Galitsie: mayn alte haym*, Buenos Aires: Tsentral-farlag fun poilishe yidn in Argentine, 1952 [Series: *Dos poilishe yidntum* 87].

Ussishkin, Shmuel, *Ima Odesah: zikhronot yaldut u-neurim, 1904–1919*, Jerusalem: ha-Sifriyah ha-Tsionit al-yad ha-Histadrut ha-Tsionit ha-olamit, 1984.

Vynnychenko, Volodymyr, "Ievreis'ke pytannia na Ukraïni," *Suchasnist'* 8 (Kyiv, 1992): 116–25.

———, *Vidrodzhennia natsiï*, 4 vols., Kyiv: Vyd-vo politychnoï literatury Ukraïny, 1990 [f.p. 1920].

Zilberfarb, Moshe, *Dos idishe ministerium un di idishe avtonomie in Ukrayne (a bletl geshikhte)*, Kyiv: Idisher Folks-farlag, 1919 [English translation: Moses Silberfarb, *The Jewish Ministry and Jewish National Autonomy in Ukraine*, trans. David Lincoln, New York: Aleph, 1993].

Secondary Sources

Abramson, Henry, "Historiography on the Jews and the Ukrainian Revolution," *Journal of Ukrainian Studies* 15:2 (Edmonton, 1990): 33–46.

———, "Jewish Representation in the Independent Ukrainian Governments of 1917–1920," *Slavic Review* 50:3 (Stanford, 1991): 542–50.

———, "The Scattering of Amalek: A Model for Understanding the Ukrainian-Jewish Conflict," *East European Jewish Affairs* 24:1 (London, 1994): 39–47.

———, "Schechtman, Joseph," 4:551; "Tcherikower, Elias," 5:180; "Yiddish," vol. 5, pp. 773–74; "Zionism," vol. 5, pp. 867–68 in the *Encyclopedia of Ukraine*, Toronto: University of Toronto Press (1988–1993).

Adams, Arthur, *Bolsheviks in the Ukraine: The Second Campaign, 1918–1919*, New Haven, CT: Yale University Press, 1963.

Altshuler, Mordechai, "Ha-politika shel ha-mahane ha-dati ve-ha-haredi be-Rusyah be-shnat 1917," *Shvut* 15 (Tel Aviv, 1992): 195–234.

———, *Soviet Jewry since the Second World War: Population and Social Structure*, New York: Greenwood, 1987.

———, "Ukrainian-Jewish Relations in the Soviet Milieu in the Interwar Period," in *Ukrainian-Jewish Relations in Historical Perspective*, ed. Peter Potichnyj and Howard Aster, Edmonton: Canadian Institute for Ukrainian Studies, 1988, pp. 281–305.

Andriewsky, Olga, "*Medved' iz berlogi*: Vladimir Jabotinsky and the Ukrainian Question, 1904–1914," *Harvard Ukrainian Studies* 14:3/4 (Cambridge, MA, 1990): 249–67.

Aronson, G. et al., eds., *Di geshikhte fun Bund*, 5 vols., New York: Farlag Unzer tsait, 1968.

Aronson, I. Michael, *Troubled Waters: The Origins of the 1881 Anti-Jewish Pogroms in Russia*, Pittsburgh: University of Pittsburgh Press, 1990.

Aster, Howard and Peter Potichnyj, *Jewish-Ukrainian Relations: Two Solitudes*, 2nd edition, Oakville, ON: Mosaic, 1987.

Avrich, Paul, *Russian Rebels, 1600–1800*, New York: Schocken, 1972.

Baker, Zachary, "Megilat ha-tevah; homer le-divrei yemei ha-peraot ve-ha-tevah ba-yehudim be-Ukrainah, be-Rusiah ha-gedolah u-ve-Rusiah ha-levanah," *Toledot* 41:1–2 (New York, 1981): 19–21.

Baron, Salo, *The Russian Jew Under Tsars and Soviets*, 2nd edition, New York: Schocken, 1987.

Bazhan, M. et al., eds., *Soviet Ukraine*, Kyiv: Academy of Sciences of the Ukrainian SSR, n.d.

Bendow [Tanenbaum] Josef, *Der Lemberger Judenpogrom (November 1918–Janner 1919)*, Vienna-Brunn: M. Hickl-Verlag, 1919.

Bilinsky, Y., "The Jewish Question in Ukraine," in *The Second Soviet Republic: The Ukraine after World War II*, New Jersey: Rutgers, 1964, pp. 395–409.

Birnbaum, Henrik, "On Some Evidence of Jewish Life and Anti-Jewish Sentiments in Medieval Russia," *Viator* 4 (Berkeley, 1973): 225–55.

———, "Some Problems with the Etymology and Semantics of the Slavic *Žid* 'Jew,'" *Slavica Hierosolymitana* 7 (Jerusalem, 1985): 1–11.

Bohachevsky-Chomiak, Marta, "Jewish and Ukrainian Women: A Double Minority," in *Ukrainian-Jewish Relations in Historical Perspective*, ed. Peter

Potichnyj and Howard Aster, Edmonton: Canadian Institute for Ukrainian Studies, 1988, pp. 355–69.

Boim, Y. and A. Katz, *Felshtin: zamlbukh tsum ondenk fun di Felshtiner kedoyshim*, New York: Felshtiner farayn, 1937.

Borys, Jurij, "Political Parties in the Ukraine," in *The Ukraine, 1917–1921: A Study in Revolution*, ed. Taras Hunczak, Cambridge, MA: Harvard Ukrainian Research Institute–Harvard University Press, 1977, pp. 128–58.

———, *The Sovietization of Ukraine 1917–1923: The Communist Doctrine and Practice of National Self-Determination*, rev. ed., Edmonton: Canadian Institute of Ukrainian Studies, 1980.

Boshyk, Yury, "Between Socialism and Nationalism: Jewish-Ukrainian Political Relations in Imperial Russia, 1900–1917," in *Ukrainian-Jewish Relations in Historical Perspective*, ed. Peter Potichnyj and Howard Aster, Edmonton: Canadian Institute for Ukrainian Studies, 1988, pp. 173–202.

———, and Myron Momryk, "A New and Major Resource: The Andrii Zhuk Collection at the National Archives of Canada," *Journal of Ukrainian Studies* 25 (Edmonton, 1988): 105–114.

Bunzl, J., *Klassenkampf in der Diaspora: Zur Geshichte der jüdischen Arbeiterbewegung*, Vienna: Europaverlag, 1975.

Bykovs'kyi, L., *Solomon I. Goldelman: A Portrait of a Politician and Educator (1885–1974): A Chapter in Ukrainian Jewish Relations*, New York: Ukrainian Historical Association, 1980.

———, *Solomon Israïlevych Gol'del'man 1885–1974: bio-bibliohrafychni materiialy*, Denver, CO: Ukrainian Continental Institute, 1976.

Chamberlin, W., *The Russian Revolution*, 2 vols., Princeton: Princeton University Press, 1935.

Choulguine, Alexandre, *L'Ukraine et le Cauchemar Rouge: Les Massacres en Ukraine*, Paris: Editions Jules Tallandier, 1927.

Deak, Istvan, *Jewish Soldiers in Austro-Hungarian Society*, Leo Baeck Memorial Lecture 34, New York: Leo Baeck Institute, 1990.

"Di kdoshim fun Zhitomir," *Dos yidishe vort* 199 (New York, 1977): 28–29.

Dimanshtein, S., ed., *Yidn in FSSR: zamlbukh*, Moscow: Emes, 1935.

Diskin, I, "Be-yemei ha-mahapekha be-Rusiyah," *He'avar* 16 (Tel-Aviv, 1969): 97–101.

Dobkowski, Elie, *L'Affaire Petliura-Schwarzbard*, [Paris?]: L'Union Federative Socialiste, n.d.

Doroshenko, Dmytro, *Istoriia Ukraïny 1917–1923 rr.*, 2 vols., New York: Bulava, 1954 [reprint of Uzhhorod, 1932].

———, *A Survey of Ukrainian History*, Winnipeg: Humeniuk, 1975.

Drabkin, A. "Itse (Isaak) iz Chernigova," *Evreiskaia entsiklopediia* (St. Petersburg, n.d.).

Dubnow, Simon, *History of the Jews in Russia and Poland: From the Earliest Times until the Present Day*, 3 vols., Philadelphia: Jewish Publication Society, 1916–1920.

———, *Weltgeschichte des jüdischen Volkes*, 10 vols., Berlin: Jüdischer Verlag, 1925.

Dunlop, D. M., *The History of the Jewish Khazars*, Princeton: Princeton University Press, 1954.

Edelman, Robert, *Proletarian Peasants: The Revolution of 1905 in Russia's Southwest*, Ithaca: Cornell University Press, 1987.

Eley, Geoff, "Remapping the Nation: War, Revolutionary Upheaval and State Formation in Eastern Europe, 1914–1923," in *Ukrainian-Jewish Relations in Historical Perspective*, ed. Peter Potichnyj and Howard Aster, Edmonton: Canadian Institute for Ukrainian Studies, 1988, pp. 205–246.

Everett, L., "The Rise of Jewish National Politics in Galicia, 1915–1907," *Nationbuilding and the Politics of Nationalism: Essays on Austrian Galicia*, eds. A. Markovits and Frank Sysyn, Cambridge, MA: Harvard Ukrainian Research Institute–Harvard University Press, 1982, pp. 149–77.

Fahn, Reuven, *Geshikhte fun der yudisher natsional-oitonomie: in'm period fun der ma'arev-ukrainishher republik*, L'viv: Kultur, 1933.

Faygenberg, Rahel, *Megilat Dubovah: toldot ir she-avrah u-vatlah min ha-olam*, Tel-Aviv: La-am, 1940.

———, *Megilat yehudei Rusyah*, Jerusalem: Kiryat sefer, 1965.

Fedotov, George, *The Russian Religious Mind*, 2 vols., Belmont, MA: Nordland, 1966.

Fedyshyn, O., *Germany's Drive to the East and the Ukrainian Revolution, 1917–18*, New Jersey: Rutgers, 1971.

Ferlov, M., "Pogromen in Ukrayne," *Der Ukrayner id in Ukrayne un Amerike*, ed. V. Edlin, [New York?]: Committee of Jewish Oganizations of the Jewish Council for Russian War Relief, 1944.

Frankel, Jonathan, "The Dilemmas of Jewish Autonomism: The Case of Ukraine, 1917–1920," in *Ukrainian-Jewish Relations in Historical Perspective*, ed. Peter Potichnyj and Howard Aster, Edmonton: Canadian Institute for Ukrainian Studies, 1988, pp. 263–80.

———, *Prophecy and Politics: Socialism, Nationalism and the Russian Jews, 1862–1920*, Cambridge: Cambridge University Press, 1981.

Friedman, Philip, "The First Millenium of Jewish Settlement in the Ukraine and in the Adjacent Areas," *The Annals of the Ukrainian Academy of Arts and Sciences in the U.S.* 7:1/2 (New York, 1959): 1483–1516.

Friedman, Saul, *Pogromchik: The Assassination of Simon Petlura*, New York: Hart, 1974.

G[alant], I[llia], "Do desiatyrichchia Denikins'kykh pohromiv," *Zbirnyk prats' ievreiskoï istorychno-arkheohrafychnoï komisiï*, vol. 2, Kyiv: Vseukraïns'ka Akademiia Nauk, 1929, pp. 385–86.

———, "Do istoriï ievreis'koï samoborony," *Zbirnyk prats' ievreiskoï istorichno-arheohrafichnoï komisiï*, vol. 2, Kyiv: Vseukraïns'ka Akademiia Nauk, 1929, pp. 389–97.

Gassenschmidt, Christoph, *Jewish Liberal Politics in Tsarist Russia, 1900–1914: The Modernization of Russian Jewry*, New York: New York University Press, 1995.

Gelbard, A., *Der jüdische Arbeiter-Bund Russlands im Revolutionsjahr 1917*, Vienna: Europaverlag, 1982.

Gelber, N., "The National Autonomy of Eastern-Galician Jewry in the West-Ukrainian Republic, 1918–1919," in *A History of Polish Jewry During the Revival of Poland*, ed. Isaac Lewin, New York: Shengold, 1990, pp. 223–326.

Gergel, Nakhum., *Di lage fun di yidn in Rusland*, Warsaw: Bzshosha, 1929.

———, "Di pogromen in Ukrayne in di yorn 1918–1921," *Shriftn far ekonomik* I (Berlin, 1928): 106–113 [English version "The Pogroms in Ukraine in 1918–1920," *YIVO Annual of Jewish Social Science* 6(New York, 1951): 237–52].

Gitelman, Zvi, *A Century of Ambivalence: The Jews of Russia and the Soviet Union, 1881 to the Present*, New York: YIVO, 1988.

———, "Contemporary Soviet Jewish Perceptions of Ukrainians: Some Empirical Observations," in *Ukrainian-Jewish Relations in Historical Perspective*, ed. Peter Potichnyi and Howard Aster, Edmonton: Canadian Institute of Ukrainian Studies, 1988, pp. 437–57.

———, *Jewish Nationality and Soviet Politics: The Jewish Sections of the CPSU, 1917–1930*, Princeton: Princeton University Press, 1972.

Goberman, D., *Ievreiskie nadgrobiia na Ukraine i v Moldove*, Moscow: Image, 1993 [=*Shedevry ievreiskogo iskusstva*].

Golb, Norman and Omeljan Pritsak, *Khazarian Hebrew Documents of the Tenth Century*, Ithaca: Cornell University Press, 1982.

Golczewski, Frank, *Polnisch-Jüdische Bezieungen 1881–1922: Eine Studie zur Geschichte des Antisemitismus in Osteuropa*, Series: *Quellen und Studien zur Geschichte des Ostlichen Europa* 14, Wiesbaden: Franz Steiner, 1981.

Goldelman, Solomon, *Lost der Kommunismus die Judenfrage? Rote Assimilation und Sowjet-Zionismus*, Vienna: Glanz, 1937.

Greenbaum, Alfred A., "Jewish Historiography in Soviet Russia," *American Academy for Jewish Research* 28 (New York, 1959): 57–77.

Greenberg, Louis, *The Jews in Russia: the Struggle for Emancipation*, 2 vols., New York: Schocken, 1976.

Gringauz, S., "The Jewish National Autonomy in Lithuania, Latvia and Estonia," in *Russian Jewry 1917–1967*, ed. G. Aronson et al., New York: Yoseloff, 1969, pp. 58–71.

Gurevitz, Baruch, "The Bolshevik Revolution and the Foundation of the Jewish Communist Movement in Russia," *Slavic and Soviet Studies* 4 (Tel-Aviv, 1976): 3–20.

———, *National Communism in the Soviet Union 1918–1928*, Pittsburgh: University of Pittsburgh, 1980.

Gusev, V., "Tsentral'na Rada i Bund (lystopad 1917–kviten' 1918 rr.)," *Ukraïns'kyi istorychnyi zhurnal* 10–11(379–380) (Kyiv, 1992): 24–34.

Gusev-Orenburgskii, Sergei, *Bagrovaia kniga: pogromy 1919–1920 gg. na Ukraine*, New York: Izd-vo Ladoga, 1983.

Guthier, Steven, "The Popular Base of Ukrainian Nationalism in 1917," *Slavic Review* 38:1 (1979): 30–47.

———, "Ukrainian Cities in the Revolution and Interwar Era," in *Rethinking Ukrainian History*, ed. Ivan Rudnytsky and John-Paul Himka, Edmonton: Canadian Institute of Ukrainian Studies, 1981, pp. 156–73.

Haberer, Erich, "Cosmopolitanism, Antisemitism, and Populism: A Reappraisal of the Russian and Jewish Socialist Response to the Pogroms of 1881–1882," in *Pogroms: Anti-Jewish Violence in Modern Russian History*, ed. John Klier and Shlomo Lambroza, Cambridge: Cambridge University Press, 1992, pp. 98–134.

Hamm, Michael, *Kiev: A Portrait, 1800–1917*, Princeton: Princeton University Press, 1993.

Herlihy, Patricia, "Ukrainian Cities in the Nineteenth Century," in *Rethinking Ukrainian History*, ed. Ivan Rudnytsky and John-Paul Himka, Edmonton: Canadian Institute of Ukrainian Studies, 1981, pp. 135–55.

Hertz, Y. Sh., *Di Geshikte fun Bund*, 5 vols., New York: Unzer tsayt, 1960.

Hewko, J., "The Ukrainian-Jewish Political Relationship During the Period of the Central Rada—March 1917 to January 1918," unpublished M.Litt thesis, St. Anthony's College (Oxford), 1981.

Himka, John-Paul, "The Background to Emigration: Ukrainians of Galicia and Bukovyna, 1848–1914," in *A Heritage in Transition: Essays on the History of the Ukrainians in Canada*, ed. M. Lupul, Toronto: McClelland and Stewart, 1982, pp. 11–31.

———, *Galician Villagers and the Ukrainian National Movement in the Nineteenth Century*, Edmonton: Canadian Institute of Ukrainian Studies, 1988.

———, "The National and the Social in the Ukrainian Revolution of 1917–1920: The Historiographical Agenda," *Archiv für Sozialgeschichte* 34 (1994): 95–110.

———, "Ukrainian-Jewish Antagonism in the Galician Countryside During the Late Nineteenth Century," in *Ukrainian-Jewish Relations in Historical Perspective*, ed. Peter Potichnyj and Howard Aster, Edmonton: Canadian Institute for Ukrainian Studies, 1988, pp. 111–58.

Holubychny, Vsevolod, *Selected Works of Vsevolod Holubychnyj*, ed. I. Koropeckyj, Edmonton: Canadian Institute of Ukrainian Studies, 1982.

Hrushevs'kyi, Mykhailo, *Istoriia Ukraïny-Rusy* 8 vols. New York: Knyhospilka, 1954.

———[Mikhailo Hrushevsky], *A History of Ukraine*, [New York?]: Archon, 1970.

Hunczak, Taras, "Communications," *Jewish Social Studies* 32:3 (July 1969): 246–53.

———, "A Reappraisal of Symon Petliura and Ukrainian-Jewish Relations, 1917–1921," *Jewish Social Studies* 31:3 (July 1969): 163–83.

———, ed., *The Ukraine, 1917–1921: A Study in Revolution*, Cambridge, MA: Harvard Ukrainian Research Institute–Harvard University Press, 1977.

Jablonski, Henryk, *Polska Autonomia Narodowa na Ukrainie 1917–1918*, Warsaw: Nakladem Towarzystwa Milosnikow Histor i z zasilku Ministerstwa Oswiaty, 1948.

Janowsky, Oscar, *The Jews and Minority Rights (1898–1919)*, New York: Columbia University Press, 1933.

Kahan, Arcadius, "The Impact of Industrialization in Tsarist Russia on the Socioeconomic Conditions of the Jewish Population," in *Essays in Jewish Social and Economic History*, ed. Roger Weiss, Chicago, 1986, pp. 1–69.

Kamenetsky, Ihor, "Hrushevskyi and the Central Rada: Internal Politics and Foreign Interventions," in *The Ukraine, 1917–1921: A Study in Revolution*, ed. Taras Hunczak, Cambridge, MA: Harvard Ukrainian Research Institute–Harvard University Press, 1977, pp. 33–60.

Karniel, Joseph, *Die Toleranzpolitik Kaiser Josephs II*, trans. Leo Koppel, Series: Schrifterreihe des Instituts für Deutsche Geschichte Universität Tel-Aviv Stuttgart: Bleicher Verlag, 1986.

Katz, Shmuel, *Lone Wolf: A Biography of Vladimir (Ze'ev) Jabotinsky*, 2 vols., New York: Barricade Books, 1996.

Kautskii, K., *Evreiskie pogromy i evreiskii vopros v Rosii*, Petersburg: Antei, 1919.

Kenez, Peter, *Civil War in South Russia, 1919–1920: The Defeat of the Whites*, Berkeley: University of California Press, 1977.

Khurbn Proskurov: Tsum andenken fun di heilige neshomes vos zaynen umgekumen in der shreklikher shkhitakh, vos iz ongefirt gevorn durkh di Haidamakes, New York: Proskurover relief farayn, 1924.

Kleiner, Israel, "Urok vtrachenykh mozhlyvostei," *Suchasnist'* 8 (Kyiv, 1992): 55–75.

Kiel, Mark W., "The Ideology of the Folks-Partey," *Soviet Jewish Affairs* 5:2 (London, 1975): 75–89.

Klier, John, "The Concept of 'Jewish Emancipation' in a Russian Context," in *Civil Rights in Imperial Russia*, ed. Olga Crisp and Linda Edmondson, Oxford: Clarendon Press, 1989, pp. 121–44.

———, "The Pogrom Paradigm in Russian History," in *Pogroms: Anti-Jewish Violence in Modern Russian History*, ed. John Klier and Shlomo Lambroza, Cambridge: Cambridge University Press, 1992, pp. 13–38.

———, *Russia Gathers her Jews: The Origins of the Jewish Question in Russia, 1772–1825*, Dekalb: Northern Illinois University Press, 1986.

———, "*Zhid*: Biography of a Russian Epithet," *Slavonic and East European Review* 60:1 (London, 1982): 1–15.

———and Shlomo Lambroza, eds. *Pogroms: Anti-Jewish Violence in Modern Russian History*, Cambridge: Cambridge University Press, 1992.

Koroliv, V. [V. Staryi], *Symon Petliura: Ukraïns'kyi narodnyi heroi*, Kyiv-Prague, Chas, 1919.

Kotik, Meir, *Mishpat Shvartsbard: restah-nakam 'al reka' ha-pogromim be-Ukrainah*, [Hadera]: Hotsaat mifale Hadera, 1972.

Kransky, Yosef, *Barikht iber der lage fun di ukrayner flikhtige un yisomim*, New York: Der Administrativ Komitet fun der Natsionaler Federatsie fun ukrayner idn in amerike, n.d.

Krawchenko, Bohdan, "The Social Structure of the Ukraine in 1917," *Harvard Ukrainian Studies* 14:1/2 (Cambridge, MA): 97–112.

———, *Social Change and National Consciousness in Twentieth-Century Ukraine*, Oxford: Macmillan, 1985.

Kruk, Yosef, "Moshe Zilberfarb (meah shanah le-huladeto)," *He'avar* (Tel-Aviv, 1977): 276–79.

Kuras, I. F. et al., eds. *Velykyi zhovten' i hromadians'ka viina na Ukraini: entsiklopedychnyi dovidnyk*, Kyiv: Redaktsiia ukraïns'koï radians'koï entsiklopediï, 1987.

Landau, Moshe, "Ha-yehudim ke-miut leumi bi-shnoteha ha-rishonot shel Polin ha-atsmait (1918–1926), Ph.D. dissertation, Hebrew University, Jerusalem, 1972.

Latski-Bertoldi, Wolf, *Gzeyrat Denikin*, Berlin: Klal-ferlag, 1922.

Lecache, Bernard, *Quand Israel meurt...*, Paris: Progres Civique, 1927.

Lederhendler, Eli, *The Road to Modern Jewish Politics: Political Tradition and Political Reconstruction in the Jewish Community of Tsarist Russia*, New York: Oxford, 1989.

Leggett, George, *The Cheka: Lenin's Political Police*, Oxford: Oxford University Press, 1981.

Lerski, George and Hanna Lerski, *Jewish-Polish Coexistence, 1772–1939: A Topical Bibliography*, New York: Greenwood, 1986 [=Bibliographies and Indexes in World History, 5].

Lestschinsky, Jacob, *La Situation Economique des Juifs depuis la guerre mondiale*, Paris: Rousseau, 1934.

———, "Der shrek fun tsifern," *Di tsukunft* 27:9 (New York, 1922): 528–32.

———, "Di sotsial-ekonomishe antviklung fun ukraynishn yidntum," *Yidn in Ukrayne*, 2 vols., New York: Andenk fun ukrainisher yidn, 1961.

———, *Dos sovetishe idntum: zayn fargangenhayt un kegnvart*, [New York?]: Yidishe Kemfer, 1941.

Levene, Mark, "Frontiers of Genocide: Jews in the Eastern War Zones, 1914–1920 and 1941," in *Minorities in Wartime*, ed. Pankos Panayi, Oxford: Berg, 1993, pp. 83–117.

Levitats, Isaac, *The Jewish Community in Russia, 1772–1844*, New York: Columbia, 1943.

———, *The Jewish Community in Russia, 1844–1917*, Jerusalem: Posner, 1981.

Lewis, R., R. Rowland and R. Clem, *Nationality and Population Change in Russia and the USSR: An Evaluation of Census Data, 1897–1970*, New York: Praeger, 1976.

Liber, George, "Ukrainian Nationalism and the 1918 Law on National-Personal Autonomy," *Nationalities Papers* 15:1 (Charleston, Ill., 1987): 22–42.

Lichten, Joseph, "A Study of Ukrainian-Jewish Relations," *Annals of the Ukrainian Academy of Arts and Sciences in the U.S.* 5:2/3 (New York, 1956): 1160–1177.

Litvinov, V. *Nestor Makhno et la question juive*, Paris: Groupe Fresnes-Antony, Federation Anarchiste, 1984.

Lohrmann, Klaus, *Das österreichische Judentum zur Zeit Maria Theresias und Josephs II*, Eisenstadt: Roetzer, 1980 [=Studia Judaica Austriaca, 7].

Löwe, Heinz-Dietrich, *The Tsars and the Jews: Reform, Reaction, and Anti-Semitism in Imperial Russia, 1772–1917*, New York: Harwood Academic Publishing, 1993.

Mace, James, *Communism and the Dilemmas of National Liberation: National Communism in Soviet Ukraine, 1918–1933*, Cambridge, MA: Harvard Ukrainian Research Institute, 1983.

Magocsi, Paul Robert, *Ukraine: A Historical Atlas*, (Geoffrey Matthews, cartographer), Toronto: University of Toronto Press, 1985.

———, *A History of Ukraine*, Seattle: University of Washington Press, 1996.

Mark, Rudolf, "Social Questions and National Revolution: The Ukrainian National Republic in 1917–1920," *Harvard Ukrainian Studies* 14:1/2 (Cambridge, MA, 1990): 113–31.

———, "Symon Petljura und die UNR. Vom Sturz des Hetmans Skoropadskyj bis zum Exil in Polen," *Forschungen zur osteuropäischen Geschichte* 40 (Berlin, 1988): 7–228.

Markovits, A. and Frank Sysyn, eds., *Nationbuilding and the Politics of Nationalism: Essays on Austrian Galicia*, Cambridge, MA: Harvard Ukrainian Research Institute–Harvard University Press, 1982.

Mawdsley, E., *The Russian Civil War*, Boston: Allen and Unwin, 1987.

Mendelsohn, Ezra, *Class Struggle in the Pale: The Formative Years of the Jewish Workers' Movement in Tsarist Russia*, Cambridge: Cambridge University Press, 1970.

———, *The Jews of East-Central Europe Between the World Wars*, Bloomington: Indiana University Press, 1983.

———, ed., *Essential Papers on Jews and the Left*, New York: New York University, 1997.

Miller, M., "The Ukraine Commission of the Joint Distribution Committee, 1920, with Insight from the Judge Harry Fisher Papers," *Jewish Social Studies* 49 (New York, 1987): 53–59.

Minc, Matityahu, "Kiev Zionists and the Ukrainian National Movement," in *Ukrainian-Jewish Relations in Historical Perspective*, ed. Peter Potichnyj and Howard Aster, Edmonton: Canadian Institute for Ukrainian Studies, 1988, pp. 247–62.

———[Mintz], "The Recruitment of Jews for Ukrainian National Units in 1917, as reflected in the minutes of the Provisional Jewish Council," *Jews and Jewish Topics in the Soviet Union and Eastern Europe* 2:12 (Jerusalem, 1990): 8–14.

——— [Mintz], "The Secretariat of Internationality Affairs (*Sekretariiat mizhnatsional'nykh sprav*) of the Ukrainian General Secretariat (1917–1918)," *Harvard Ukrainian Studies* 6:1 (Cambridge, MA, 1982): 25–42.

Mishkinsky, Moshe, "The Attitudes of the Ukrainian Socialists to Jewish Parties in the 1870s," in *Ukrainian-Jewish Relations in Historical Perspective*, ed. Peter Potichnyj and Howard Aster, Edmonton: Canadian Institute for Ukrainian Studies, 1988, pp. 57–68.

———, "'Black Repartition' and the pogroms of 1881–1882," in *Pogroms: Anti-Jewish Violence in Modern Jewish History*, ed. John Klier and Shlomo Lambroza, Cambridge: Cambridge University Press, 1992, pp. 62–98.

———, "Regional Factors in the Formation of the Jewish Labor Movement in Czarist Russia," in *Essential Papers on Jews and the Left*, ed. Ezra Mendelsohn, New York: New York University Press, 1997, pp. 78–100.

Mosse, W.E., "A.F. Kerensky and the Emancipation of Russian Jewry," *Bulletin on Soviet and East European Jewish Affairs* 6 (London, 1970): 33–38.

Mykhal'chyk, Vasyl, *Symon Petliura ta ukraïns'ka natsional'na revoliutsia*, Kyiv: Rada, 1995.

Nadel, B. *Yidn in Mizrekh-Eyropa fun di elteste tsaytn biz der mongolisher invazie (1240)*, Warsaw: Yidish bukh, 1960.

Nahayewsky, I., *History of the Modern Ukrainian State 1917–1923*, Munich: Ukrainian Free University and the Academy of Arts and Sciences, 1966.

Nevada, Joseph, *Trotsky and the Jews*, Philadelphia: Jewish Publication Society, 1972.

Orbach, Alexander, "Zionism and the Russian Revolution of 1905: The Committment to Participate in Domestic Political Life," *Bar-Ilan Studies in the History and Cultre of East European Jewry* 24–25 (1989): 7–23.

Palij, Michael, *The Ukrainian-Polish Defensive Alliance: An Aspect of the Ukrainian Revolution*, Edmonton: Canadian Institute of Ukrainian Studies, 1995.

Peled, Y., *Class and Ethnicity in the Pale: The Political Economy of Jewish Workers' Nationalism in late Imperial Russia*, London: Macmillan, 1989.

Pidhainy, Oleh, *The Formation of the Ukrainian Republic*, Toronto: New Review, 1966.

Pinkus, Benjamin, *The Jews of the Soviet Union: The History of a National Minority*, Cambridge: Cambridge University Press, 1988.

Pipes, Richard, "Catherine II and the Jews: The Origins of the Pale of Settlement," *Soviet Jewish Affairs* 5:2 (London, 1975): 3–20.

———, *The Formation of the Soviet Union: Communism and Nationalism, 1917–1923*, Cambridge, MA: Harvard University Press, 1964.

———, *Russia under the Bolshevik Regime*, New York: Alfred A. Knopf, 1993.

Pliguzov, Andrei, "Archbishop Gennadii and the Heresy of the Judaizers," *Harvard Ukrainian Studies* 16:3–4 (1992): 269–88.

Pliushch, Leonid, "Borot'ba z ievreiamy—tse borot'ba z namy..." *Suchasnist'* 8 (Kyiv, 1992): 89–100.

Podskalsky, Gerhard, *Christentum und Theologische Literatur in der Kiever Rus' (988–1237)*, Munich: C. H. Beck, 1982.

Polin, vol 2: *Eastern Galicia*, eds. Danuta Dombrovska, Avraham Vayn, Avraham Weiss, Jerusalem: Yad Vashem, 1980 [=*Pinkas ha-Kehilot: Entsiklopedyah shel ha-yishuvim ha-yehudim le-min hivasdam ve-ad le-ahar shoat milhemet ha-olam ha-sheniya*].

Potichnyi, Peter and Howard Aster, eds., *Ukrainian-Jewish Relations in Historical Perspective*, Edmonton: Canadian Institute of Ukrainian Studies, 1988.

Pritsak, Omeljan, "The Pre-Ashkenazic Jews of Eastern Europe in Relation to the Khazars, the Rus' and the Lithuanians," in *Ukrainian-Jewish Relations in Historical Perspective*, ed. Peter Potichnyj and Howard Aster, Edmonton: Canadian Institute for Ukrainian Studies, 1988, pp. 3–22.

Radkey, Oliver, *The Election to the Russian Constituent Assembly of 1917*, Cambridge, MA: Harvard University Press, 1950.

Raisin, Jacob, *The Haskalah Movement in Russia*, Philadelphia: The Jewish Publication Society of America, 1913.

Ravage, Marcus E., *The Jew Pays: A Narrative of the Consequences of the War to the Jews of Eastern Europe, and of the Manner in which Americans Have Attempted to Meet Them*, New York: Knopf, 1919.

Reshetar, John, *The Ukrainian Revolution, 1917–1920: A Study in Nationalism*, New York: Arno, 1972.

Resnick, Salomon, *Cinco Ensayos Sobre Temas Judios*, Buenos Aires: Editorial Judaica, 1943.

Rigby, Thomas H., *Communist Party Membership in the USSR 1917–1967*, Princeton: Princeton University Press, 1968.

Rosental, D., *Megilat ha-tevah*, 3 vols. Jerusalem: n.p., 1929–1931.

Rosman, Moshe, *The Lords' Jews: Magnate-Jewish Relations in the Polish-Lithuanian Commonwealth during the 18th Century*, Cambridge, MA: Harvard Ukrainian Research Institute and Harvard Center for Jewish Studies–Harvard University Press, 1990.

Rudnytsky, Ivan, "Drahomanov as a Political Theorist," *Essays in Modern Ukrainian History*, ed. P. Rudnytsky, Edmonton: Canadian Institute of Ukrainian Studies, 1987, pp. 203–253.

———, "Mykhailo Drahomanov and the Problem of Ukrainian-Jewish Relations," in *Essays in Modern Ukrainian History*, ed. P. Rudnytsky, Edmonton: Canadian Institute of Ukrainian Studies, 1987, pp. 283–98.

———, "The Problem of Ukrainian-Jewish Relations in Nineteenth-Century Ukrainian Political Thought," in *Essays in Modern Ukrainian History*, ed. P. Rudnytsky, Edmonton: Canadian Institute of Ukrainian Studies, 1987, pp. 299–313.

———, "Ukrainian-Jewish Relations in Nineteenth Century Political Thought," in *Ukrainian-Jewish Relations in Historical Perspective*, ed. Peter Potichnyj and Howard Aster, Edmonton: Canadian Institute for Ukrainian Studies, 1988, pp. 69–84.

———, "The Ukrainians in Galicia under Austrian Rule," in *Nationbuilding and the Politics of Nationalism: Essays on Austrian Galicia*, ed. Andrei Markovits and Frank Sysyn, Cambridge, MA: Harvard Ukrainian Research Institute–Harvard University Press, pp. 23–67.

Schapiro, Leon, "The Role of the Jews in the Russian Revolutionary Movement," in his *Russian Studies*, London: Collins Havrill, 1986, pp. 266–89.

Schechtman, Joseph, *Pogromy dobrovol'cheskoi armii na Ukraine*, Berlin: Ostjüdisches Historisches Archiv, 1932.

———, "A 'Reappraisal' of Symon Petliura," *Midstream* 15:9 (New York, 1969): 59–61.

———, *Ver iz farantvortlikh far di pogromen in Ukrayne: loyt naye nit farefntlikhte materiyaln un dokumentn*, Paris: Imprimerie Scientifique et Commerciale, 1927.

Schneerson, Fischel, *Die Katastrophale Zeit und die Heranwachsende Generation (Die Wirkung von Katastrophen auf die Seele des normalen und abnormalen Kindes)*, Berlin: C. A. Schwetschke, 1924.

Schulman, Elias, "The Pogroms in the Ukraine in 1919," *The Jewish Quarterly Review*, 57:2 (Philadelphia, 1966): 159–66.

Schwarz, Solomon, *The Jews in the Soviet Union*, Syracuse: Syracuse University Press, 1951.

Sefer Galitsie, ed. Yosef Akroni, Buenos Aires: Tsentral Farband fun Galitsianer Yidn in Buenos Aires, 1968.

Serbyn, Roman, "The Sion-Osnova Controversy of 1861–1862," in *Ukrainian-Jewish Relations in Historical Perspective*, ed. Peter Potichnyj and Howard Aster, Edmonton: Canadian Institute for Ukrainian Studies, 1988, pp. 85–110.

Shankowsky, L., "Russia, the Jews and the Ukrainian Liberation Movement," in *Ukrainians and Jews*, ed. W. Dushnyk, New York: Ukrainian Congress Committee of America, 1966, pp. 65–96.

Shmidl, Erwin, *Juden in der k.(u.)k. Armee 1788–1918*, Eisenstadt: Österreichisches Jüdisches Museum, 1989 [=Studia Judaica Austriaca, 11].

Shtif, N. I., *Pogromy na Ukraine (period Dobrovol'cheskoi Armii)*, Berlin: Wostok, 1922 [=Yiddish version: *Pogromen in Ukraine: di tsait fun der frayviliger armey*, Berlin: Wostok, 1923].

Skava, A. et al., eds. *Ukraïns'ka RSR v period hromadians'koï viiny 1917–1920 rr.*, 3 vols., Kyiv: Vyd-vo politychnoï literatury Ukraïny, 1968.

Skvirer khurbn, New York: Skvirer Yugent Farayn in Nyu York, 1923.

Slutsky, Y., "Bayat ha-aharayut le-peraot Ukrainah," *He'avar* 17 (Tel Aviv, 1970): 27–43.

Stachiw, M. and J. Sztendera, *Western Ukraine at the Turning Point of Europe's History, 1918–1923*, 2 vols., New York: Shevchenko Society, 1971.

Stillschweig, K., "Nationalism and Autonomy among Eastern European Jewry: Origin and Historical Development up to 1939," *Historica Judaica* 6 (New York, 1944): 27–68.

———, "Zur neueren Geschichte der jüdischen Autonomie," *Monatsschrift für Geschichte und Wissenschaft des Judentums* 83 (Berlin, 1939): 509–532.

Stites, Richard, *The Women's Liberation Movement in Russia: Feminism, Nihilism, and Bolshevism, 1860–1930*, Princeton: Princeton University Press, 1978.

Stojko, Wolodymyr, "Ukrainian National Aspirations and the Russian Provisional Government," in *The Ukraine 1917–1920: A Study in Nationalism*, ed. Taras Hunczak, Cambridge, MA: Harvard Ukrainian Research Institute–Harvard University Press, 1977.

———, "Z"ïzd narodiv v Kyievi 1917 roku," *Ukraïns'kyi istoryk* 3–4 (55–56) (New York, 1977): 14–25.

Subtelny, Orest, *Ukraine: A History*, Toronto: University of Toronto Press, 1988.

Suprunenko, N. et al., eds. *Istoriia ukrainskoi SSR: Velikaia oktiabrs'kaia sotsialisticheskaia revoliutsiia i grazhdanskaia voina na Ukraine (1917–1920)*, Kyiv: Naukova Dumka, 1984.

Szajkowski, Zosa, "Communications," *Jewish Social Studies* 32:3 (1970): 253–63.

———, *An Illustrated Sourcebook of Russian Antisemitism, 1881–1971*, 2 vols., New York: Ktav, 1980.

———, "Parashat Petliurah," *He'avar* 17 (Tel-Aviv, 1970): 5–26.

———, "'A Reappraisal of Symon Petliura and Ukrainian-Jewish Relations, 1917–1921:' A Rebuttal," *Jewish Social Studies* 31:3 (1969): 184–213.

Tarnopoler, L., "Avraham Revutsky—itonai, hoker ve-lokhem," *He'avar* 17 (Tel-Aviv, 1970): 217–28.

Taube, Moshe, "The 'Poem on the Soul' in the *Laodicean Epistle* and the Literature of the Judaizers," *Harvard Ukrainian Studies* 19 (1995): 671–85.

Tcherikower, Elias, *Di ukrayner pogromen in yor 1919*, New York: YIVO, 1965.

Tenenbaum, Jozef, *Żydowskie Problemy Gospodarcze w Galicyi*, Wieden: Nakładem Dr. Wilhemina Berkelhammera ("Moria"), 1918.

Tobias, Henry, *The Jewish Bund in Russia: From its Origins to 1905*, Stanford: Stanford University Press, 1972.

Toews, J., *Czars, Soviets and Mennonites*, Newton, KS: Faith and Life Press, 1982.

Tolochko, Petro, "Volodimer Svjatoslavič's Choice of Religion: Fact or Fiction?" *Harvard Ukrainian Studies* 12/13 (Cambridge, MA, 1988–1989): 816–29.

Torrés, Henri, *Les Procès des Pogromes*, Paris: Les Editions de France, 1928.

Troper, Harold and Morton Weinfeld, *Old Wounds: Jews, Ukrainians and the Hunt for Nazi War Criminals in Canada*, Toronto: Viking, 1988.

Trotzky, I., "Jewish Pogroms in the Ukraine and in Byelorussia," in *Russian Jewry 1917–1967*, ed. G. Aronson et al., New York: Yoseloff, 1969, pp. 72–88.

Vays, Sh., *Der shos oyf Petliura (Shvartsbard-protses)* Warsaw: Farlag "Groshn-bibliotek," 1933.

Vikhnovich, Vsevolod, "From the Jordan to the Dnieper," *Jewish Studies/Madaei ha-Yahadut* 31 (Jerusalem, 1991): 15–24.

Weinreich, Max, *History of the Yiddish Language*, trans. S. Noble (Chicago, 1980).

Weinryb, Bernard, "The Beginnings of East-European Jewry in Legend and Historiography," in *Studies and Essays in Honor of Abraham A. Neuman*, ed. Meir Ben-Horin, Bernard Weinryb, and Solomon Zeitlin, Philadelphia: E. J. Brill for Dropsie College, 1962, pp. 445–502.

———, "Hebrew Chronicles on Bohdan Khmel'nyts'kyi and the Cossack-Polish War," *Harvard Ukrainian Studies* 1 (Cambridge, MA, 1977): 153–77.

———, *The Jews of Poland: A Social and Economic History of the the Jewish Community in Poland from 1100 to 1800*, Philadelphia: Jewish Publication Society of America, 1973.

Weissler, Chava, "Prayers in Yiddish and the Religious World of Ashkenazic Women," in *Jewish Women in Historical Perspective*, Detroit: Wayne State University Press, 1991, pp. 159–81.

Yidn in Ukrayne, 2 vols., New York: Andenk fun Ukrayner Yidn, 1961.

Zaidman, A., "Ha-avtonomia ha-leumit ha-yehudit be-Ukrainah ha-atsmait ba-shanim 1917–1919," Ph.D. thesis, Tel-Aviv University, 1980.

Zamorski, Krzysztof, *Transformacja demograficzna w Galicji na tle przemian ludnościowych innych obszarów Europy środkowej w drugiej połowie XIX i na początku XX w.*, Cracow: Uniwersytet Jagielłoński, 1991.

Zborowski, M. and E. Herzog, *Life is With People: The Culture of the Shtetl*, New York: Schocken, 1952.

Zenner, Walter, "Middleman Minorities and Genocide," in *Genocide and the Modern Age: Etiology and Case Studies of Mass Death*, ed. Isidor Walliman and Michael Dobkowski, New York: Greenwood, 1989 [=Contributions to the Study of World History, 3].

———, *Minorities in the Middle: A Cross-Cultural Analysis*, Albany: SUNY Press, 1991 [=SUNY Series in Ethnicity and Race in American Life, ed. John Sibley Butler].

Zinger, L., *Dos banayte folk (tsifern un faktn vegn di yidn in FSSR)*, Moscow: Emes, 1941.

Zozulia, Iakiv, *Velyka ukraïns'ka revoliutsiia (materiialy do istoriï vidnovlennia ukraïns'koï derzhavnosty)*, New York: Ukraïns'ka Vil'na Akademiia Nauk u SShA, 1967.

Index

Other Titles of Interest

The Lords' Jews: Magnate-Jewish Relations in the Polish-Lithuanian Commonwealth during the 18th Century. M. J. Rosman. Clothbound, ISBN 0-916458-18-0. Softcover, 0-916458-47-4.

Kistiakovsky: The Struggle for National and Constitutional Rights in the Last Years of Tsarism. Susan Heuman. Clothbound, ISBN 0-916458-61-X.

The Great Soviet Peasant War. Bolsheviks and Peasants, 1917–1933. Andrea Graziosi. Softcover, ISBN 0-916458-83-0.

Carpatho-Ukraine in the Twentieth Century: A Political and Legal History. Vincent Shandor. Clothbound, ISBN 0-916458-86-5.

Nationalim, Marxism, and Modern Central Europe. A Biography of Kazimierz Kelles-Krauz (1872–1905). Timothy Snyder. Softcover, ISBN 0-916458-84-9.

Communism and the Dilemmas of National Liberation: National Communism in Ukraine, 1918–1933. James Mace. Clothbound, ISBN 0-916458-09-1.

Available from:

Harvard University Press
79 Garden Street
Cambridge, MA 02138 USA
tel. 1-800-448-2242 (US & Canada), 1-617-495-2480 (all others)
fax. 1-800-962-4983 (US & Canada), 1-617-495-8924 (all others)
SAN: 200-2043
www.hup.harvard.edu

Typeset at the Harvard Ukrainian Research Institute in Goudy, utilizing Adobe PageMaker® and Adobe Illustrator® for the Macintosh and Harvard Graphics® for DOS. Graphs by the author. Cartography by R. De Lossa, based on maps by Adrian Hewryk. Cover, jacket, and interior layout by R. De Lossa.